Linking Quality to Profits

Also available from ASQ Quality Press

Full-Cycle Corrective Action: Managing for Quality and Profits
Thomas M. Cappels

*Principles of Quality Costs: Principles, Implementation, and Use,
Second Edition*
ASQ Quality Costs Committee, Jack Campanella, editor

Quality Costs: Ideas and Applications, Volume 1, Second Edition
ASQ Quality Costs Committee, Andrew F. Grimm, editor

Quality Costs: Ideas and Applications, Volume 2
ASQ Quality Costs Committee, Jack Campanella, editor

The ASQ Total Quality Management Series

> *TQM: Leadership for the Quality Transformation*
> Richard S. Johnson

> *TQM: Management Processes for Quality Operations*
> Richard S. Johnson

> *TQM: The Mechanics of Quality Processes*
> Richard S. Johnson and Lawrence E. Kazense

> *TQM: Quality Training Practices*
> Richard S. Johnson

To request a complimentary catalog of publications,
call 800-248-1946.

Linking Quality to Profits

Quality-Based Cost Management

Hawley Atkinson
John Hamburg
Christopher Ittner

ASQ Quality Press
Milwaukee, Wisconsin

Institute of Management Accountants
Montvale, New Jersey

Linking Quality to Profits: Quality-Based Cost Management
Hawley Atkinson, John Hamburg, and Christopher Ittner

Library of Congress Cataloging-in-Publication Data
Atkinson, John Hawley.
     Linking quality to profits: quality-based cost management / Hawley
Atkinson, John Hamburg, Christopher Ittner.
        p. cm.
     Includes bibliographical references and index.
     ISBN 0-87389-189-9
     1. Quality of products—Cost effectiveness. 2. Quality control—
Costs. I. Hamburg, John.   II. Ittner, Christopher
III. Title.
HF5415.157.A87   1994

94-17503
CIP

10 9 8 7 6 5 4

ISBN 0-87389-189-9

Acquisitions Editor: Susan Westergard
Project Editor: Jeanne W. Bohn
Production Editor: Annette Wall
Marketing Administrator: Mark Olson
Set in Bodoni and Futura Condensed by Montgomery Media, Inc.
Cover design by Montgomery Media, Inc.
Printed and bound by BookCrafters, Inc.

ASQ Mission: To facilitate continuous improvement and increase customer satisfaction by identifying, communicating, and promoting the use of quality principles, concepts, and technologies; and thereby be recognized throughout the world as the leading authority on, and champion for, quality.

For a free copy of the ASQ Quality Press Publications Catalog, including ASQ membership information, call 800-248-1946.

IMA Mission: To provide to members personal and professional development opportunities through education, association with business professionals, and certification in management accounting skills; to ensure that IMA is universally recognized by the financial community as a respected institution influencing the concepts and ethical practices of management accounting.

To receive a free copy of the IMA Publications Catalog, call 800-638-4427.

Printed in the United States of America

 Printed on acid-free recycled paper

American Society for Quality

Quality Press
611 East Wisconsin Avenue
P.O. Box 3005
Milwaukee, Wisconsin 53201-3005

INSTITUTE of
MANAGEMENT
ACCOUNTANTS
CERTIFIED MANAGEMENT ACCOUNTANT PROGRAM

10 Paragon Dr., Montvale, N.J. 07645

To my father, mother, and wife JoAnn Marie—Hawley Atkinson

To my father, mother, and wife Shelley—John Hamburg

To my wife Caroline—Chris Ittner

Contents

Publisher's Foreword

Total quality management (TQM) is a proven approach to eliminating waste and nonvalue-adding activities. Quality-based cost management (QBCM) is a spin on TQM that adds a financial dimension to the quality process. The authors of *Linking Quality to Profits* report on how more than 30 manufacturing and service companies are able to improve customer satisfaction and financial performance by managing the quality process with QBCM. The quality tools and techniques the companies use are illustrated so they can be copied.

The essence of what the authors are conveying through their experiences working with these companies is stated in W. Edward Deming's obituary in the *New York Times* (December 21, 1993).

> *Mr. Deming's theories were based on the premise that most product defects resulted from management shortcomings rather than careless workers, and that inspection after the fact was inferior to designing processes that would produce better quality. He argued that enlisting the efforts of willing workers to do things properly the first time and giving them the right tools were the real secrets of improving quality—not teams of inspectors.*

The Institute of Management Accountants (IMA) is continuing its support of the concept of quality by collaborating on the publication of this book. The institute itself has published two research studies on quality, *Measuring, Planning, and Controlling Quality Costs* and *Current Trends in Cost of Quality: Linking the Cost of Quality and Continuous Improvement,* as well as Statement on Management Accounting No. 4R, *Managing Quality Improvements.* The IMA regularly publishes numerous articles on quality in its magazine, *Management Accounting,* which add a significant dimension to the literature on the subject. In addition, the IMA has established a Continuous Improvement Center (CIC) built around benchmarking, best practices in forum settings, and recognition.

There are really two crucial quality-related roles for the management accountant: (1) within the accounting/finance organization quality initiative and (2) within the company-wide quality initiative. *Linking Quality to Profits* will be particularly useful to managers who are struggling with the quality process and want to show bottom-line improvement to management. The book will give managers a better methodology for applying quality costs to company strategic plans, business goals, and efforts to increase customer satisfaction. Those who are dedicated to eradicating waste, expanding value-added activities, and maximizing profits while increasing the company's market share will find *Linking Quality to Profits* of great value.

The IMA appreciates the efforts of ASQC in furthering the pursuit of quality. IMA's Committee on Research is proud to be associated with ASQC and believes that this collaboration will enrich IMA members' understanding of the importance of managing quality.

This report reflects the views of the researchers and not necessarily those of the institute or the Committee on Research.

Julian Freedman
Director of Research
Institute of Management Accountants

Foreword

The use of the quality costs concept as applied to the management of an organization is not as widespread as one would think. This state of affairs can be related to a number of factors. Misunderstanding of the concept and subsequent misapplication to managing the quality process can result in the rejection of the tool by those companies that have tried and failed. Further, as found in various surveys, a vast majority of companies have either overlooked the use of the concept or were completely unaware of its existence. This may change rapidly as more companies investigate the ISO 9000 series of standards, which details a requirement for a quality cost system.

However, this system may be advantageous. By applying the suggestions contained in this book, many of which are improvements to the classical approach, companies could become more profitable by implementing a successful system. Engaging a different perspective of quality costs, that is, the cost of poor quality, the authors propose a methodology that will result in positive effects on the bottom line. These results are proven by the experiences of companies described in case studies. These case studies back up the main theme of the book: linking quality to profits.

What does this book do for you? The interested reader can gain insights into introducing a new system. The authors establish the relationship of the quality process to business planning. They define the cost of poor quality concept and its application to quality improvement of the quality process. They provide an in-depth description of a quality-based cost management system. This new model is important for those who have not used the quality cost concept before and are continuously looking for means of improving the quality process within their operations. It provides a system that has been proven successful. More important, the model can be used by those who have failed before but want to try again.

Andrew F. Grimm
ASQC Fellow
Automotive Division—
Strategic Planning Committee Chair

The Goals
of This Book

The first goal of this book is to examine the approaches that market and industry leaders have developed to use quality tools and techniques to add a financial dimension to the quality process. The strengths and weaknesses of existing quality implementations in more than 30 companies were assessed to determine the practices that have the greatest positive impact on financial performance. The assessment of quality-based cost management implementations and the synthesis of best practices were completed over a four-year period and consisted of more than 150 interviews with key managers and personnel from a wide variety of industries, functions, and disciplines. Participating companies made detailed implementation documentation available, provided insights into their management and implementation practices, and generously shared the results of their efforts.

The second goal is to present a framework and methodology, synthesized from the best practices of the companies that participated in the study, that link the quality process to improved financial performance. A general framework for strategic quality planning is provided to help companies align the quality process with overall business objectives. A detailed methodology for implementing quality-based cost management is then presented for companies to follow as they begin to improve financial performance through quality improvement.

Whether the reader is a senior manager, quality professional, financial executive, or someone who is simply interested in increasing customer satisfaction and financial performance, we will have reached our goals if this book helps you to reach yours.

Acknowledgments

We are deeply indebted to all of the companies that participated in the study. Although many of the individuals and companies cannot be identified by name due to confidentiality agreements, we wish to recognize them not only for the data they provided but also for the time so generously given. We are especially grateful to H.J. Heinz Company and Westinghouse Electric Corporation for agreeing to participate as detailed case studies.

At H.J. Heinz Company, we would like to thank Dr. Frank Adamson and Mary Ann Bell from World Headquarters; Dick Wamhoff from the Star-Kist Seafood Company; and Jim Kurt from Heinz Pet Products. At Westinghouse Electric Corporation, we would like to thank Carl Arendt, Nate Moore, and Alan Cooper from the Westinghouse Productivity and Quality Center, and Moti Khemlani from the Power Generation Business Unit.

We are especially indebted to Professor Lawrence P. Carr from Babson College for his assistance in preparing the Xerox United States Customer Operations case study.

We also would like to thank the Division of Research at Harvard Business School and the Wharton School at the University of Pennsylvania for providing financial support that made portions of this study possible.

Finally, we would be remiss in not expressing our appreciation and thanks to individuals who contributed to our efforts over the last four years: Bill Ainsworth from KPMG Peat Marwick, Atlanta; L. Douglass Piggott from L. D. Piggott and Associates, Atlanta; David Allen from Buccino & Associates, Inc., Chicago; Dennis Simon from Price Waterhouse, Century City, California; David Hunter from AMS, Inc., Norwell, Massachusetts; and Michael Schuster from The Center for Professional Development, Scottsdale, Arizona.

Part I

**The Enterprise-Wide Approach
to Quality Management**

1 Evolution of the Traditional Quality Management Approach _____

Executive Summary

The interest and involvement of top management in the quality process have grown significantly as companies have realized that the impact of poor quality is lost profitability and competitiveness. Presidents and chief executive officers (CEOs) have begun to view quality as a competitive tool and have attempted to integrate quality into the business strategy. Top managers are now focusing on quality improvement as a means to build a sustainable competitive advantage and improve financial performance through lower costs, improved productivity, and increased profitability.

This top management focus creates an entirely new and different set of demands and requirements for quality processes. Top management is pressing participants in the quality process to contribute to the achievement of broader business goals. Quality initiatives, on the other hand, continue to emphasize results such as conformance to requirements, the number of teams deployed, or the number of suggestions received from employees or quality circles without linking the achievement of these goals to the overall requirements of the business.

For many companies, it is only a matter of time before the priorities and objectives of the quality process became disconnected from those of the business. Reports in the business press now chronicle the failure of many quality processes to deliver meaning-ful results. The leading cause of these failures is the weak and unclear connection between the strategic objectives set by top man-agement and the results emphasized by the quality process. The failure of quality processes is the inability to deliver results that are meaningful to top managers who are searching for ways to improve profitability and increase customer satisfaction.

The inability to bridge effectively from the strategic vision of the business to the quality plan almost guarantees that the results of quality improvement efforts will be of little value to top management, shareholders, or investors. As Garvin points out, "Many companies have unknowingly fallen short here: they provide training in the tools of quality control but have failed to emphasize quality's connection with basic business objectives. The resulting processes have been long on technique but lacking in motivation and purpose."[1]

In sharp contrast to the failure of many companies are the stun-ning competitive successes of industry and market leaders—world-class companies—that credit their quality improvement process as a source of success. These companies have taken a different approach to managing their quality process by blending the strate-gic requirements of top management with the more traditional per-spectives of quality control. A common element within many of the successful companies is the use of more powerful cost of poor qual-ity concepts in the selection and management of improvement pro-jects that simultaneously improve financial performance and customer satisfaction.

EVOLUTION OF THE TRADITIONAL QUALITY MANAGEMENT APPROACH

More than a decade ago the Japanese introduced a competitive strat-egy that combined competition based on price from the 1960s with competition based on higher quality from the 1970s. Long-standing truths about the tradeoffs between quality, cost, productivity, reliabil-ity, and flexibility were shattered when the Japanese accomplished the impossible—producing higher quality products at a lower cost.[2]

By offering customers higher quality and lower cost products, the Japanese added a new dimension to the concept of quality and changed customers' perceptions of superior quality from defect free to superior value. The perception of superior quality as superior value allowed the Japanese to achieve a significant competitive advantage in the world marketplace. The shortfall in perceived value between Japanese products and all others represented a value gap that grew steadily throughout the 1980s.

Higher Quality Gives Way to Superior Value

Consumers initially learned of this value gap through products like automobiles, cameras, and consumer electronics. After more than a decade of experience with a broad range of products that offered superior value, customers and buyers now routinely expect greater value in the products they buy.[3] The products winning in the marketplace today are winning on the basis of providing higher quality at a lower price or cost.

Companies face a difficult challenge competing in a marketplace where quality is judged in relation to price. In a world where customers can now demand and get products and services that provide both higher quality and lower costs, surviving will require companies to adapt their strategies and priorities to meet this new challenge. Success will require companies to align the priorities and objectives of the quality process with the priorities and objectives of the business to compete on the basis of superior value. The most difficult aspect of this alignment is shifting the focus of the quality process from its traditional emphasis on merely delivering higher conformance to requirements to delivering both higher conformance *and* lower costs.

The traditional quality strategy of conformance to requirements is no longer an adequate competitive strategy in today's value-driven marketplace because it emphasizes tools, techniques, and processes over observable results such as lower costs and increased profits.[4] Detached from the results-oriented strategies and decision making of those responsible for running the business, the quality improvement vision is incomplete and cannot provide the competitive edge that companies seek.

Many quality programs are struggling to produce meaningful business results because they lack a management approach that is equal in scope and breadth to the challenge of today's business requirements. Without a strategy and logical framework that links quality improvement to the broader requirements of the business and upper management—lower costs, improved profitability, increased market share—most quality programs will continue to struggle and exist outside the mainstream of management decision making.

In order to close the value gap, businesses must overcome the barriers that arise when (1) higher quality is emphasized without explicitly linking the improvement initiative to the business strategy and (2) unstructured approaches are used to manage the quality process. This requires that businesses first challenge the quality process to improve financial performance as well as increase conformance. Companies need to adopt a more modern quality strategy that embraces the business vision and guides the quality process. The goals and objectives of the quality process must be directly aligned with the achievement of broader business goals and objectives.

Companies need to develop a structured management approach to implementing a quality process that is driven by the business vision. Day-to-day quality improvement priorities must reflect the needs of the business. Most quality processes lack the capability to identify and quantify the nonvalue-added activities and waste driven by poor quality, and are consequently unable to demonstrate logically the cause-and-effect relationships between quality and profitability, to select projects that improve financial performance as well as nonfinancial performance, or to judge the effectiveness of the quality process using the same financial indicators that businesses apply every day to measure return on investment.

Companies that are today's market and industry leaders recognized early on that success in a changing competitive world would require updated quality strategies and structured quality management practices. These market and industry leaders evolved beyond traditional quality strategies and implementation practices to develop an enterprise-wide approach that focuses quality efforts on the achievement of improved profitability and sustained competitive advantage. Their quality strategies and implementations emphasize the elimination of the nonvalue-added activities and waste driven by poor quality as the means to increase productivity, improve profitability, and increase customer satisfaction.

The Enterprise-Wide Approach to Quality Management

The enterprise-wide approach to quality management that we observed has two major thrusts.

1. Strategic quality planning. The requirements of the business are closely tied to the quality process. The interplay of four elements—the quality vision, improvement goals, competitive environment, and the quality strategy—guides the implementation priorities of the quality improvement process.
2. Quality-based cost management. Implementation of the quality process blends the tools and techniques of quality improvement with a focus on cost-effective elimination of nonvalue-added activities and waste caused by poor quality. By adding a financial dimension to the quality process, case study companies have developed an enhanced capability to improve financial performance.

Strategic quality planning demonstrates how, when, and why the quality process should be a part of an organization's overall competitive strategy, and is necessary for gaining the confidence and sustaining the commitment of upper management. Quality-based cost management—the use of quality tools and techniques to manage costs—serves as the structured framework to identify, select, and implement improvement projects that can provide the greatest financial return, allowing companies to increase customer satisfaction and profitability simultaneously.

Do You Really Have a Choice?

The perception of superior quality as superior value establishes the new "ground floor" for competing in today's marketplace. The short- and long-term implications of competing on the basis of superior value are clear: A business has to be *profitably* moving toward 100 percent quality.

For the company that is already involved in quality improvement, the enterprise-wide approach provides an opportunity to step back and ensure that the priorities, resources, and objectives of the quality process are aligned with the key issues of the business. Quality-based cost management offers companies with an established quality improvement process a proven methodology to identify and quantify the "vital few" opportunities for reducing and eliminating poor quality and its related costs. For the company just beginning the quality journey, quality-based cost management is a powerful tool to educate and demonstrate to top management the significant benefits from higher customer satisfaction, increased productivity, and improved financial performance that are available from investments in the quality process.

Linking quality to profits is accomplished by using poor quality costs as a focal point for coordinating and communicating the need for action and the setting of priorities. The updated poor quality cost applications developed by the case study companies provide the financial information required to select improvement projects on the basis of payback and return on investment.

For those responsible for managing the quality process, quality-based cost management allows them to "put their stake in the ground" by preparing a quality plan that is substantiated by poor quality cost reductions and worthy of being made a part of the overall strategy for the business.[5] The elimination of poor quality costs using quality-based cost management is a proven competitive strategy that is just now beginning to be widely understood and embraced.

Evolving Beyond the Traditional Approach to Quality Management

Articles in prominent business and quality publications describe the failure of many quality processes to produce meaningful results. A variety of industry surveys confirm that quality improvement processes are not delivering as expected. The articles and surveys call attention to the question of whether or not the results from quality improvement justify the investments. Unable to increase competitiveness from their investment in quality improvement, some companies now suggest that they may jettison quality improvement efforts in favor of other business alternatives.

The headline from a recent article in the Wall Street Journal sums up the problem for many companies: *Quality Programs Show Shoddy Results.*[6] The article describes the results of an American Quality Foundation survey of 584 companies in the United States, Canada, Germany, and Japan. The article goes on to say, "despite plenty of talk and much action, many American companies are stumbling in their implementation of quality-improvement efforts.... Many quality management plans are simply too amorphous to generate better products and services."

The study maintains that many quality implementations fail because quality efforts are diluted by addressing too wide a spectrum of quality problems. Companies read books, conduct numerous training programs, deploy teams, and implement a multitude of new practices all at the same time. Firms are trying to do too much too soon, and they are ending up with very modest results.

An article in the *Harvard Business Review* highlights the results from a 1991 survey of more than 300 companies conducted by the American Electronics Association.[7] Nearly two-thirds of the companies with quality processes reported that the quality initiatives had failed to reduce defects by even 10 percent.

The March 1990 issue of *Quality* describes circumstances where[8]

companies have trained tens of thousands of employees, launched numerous quality processes in location after location, and have been disappointed in the results.

Despite their best intentions, despite numerous success models, these companies have floundered. These companies have recognized the need for annual quality improvement at a revolutionary rate, but have not achieved what they set out to achieve. Why have they failed? What went wrong?

A different study of 30 quality processes by the consulting firm of McKinsey & Company found that nearly two-thirds had either stalled or fallen short of delivering real improvements. The study attributes the dismal results to the sheer size of many quality efforts. McKinsey & Company concludes that most quality processes require so much groundwork before results are realized that the quality processes are doomed to fail before they begin.

Surveys by other consulting organizations confirm the results of the McKinsey study. Rath & Strong released a survey detailing how companies graded their total quality management (TQM) processes in terms of their ability to improve market share, reduce costs, and satisfy customers. Most TQM processes rated only Ds and Fs. In a survey of 500 companies, the Boston consulting firm of Arthur D. Little came up with similar results—barely one-third of the companies credited their TQM processes with having "a significant impact" on improving competitiveness.[9]

The level of frustration and impatience is growing in companies that have invested in quality improvement to increase profits, improve customer satisfaction, and enhance competitiveness, but have little to show for their time, effort, and costs. Top management envisioned investments in quality that would complement the company's competitive strategy and build a sustainable advantage, thereby helping companies become more profitable and competitive. For the most part, however, the connection from quality improvement to the strategic and financial imperatives of top management has not been stressed by the consultants and experts brought in to assist in developing a quality process.

Schaffer and Thomson identify six major reasons why many quality efforts are doomed to fail.[10]

1. Not keyed to specific results. *Many improvement activities and initiatives focus on reforms in management-employee relationships, worker training, new measure-*

ment schemes, and increased employee awareness of customer attitudes, with the expectation that these steps will inevitably lead to better business performance. However, senior managers rarely make explicit how these activities lead to improved bottom-line results. Because management never specifies which performance parameters it wants to improve—that is, cost, defect rates, margins, sales, on-time delivery—there is no way to determine whether there is any link between the improvement activities and specific measurable results.

2. Too large scale and diffused. *Most companies choose to involve the organization in a hodgepodge of small improvement activities. With so many local projects proceeding concurrently, management is unable to determine which, if any, of the initiatives are delivering meaningful results to the organization as a whole.*

3. Results is a four-letter word. *The failure of quality processes to produce tangible improvements in financial or operational performance is frequently rationalized by stating that the gains from quality improvement can only be realized in the long term. Managers attempting to establish direct links between the investment in quality and improved financial or operational results find themselves subject to the criticism that they are sacrificing the company's long-term viability for short-term results.*

4. Delusional measurements. *Financial and operational performance measures linking the quality process to business goals and critical success factors are rejected in favor of performance measures that have little or no connection with the organization's goals or objectives. Nonfinancial measures such as the number of people trained, the number of teams deployed, and absentee rates are substituted for performance measures linked to business objectives such as higher profitability, lower costs, increased sales, or improved cash flow. The crucial fact these companies miss is that nonfinancial measures of quality process implementation do not necessarily translate into improved financial or operational performance.*

5. Staff and consultant driven. *Quality processes designed by staff personnel or consultants rather than operational personnel tend to concentrate on a variety of generic activities that add little to operational improvements. Past studies have shown that organizational change programs that have been implemented or managed by staff personnel are generally ineffective; quality improvement efforts are no exception.*[11]

6. Bias to orthodoxy, not empiricism. *Relying on faith rather than evidence, quality process proponents—convinced that they have the "cure" for the company's ills—urge participants to follow the "right" steps without attempting to find out if*

these steps actually yield results. Because no attempt is made to evaluate what did or did not work, it is difficult for companies to develop an understanding of the true cause-and-effect relationships between improvement activities and financial or operational results. With no empirically tested cause-and-effect framework in place, quality process participants have little opportunity to learn useful lessons that can be applied on a wider scale.

Most of the surveys and studies suggest remedies for struggling quality processes. The antidote prescribed by the *Quality* magazine article is to implement a strategic quality plan based on four critical elements: leadership, structure, technology, and customer focus. The essence of the solution is top management's role in strategic quality planning and the need for these executives to establish the structure necessary to make quality happen throughout the company, set realistic but challenging goals, provide visible leadership, select meaningful improvement projects that can make a competitive difference, and provide the incentive for action and other types of support to make the improvements permanent.[12]

The American Quality Foundation's survey of 584 companies concludes that companies should "target their quality efforts more tightly." The *Wall Street Journal* article entitled "Quality Programs Produce Shoddy Results" cites Johnson & Johnson as an example of a company that has been successful by narrowing the focus of its quality process and establishing more explicit quality goals: increasing customer satisfaction, reducing the time required for product introduction, and cutting costs. The quality emphasis at Johnson & Johnson has shifted to "do[ing] fewer things better."

The view that quality processes are struggling has also been put forth by a number of notable business scholars. They provide additional insights into the reasons that quality processes have faltered. In general, the research by business scholars arrives at the same conclusion: *Many quality processes do not deliver meaningful results, and the fundamental failure is an unfocused implementation approach that fails to reflect the strategic requirements of the business.*

The Appearance of Strategic Quality Management

Over the past century, the quality process has evolved in response to changes in the competitive environment, technology, communications, manufacturing and management philosophies, and customer expectations, to name just a few. Quality initiatives have gone through three phases and are now entering a fourth phase, with each phase possessing distinct characteristics. The first phase, beginning at the turn of the century and lasting into the 1930s, was characterized by detection of defects as its primary concern. The second phase lasted into the mid-1950s and was characterized by a shift in focus from detection to control, as evidenced by the development of statistical tools and techniques. The third phase is characterized by a primary concern with reaching higher levels of quality assurance. This phase emphasizes quality across the entire organization and concentrates on building quality into products.

Garvin refers to the integration of the quality process into the strategic requirements of the business as the fourth phase of the quality movement. In contrast to earlier stages, the distinguishing characteristic of this phase is the emphasis on developing the strategic elements of the quality process and linking quality to competitive market advantage.[13] Blending the tools and techniques of quality assurance and control with the strategic requirements of top management, however, has proven to be a more difficult task than companies anticipated. Garvin describes this complication.[14]

> *Strategic quality management, then, is more an extension of its predecessors than a denial of them. . . . The strategic approach to quality is more comprehensive than its predecessors, more closely linked to profitability and basic business objectives, more sensitivity to competitive needs and the consumer's point of view, and more firmly tied to continuous improvement. Many companies mistakenly think that they have adopted the new [strategic] approach when their processes merely include elements of quality assurance and quality control. For the most part, these companies are still thinking defensively about quality. They have yet to see its competitive potential.*

A closer look at the criticisms launched against many quality programs supports Garvin's observation that quality processes fail to satisfy strategic requirements.

Organization	Predominant Failure Cited
Rath & Strong	Failed to increase market share, manage costs, and satisfy customers
Arthur D. Little	Failed to increase competitiveness
American Quality Foundation	Failed to achieve results and business objectives
American Electronics Association	Failed to reduce defects by 10 percent
Quality magazine	Failed to achieve what they set out to achieve
McKinsey & Company	Stalled or fallen short of delivering real improvements

One of the primary reasons for these failures is that approaches to quality management are not designed to meet the strategic demands of top management but, instead, concentrate on the more limited aspects of quality assurance and control. Most quality processes lack a mechanism to link day-to-day quality activities with the achievement of business goals and objectives, thereby causing the priorities of the business and the quality process to be uncoordinated. Without such a linking mechanism, it is impossible to specify how and when most quality processes will contribute to the accomplishment of broader business goals and objectives.

Quality Management and Measuring the Cost of Poor Quality

Cost of quality is the tool that many have called the missing link between the quality process and strategic results, particularly the financial goals and objectives of the firm. The cost of quality, or more accurately the cost of poor quality, is described by Juran as "the sum of all costs that would disappear if there were no quality problems."[15]

In order to maintain a sharp focus on the objective of improving financial performance, as well as to remain consistent with the views of other experts such as H. James Harrington and Frank M. Gryna, the remainder of this book uses the term cost of poor quality in place of quality costs or the cost of quality.[16] Use of the cost of poor quality terminology speaks directly to the real issue and challenge at hand: reducing and eliminating the nonvalue-added costs and waste associated with poor quality. The cost of poor quality comprises the following four categories.

1. *Prevention costs.* The sum of all costs associated with the activities designed to prevent defects through the identification and elimination of the causes of failure. By preventing the defective component, service, or transaction from occurring or recurring, the additional processing and handling costs associated with appraisal or failure are not incurred. Examples of prevention costs include quality process implementation and maintenance, quality-related training, quality planning, and root-cause analysis to eliminate the sources of defects and failures.

2. *Appraisal costs.* The sum of all costs associated with activities to measure, evaluate, or audit products, processes, or services to ensure conformance to either internal or external customer requirements. Appraising the production and service delivery processes allows a company to adjust the processes if they are not in a stable and predictable state. Examples of appraisal costs include the cost of tests or evaluations to determine and ensure the acceptability of a product or service; cost of testing the timeliness, accuracy, and responsiveness of a customer delivery system; and cost of evaluation activities to determine the performance of personnel in relation to expected performance such as pre-established standards and requirements.

3. *Internal failure costs.* The sum of all costs incurred prior to shipment due to the failure of a product or service to meet customer requirements. Internal failure costs include the cost of all activities or processes required to evaluate, dispose of, and correct or replace defective or deficient products or services prior to delivery to the internal or external customer. Examples of internal failure costs include scrap, rework, corrective actions and downtime due to failure, and costs needed to complete or correct a service deficiency.

4. *External failure costs.* The sum of all quality-related costs incurred after a product or service failure is shipped or delivered to the customer. Product-related examples of external failure costs include postproduct release engineering changes and tool improvements, warranty claims, returned goods, liability insurance and claims, penalties, and lost sales. Service-related examples include the cost of replacing or correcting a service failure, complaint investigation, lost sales due to a damaged reputation, and cost of price discounts due to quality problems.

The use of the cost of poor quality as a quality measurement tool was introduced by Juran in 1952 in his *Quality Control Handbook,* in which he presented the analogy that poor quality and its related costs are "gold in the mine."[17] For the past 40 years, Juran has emphasized the quantification of quality costs as a means to sensitize senior management about the profit potential of quality improvement. Juran contends that quality managers should assess the cost of poor quality to determine the potential of a quality control system, and then use subsequent cost of poor quality assessments to measure the progress achieved by the improvement process.

Feigenbaum broadened Juran's view on the use of poor quality costs in a 1957 article that highlighted how investments in prevention costs can reduce the costs associated with both appraisal and failure.[18] In the same year, an article published by Masser focused on the role of quality cost measurement, with an emphasis on five major uses.[19]

1. *As a measure of overall business quality performance*
2. *As an analytical tool to indicate where quality dollars are being spent*
3. *As a method to determine the "when, where, and how of quality improvement"*
4. *As a budgetary tool for forecasting realistic needs for quality improvement*
5. *As a means to determine the quality level that would provide "optimum benefit to the business and to the customer"*

Like Juran, the early work of both Feigenbaum and Masser stressed the value of cost of poor quality measurement and reporting to gain and maintain top management's interest in quality improvement.

By 1963, the Department of Defense had issued the military standard entitled *Quality Program Requirements*, creating widespread interest in quality costs as a management approach within the defense industry. The Air Force Systems Command subsequently developed the Quality Improvement Through Cost Optimization (QUICO) system in 1964 and published the *Quality Cost Analysis Implementation Handbook*. These publications were based on an extensive research program that was funded by the government and conducted by Stanford University.

The work by Stanford University provided the foundation for later publications that included *A Guide to Quality Cost Analysis* by the Office of the Assistant Secretary of Defense for Installations and Logistics and *Quality Costs—What and How* by the American Society for Quality Control (ASQC). These pioneering publications provide the traditional framework for managing quality improvement processes using quality cost systems.

Updating the Cost-of-Poor-Quality Approach

While cost-of-poor-quality measurement has proven to be a useful tool for focusing management attention on the profit impact of poor quality, its ongoing role in the strategic quality initiatives of the 1990s has been questioned.[20] Professors Plunkett and Dale, for example, reviewed the existing literature on cost-of-poor-quality measurement and concluded that the concept developed in the mid-1960s fails to reflect the philosophical changes that have occurred in the transition from quality control and assurance to strategic quality management.[21]

Similarly, John Hagan, director-quality measurement at ITT Corporation, noted that less than 15 percent of the opportunities for applying poor quality cost techniques in manufacturing companies are pursued in a profitable manner.[22] Hagan added that the time is ripe to learn from experience to develop new methods that allow the full potential of cost-of-poor-quality systems to be achieved.

In response to questions about the role of cost-of-poor-quality measurement in today's strategic quality management initiatives, we visited more than 30 companies that have used cost-of-poor-quality systems to help manage their quality processes, including recognized quality leaders such as Xerox, Westinghouse, Texas Instruments, H. J. Heinz, and Hewlett-Packard. Interviews were conducted with over 150 corporate and plant representatives from accounting, quality, operations, and engineering to better understand the strengths and weaknesses of cost of poor quality programs.

Our study found that traditional cost-of-poor-quality systems serve as useful tools during the early stages of a quality process to highlight the importance of quality improvement to bottom-line performance. As the quality processes matures, however, many companies abandon or de-emphasize poor quality cost measurement. The interviews uncovered a number of shortfalls to explain why the traditional cost-of-poor-quality concept has not provided more useful support for quality improvement processes.

1. *Cost-of-poor-quality programs have not kept pace with the strategic management requirements or initiatives of the 1990s.* The period since the late 1960s has been one of rapid changes in technology, dramatic shifts in economic power and concentration, alterations of competitive strategies based on world-class competencies, and unprecedented increases in the expectations of customers

with regard to quality and price. Cost-of-poor-quality processes, on the other hand, have continued to focus on reductions in scrap and rework. As a result, many companies have replaced the cost of poor quality and other financial performance measures with nonfinancial measures of quality that are more closely related to the strategic quality imperatives of today's quality processes.

Nonfinancial measures such as defect reductions, customer satisfaction indices, and the number of improvement teams are often used to assess performance in important aspects of the quality process. Many companies have assumed that improvement in these same nonfinancial measures will automatically translate into better financial performance, often with little proof. The use of nonfinancial performance measures as proxies for financial performance measures has created a dilemma for many companies: They cannot explicitly link improvements in nonfinancial measures to the bottom line. The reliance on nonfinancial quality measures leaves a number of strategic questions open, such as the following:

- How does the quality process contribute directly to the achievement of financially oriented business goals and objectives?
- How can the priorities of the quality process be more closely aligned with business priorities?
- How can a quality improvement process be monitored and measured to evaluate the gains and benefits produced?
- How can the cost effectiveness of potential projects be accurately determined and used to set improvement priorities?
- How does higher quality generate increased productivity? How can that process be better managed for greater competitiveness?
- How is increased productivity related to improved profitability? How can that relationship be better managed for greater competitiveness?
- How can the financial effects of cross-functional problem solving be more effectively identified, prioritized, and communicated?

- How can the activities of cross-functional improvement teams be more efficiently coordinated, monitored, and measured?
- How should improvement priorities balance the requirements of the voice of the customer and the voice of the business?
- How do managers distinguish between the vital few and the useful many?
- How can a company establish a logical cause-and-effect relationship among quality, productivity, profitability, and competitiveness?

Unable to align the objectives and priorities of the quality process with the objectives and priorities of the business, many quality processes have failed to deliver improved financial performance. Because so many companies lack an effective approach that focuses quality improvement on producing meaningful financial results, a general consensus is beginning to build that the total quality movement may be floundering.

2. *White-collar costs are omitted by most cost-of-poor-quality systems.* Companies rarely conduct cost-of-poor-quality assessments for the white-collar, service, and support areas of the company, thereby overlooking significant improvement opportunities. Critics of cost-of-poor-quality systems charge the total cost of poor quality is so grossly underestimated that managers are led into making improper, suboptimal, and potentially harmful decisions.[23]

A number of prominent quality experts maintain that the inability of quality cost systems to capture white-collar and indirect quality costs is a fatal shortcoming. Deming, for instance, argues that quality cost systems typically focus on direct effects of poor quality such as scrap, rework, and warranty claims while ignoring significant indirect effects such as disruptions in operations due to out-of-conformance purchases and production, excessive inventory levels held to accommodate poor quality, quality-related schedule changes and downtime, and the opportunity costs of lost consumer goodwill.[24]

Studies estimate that the cost of poor quality for white-collar areas of the business can be as high as 50 percent of the areas' total budgets, yet most companies have little or no capability to track white-collar quality costs.[25] By ignoring the impact of poor quality and its costs on the white-collar functions, companies have severely limited their ability to assess accurately the true cost of poor quality, identify the causes of poor quality, communicate the need for quality improvement to functions and departments outside of manufacturing, or coordinate problem-solving efforts that involve the white-collar areas of the organization.

Given most firms' inability to reasonably estimate the impact of poor quality, it is not surprising that companies consistently underestimate the benefits from quality improvement.[26] Studies indicate that the cost of poor quality in indirect and white-collar areas, which are typically hidden from the view of top management, can exceed the commonly reported direct costs by 300 percent to 500 percent. A survey of companies by the Illinois Manufacturers' Association illustrates the differences between the direct costs of poor quality that are reported by most firms and the actual costs of poor quality, which include the impact of poor quality on white-collar and indirect functions.[27] The survey provided definitions and examples of major categories of poor quality costs. Each company was then asked to estimate the total dollar value associated with the major cost categories, as well as to provide other financial data such as sales and cost of goods sold.

A comparison of the initial survey responses and subsequent in-depth research shows a significant margin of error between the estimated and actual costs of poor quality.

Initial Survey Results	Follow-up Research Results	Margin of Error
6%	25%	400%

Detailed cost-of-poor-quality assessments conducted as a part of the follow-up research found that the actual cost of poor quality for a typical Illinois manufacturer is much closer to 25 percent of sales, rather than the 6 percent of sales reported in the survey, indicating that more than 75 percent of the total cost of poor quality is "hidden" from view. Further research showed that substantially all of the "hidden" costs related directly to failure costs in white-collar areas.[28]

One reaction of management to the costs reported by most cost-of-poor-quality systems is to assume there is no real problem when, in fact, the opposite is true. In a poll commissioned by ASQC, more than 70 percent of the executives responding believed that the cost of poor quality in their companies was less than 10 percent. Twenty-seven percent admitted they had no idea what the cost of poor quality was. David Kearns, chairman of Xerox at the time the survey was conducted, commented, "The survey shows that many people still do not understand the connection between cost and quality. You will not change the culture with that kind of data or those kinds of perceptions."[29]

Examples of the hidden costs of poor quality include

- The costs of poor quality in supplier organizations that are passed on to the buyer in the form of higher prices because of the supplier's poor quality; costs incurred by the customer to solve problems caused by defective or nonconforming products or services; and the loss of sales and reputation from a product failure due to a faulty purchased part.
- The cost of errors and nonvalue-added and redundant activities in service and support departments and functions such as sales, marketing, purchasing, accounting, advertising, logistics, data processing, production control, and engineering. Poor quality products and services provided by internal suppliers to internal customers create the same negative impact on costs and performance as poor quality products and services provided by the external suppliers.
- Excess allowances for material, labor, and expenses that are built into a company's standards and operating procedures. Examples include allowances for scrap, acceptable levels of customer returns, annual inventory write-downs, and accounts receivable write-offs.

A number of common reasons have led to a significant proportion of poor quality costs remaining hidden.

- Companies have had difficulty measuring poor quality costs that are not routinely reported by financial or manufacturing systems. Existing accounts typically capture less than 20 percent of the total costs of poor quality, leaving the company unaware of the true magnitude of nonvalue-added activities and waste driven by poor quality.
- Many of the hidden poor quality costs are institutionalized and are considered acceptable even though the costs are a result of poor quality practices. This is especially common as organizations adopt standards or allowances that exclude these costs from efficiency measurements, thereby signaling management's acceptance of these poor quality costs as a routine cost of doing business.
- Most companies lack the budgetary and financial controls to provide management information once a cost crosses a departmental or functional boundary.

> This is all too natural a phenomenon in organizations that are never fully charged with all the inefficiencies—because some of the inefficiencies are hidden and not measured—and thus are able to maintain an illusion of effective management. In this kind of an [organization], departments that cause inefficiencies in areas besides their own frequently get off scot-free because the problems they create, and their responsibility for them, are never properly identified.[30]

3. *Lost sales opportunities due to poor quality are omitted from reported poor quality costs.* Few companies attempt to measure or estimate the impact of poor quality on current or future sales. Studies sponsored by the U.S. Department of Commerce, however, indicate that the opportunity costs of defects and failures that reach the customer may greatly exceed the poor quality costs reported by most systems.

Consumer surveys have found the expected repurchase rate for a consumer facing a quality problem with an expected financial loss of $1 to $5 is 71 percent if the complaint is satisfactorily resolved. When the estimated financial loss is $100 or more, the expected repurchase rates falls to 54 percent if the complaint is satisfactorily resolved or to 19 percent if the complaint is not satisfactorily resolved. Moreover, while satisfied customers tell an average of 5 others about their experience with the product, dissatisfied customers tell 19 others.[31] The resulting loss of sales can be enormous.

Instead of attempting to measure the opportunity costs of lost sales, many companies rely on nonfinancial measures such as returns and customer complaints to gauge the impact of poor quality on revenues. Unfortunately, these measures provide no indication of the financial magnitude of lost sales due to various quality problems. For example, small visual defects such as scratches may cause a customer to return a product but may not discourage the person from purchasing the product again in the future. Infrequent functional failures that cause a customer great inconvenience, on the other hand, may cost a company not only that customer in the future but also others who learned of the original consumer's dissatisfaction with the product. Consequently, by prioritizing improvement opportunities based on nonfinancial measures, many companies are unable to distinguish problems with the greatest frequency of complaints from those causing the greatest financial loss.

4. *Reported poor-quality costs are frequently inadequate for problem solving and management decision making.* Several substantial limitations were observed in the use of reported poor-quality costs for problem solving and management decision making: (1) cost-of-poor-quality reporting periods are too long to provide meaningful feedback to identify and eliminate the sources of problems; (2) the cost-of-poor-quality reports aggregate data at too high a level, making it difficult for managers to identify problems at lower levels in the

organization; and (3) reporting focuses on total poor-quality numbers rather than focusing attention on the root causes of poor quality, and consequently provides little direct support for quality improvement.

In most cases, these three limitations are related more to implementation issues than to deficiencies in the cost-of-poor-quality concept itself. For example, some companies introduce cost-of-poor-quality reporting based on the advice of consultants or textbooks without first developing a clear idea of what role the information is supposed to play in the quality improvement process or in meeting the company's strategic objectives. The resulting generic systems are frequently ill suited to meet the organization's requirements.

Other companies assume that the publication of cost-of-poor-quality costs alone will motivate improved quality. With no structured process or organizational mechanism in place for identifying and eliminating the root causes of problems, the anticipated cost reductions never appear, with the blame typically placed on the inability of the cost of poor quality reports to identify the sources of defects.

Finally, many companies have not integrated cost-of-poor-quality measurement with the other quality measurements and problem-solving tools used within the organization. As a stand-alone system, decoupled from management decision making and the quality improvement process, cost-of-poor-quality measurement suffers from the many shortcomings identified previously.

5. *Reported poor-quality costs are a poor performance measure.* Two potential shortcomings in the use of reported poor-quality costs for performance measurement were identified. First, most companies estimate at least some poor-quality cost elements. For example, a company may calculate engineering department failure costs using estimates by engineering managers of the amount of time their employees spend responding to quality problems. Though these estimates may be adequate to identify quality improvement opportunities, the measurements' use in performance

evaluation are subject to challenge on the grounds that the estimates lack credibility. This perceived lack of credibility can make poor-quality costs unsuitable as performance measures and, in some situations, jeopardize the credibility of the entire cost-of-poor-quality effort.

A second problem arises when companies attempt to control poor-quality costs using budgets or targets without first linking the financial goals to specific quality improvements targets. In these environments, people tend to view poor-quality-cost measurement as a cost reduction effort rather than a quality improvement mechanism. Consequently, poor-quality-cost reduction efforts often focus on projects that lower costs without improving the quality of the product, service, or process. For example, one company issued a corporate mandate to reduce poor-quality costs to a specified level. In response, a manufacturing plant consolidated numerous small rework areas into a larger, more efficient rework department. The consolidation lowered internal failure costs by reducing the cost per item repaired, but it had no impact on the underlying causes of rework or the quality of the products shipped to the customer—the ultimate objectives of this company's quality initiative.

Characteristics of Successful Cost-of-Poor-Quality Initiatives

Companies that successfully use cost-of-poor-quality measurement as a management tool have done so by modifying their applications to address the limitations of the conventional approach. These organizations have broadened the cost-of-poor-quality concept to meet the more strategic requirements of top management in four major areas: (1) inclusion of estimates for white-collar areas, indirect effects, and lost sales opportunities; (2) estimation of the financial payback from improvement projects using cost driver analyses to isolate the financial impact of root causes of poor quality; (3) implementation of procedures to provide for timely and accurate monitoring and measurement of progress; and (4) presentation to top management of financial and nonfinancial results from the investment in the quality process.

The following paragraphs summarize common elements that companies are using to overcome the limitations associated with quality management and cost-of-poor-quality approaches.

1. *Integration with the strategic management requirements and initiatives of the 1990s.* Successful companies recognize that achieving business objectives is a fundamental priority of the quality process. The reason is simple: Competitors are setting and then resetting customers' expectations and perceptions of superior quality. With customers defining superior quality in terms of superior value, successful companies look to their quality initiatives for assistance in achieving competitive success.

By modifying the criteria used for selecting quality improvement projects, the updated cost of poor quality approaches directly address customer requirements for superior value. As priorities shift toward selecting projects on the basis of improving both customer satisfaction *and* financial performance, companies move rapidly away from many well-intentioned but relatively unimportant projects to a few carefully selected, well-managed projects that can make a genuine difference in the competitiveness of the business.

Responsibility for project selection is elevated to higher levels within many businesses as the strategic importance of quality improvement grows. Project selection is recognized as the crucial link between strategic and financial initiatives and the quality process. As a consequence, senior management is actively involved in selecting and supporting projects that make a competitive difference.

The updated selection process requires that quality projects be evaluated and nominated on the basis of lowering costs, improving cash flow, or increasing profits. The cost of poor quality becomes the bridge between the financial requirements of top management and the selection of improvement projects. With quality improvement projects being recognized as a valuable source of cash flow and profitability—as well as a method for increasing customer satisfaction—the stature and importance of the quality initiative increases dramatically.

The business worth of quality improvement becomes clear as quality initiatives focus on generating increases in productivity, profitability, and competitiveness. As a result, the quality planning and implementation process is elevated to the same level of importance as other business functions, with quality improvement serving as the cornerstone of the competitive strategy.

2. *Assessing the costs of poor quality.* As cost-of-poor-quality assessments are expanded to include indirect and white-collar costs, companies find that the true costs of poor quality often exceed 20 percent of sales. White-collar costs of poor quality often represent as much as 75 percent of the total cost of poor quality for the entire organization. With so much at stake, successful companies have developed innovative approaches to identify and eliminate white-collar and indirect poor-quality costs to improve profitability and competitiveness.

From the beginning of their quality processes, the companies participating in the study realized the significant potential for quality-related cost reductions in direct areas. But the cost-of-poor-quality assessments in indirect and white-collar areas created an awareness and sensitivity to the impact of poor quality that typically had not existed before. The assessments helped to demonstrate that the poor-quality costs observed in one part of the organization are often created in another part of the company. Educating *all* responsible managers about the impact of poor quality on the organization as a whole is a key ingredient in using the cost of poor quality as a mechanism to facilitate more open information flows and coordinate cross-functional problem solving. By assessing the level of indirect and white-collar poor-quality costs, top management begins to understand the total impact of poor quality on productivity and profitability.

The realization that poor quality costs have no regard for organization boundaries is fundamental to effective quality-based cost management. McDonnell Douglas Corporation is the manufacturer of the C-17 military cargo aircraft. In 1992, McDonnell Douglas Aircraft published continuing results from its efforts to eliminate rework and repair costs in final assembly for the C-17 military cargo plane program.[32] The first priority was to identify and quantify the cost of poor quality, and then conduct additional analyses to isolate the high payback improvement opportunities.

The company discovered that rework and repair costs in final assembly are actually driven by "upstream" problems in engineering, planning, and tool design. Using the cost of poor quality to guide the improvement process, focus shifted away from the direct labor areas to these indirect and white-collar areas of the company. Plans were developed to address the upstream drivers of poor quality costs, mobilize resources to solve the problems, and coordinate solutions on a multifunctional basis. The cost of poor quality was used to demonstrate the impact of indirect and white-collar problems on cost, schedule, and delivery performance and to set the stage for communicating and coordinating improvement activities on a multifunctional basis. As shown in Figure 1.1, McDonnell Douglas expects to achieve significant cost reductions by using its understanding of poor quality costs to focus the quality process on eliminating the high-payback root causes of poor quality.

3. *Estimating the lost sales opportunities due to poor quality.* Even in successful companies, the opportunity costs of lost sales are rarely estimated, although companies are increasingly attempting to quantify these potentially huge costs. The companies that do estimate lost sales due to poor quality are developing valuable information about customer perceptions of quality, the importance of specific features and functions, and the impact of certain product or service failures on revenues. Quantifying the lost sales attributable to the failure of a specific feature or function allows companies to prioritize their problem-solving activities and to concentrate on reducing failures with the greatest impact on revenues.

One case study company, a manufacturer of consumer goods, has developed a "lost sales model" to prioritize its quality improvement efforts. Lost sales are estimated based on three criteria.

From the test aircraft (T-1) to the eighth production aircraft (P-8), the cost of poor quality per aircraft has been reduced by 71 percent.

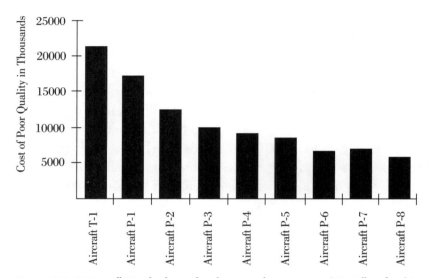

Figure 1.1 McDonnell Douglas has reduced poor-quality costs over $90 million for the C-17 transport aircraft.

1. Severity of the defect
2. Expected purchasing patterns of customers who experience a quality problem, as well as potential customers who observe the defect and choose not to buy the company's products
3. Expected purchasing patterns of customers who do not experience a quality problem

Using marketing research techniques, the company determines the level of severity that customers attach to each category of defect, and then the company rates the defects on a scale from minor to major. The probability that a customer will continue buying the company's products is assessed for each level of severity. For example, a minor cosmetic problem may drive few customers away, while a major defect that renders the product unusable may drive away the existing customer as well as potential customers who may hear of the problem.

Consumer surveys are used to estimate the average number of times a customer buys the company's products during a year. Based on the expected buying patterns of satisfied customers and the probability that dissatisfied customers will stop purchasing the product, an average level of "lost sales" per dissatisfied customer is established for each category of defect.

Defect Level Experienced	Average Annual Customer Purchases	Probability of Repurchase
High—product unusable	$100	25 percent
Medium—partially usable	$100	75 percent
Low—usable with cosmetic defect	$100	95 percent

Company experience indicates that not all consumers who experience a problem will use the warranty return program. Therefore, the number of actual warranty returns is multiplied by a factor to estimate the total number of customers who experience a defect.

Defect Level Experienced	Number of Claims Filed	Probability of Filing a Warranty Claim	Number of Customers Affected
High—product unusable	50	50 percent	100
Medium—partially usable	120	30 percent	400
Low—usable with cosmetic defect	100	20 percent	500

The estimated number of customers who experience a defect is then adjusted to account for potential customers who observe the defect and decide not to buy the company's products. For example, a customer who experiences a high-level defect typically will tell five others, one of whom will decide not to buy the product because of the observed defect.

Defect Level Experienced	Potential Customers Who Observe Each Defect	Probability of Lost Sales
High—product unusable	500	20 percent
Medium—partially usable	40	0 percent
Low—usable with cosmetic defect	10	0 percent

The total number of current and potential customers who observe the defect is then multiplied by the probability of repurchase to estimate the number of lost customers.

Defect Level Experienced	Affected Current Customers (A)	Potential Lost Customers (B)	Probability of Repurchase (C)	Total Lost Customers (A + B) (100% – C)
High	100	100	25 percent	150
Medium	400	0	75 percent	100
Low	500	0	95 percent	25

The number of lost customers per defect category times the average amount of lost sales for that category's defect severity level gives total estimated lost sales.

Defect Level Experienced	Average Annual Customer Purchases	Total Estimated Lost Customers	Total Estimated Lost Sales
High	$100	150	$15,000
Medium	$100	100	$10,000
Low	$100	25	$ 2,500

Prior to implementing the lost sales model, the company prioritized its improvement opportunities using the number of defects experienced in the field. When estimated lost sales were initially calculated for each defect category, the company found that some minor problems that occur quite frequently had relatively little impact on future sales. On the other hand, some major defects that occur less frequently have a significant impact on the probability that a customer will purchase the product again. As Figure 1.2 illustrates, the initial comparison of priorities using defect counts versus the estimated lost sales shows that category 2 defect are nearly as costly as category 1 defects, even though the number of category 2 defects in the field is 40 percent less than those in category 1. Category 3 defects rank third in frequency but only ninth in terms of estimated lost sales. Using this analysis of estimated lost sales, the company has shifted the priority of its improvement projects and internal inspections to emphasize the elimination of defects with the greatest impact on future sales.

Other examples of the impact of lost sales opportunities due to poor quality are provided in *Cost of Quality: A Guide to Application* written by the Xerox United States Customer Operations (formerly the United States Marketing Group) cost of quality team. The United States Customer Operations (USCO) approach to identifying and quantifying the cost of poor quality and lost sales opportunities is slightly different from the guidelines provided by ASQC and others.

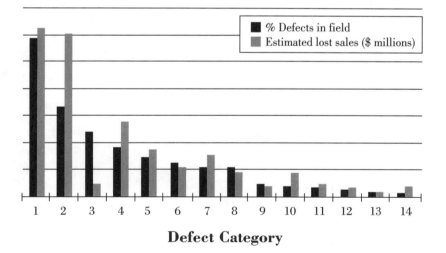

Figure 1.2 Setting improvement priorities on the basis of financial impact rather than frequency of occurrence.

In addition to the established quality cost categories of conformance (prevention and appraisal costs) and nonconformance (internal and external failure costs), USCO adds a third category, lost opportunities. The cost of lost opportunities is explained as follows:[33]

> *Lost opportunities are the profit impact of the lost revenues resulting from the purchase of competitive products and services or from cancellations of Xerox products and services because customer requirements were not met. Examples include cancellations because of inadequate service response at critical demand times, as well as the ordering of competitive products because the customer was sold equipment or services which are inadequate or unnecessary.*

The following lost sales examples, adapted from a hypothetical USCO district case study in the application guide, are used to educate USCO personnel and demonstrate the impact of poor quality and its related costs, and to help USCO improvement teams identify projects with the highest potential payback.

- Sales returns—3 percent sales returns times 3000 installation per district equals approximately 100 returns. Remanufacturing costs at $4000 plus the cost of sales representative time plus the lost profit to the district times a 50 percent lost opportunity assessment equals poor quality costs of nonconformance and lost sales opportunities from sales returns of $930,000.
- Invoice errors—administrative time plus 2 percent of lost revenue and gross profit from the sales equals poor quality costs of lost sales opportunities from invoice errors of $610,000.
- Turnover productivity—decreased sales revenue generation by lost productivity of new hires for two months times the average sales revenue generated per month by a sales representative times the turnovers per year times the profit margin equals poor quality costs of lost gross profits from sales person turnover of $500,000.

- Equipment constraints—lost revenue and profits due to equipment constraints, such as long lead times or long order-to-initial-install times, producing lost customer orders times the profit margin equals poor-quality costs of lost gross profits from equipment constraints of $420,000.

Companies that assess the impact of poor quality on revenues begin to develop broader insights into the cause-and-effect relationships among higher quality, increased sales, and improved profitability. On several occasions, these insights have provided the basis for senior management to reevaluate its investment priorities. This, in turn, has led to changes in policy that allow an increase in quality-related investments that would never have been considered under existing investment criteria. For example,[34]

under its low-cost operator programs, Heinz had cut the work force at its Star-Kist tuna canning factories in Puerto Rico and American Samoa by 5 percent. With tough competition coming in from low-wage rivals in Thailand, keeping a lid on labor costs seemed to make sense. But the fish cleaners were so overworked that they were leaving literally tons of meat on the bone every day. Says [J. Wray Connolly, the senior vice president] who heads the company's total quality management effort: "We discovered that we had to add people, not subtract them. In the past, we wouldn't have done that."

The Japanese subsidiary of a U.S. consumer products company follows a method for estimating lost sales that captures not only the cost elements contained in the USCO approach, but also an estimate of the effect of lost sales due to discontinued use. The costs of poor quality due to external defects are grouped according to the following categories.

- Cost of salesperson time for customer claims visits
- Cost of any additional customer compensation
- Cost of replacement refills
- Cost of replacement units

- Future lost sales impact for customers claiming to discontinue their use of the products

This reporting approach accounts for the costs of productivity losses—the salesperson time—as well as the opportunity costs arising from the loss of a customer. Coupled with product failure reports that are linked to the sources of lost sales, the subsidiary is able to build insights into the failures that are the most costly to the business.

4. *Integrating the cost of poor quality into the organization's management decision-making and problem-solving processes.* The firms in our study found that cost-of-poor-quality techniques cannot be used in isolation, but instead must be integrated with both the strategic objectives of the business and the other elements in the quality improvement process. Only by explicitly integrating cost of poor quality reporting into the broader operations and objectives of the business can the tool successfully support problem solving and management decision making.

Pacific Bell provides a useful example to illustrate how one company links the cost of poor quality to the organization's overall business objectives and quality process.[35] In the 1980s, Pacific Bell management realized that the company needed to change the way it did business if it was to succeed in the newly deregulated and increasingly competitive telecommunications market. The company responded by placing increased emphasis on customer satisfaction and improved productivity. As stated in Pacific Bell's business plan, "Earning our customers' business means all employees are looking at everything they do with the question, 'How can I do this to add value or reduce costs?'"

The total quality initiative provides the framework for achieving the company's vision of being the customer's choice by offering higher value and lower cost products and services than the competition. To achieve this vision, a set of challenging "bold goals" has been established to provide clear priorities to everyone in the company. These targets focus on critical areas that provide the opportunity for dramatic gains in both customer satisfaction and corporate growth. By 1995 Pacific Bell intends to

- Increase customer satisfaction to at least 95 percent excellent or good ratings, as measured by its telephone and mail surveys.
- Reduce customer appeals to the California Public Utilities Commission, Federal Communications Commission, and executive management by 60 percent.
- Reduce customer trouble reports by 30 percent.
- Reduce service order defects by 50 percent.
- Increase employee satisfaction to at least 80 percent, as measured by Pacific Bell's job fulfillment assessment.
- Increase selected product revenue and network usage significantly.

By identifying the improvement opportunities that offer the greatest leverage and profitability potential, cost-of-poor-quality analysis serves as a planning tool to link the bold goals with the organization's quality improvement activities. Consider, for example, the company's use of cost of poor quality information in addressing the service order defects bold goal. A service order is a document or system record to register and transmit a customer's request to establish, rearrange, or discontinue a Pacific Bell product or service. A failure is defined as any service order entry, omission, or distribution failure that falls short of customer expectations, that results in unnecessary manual intervention in system processes, or that fails to establish accurate postcompletion records.

In analyzing prior service order improvement efforts, the quality improvement team working on the bold goal identified four obstacles that tended to limit success.

1. Efforts did not identify, include, or completely account for organizational root-cause issues and relationships.

2. Action plans tended to be fragmented and functional in nature, and were not targeted at systematic issues that cut across the entire service order process.
3. A quality improvement process was not put in place to ensure accountability, follow-up, and continuous process improvement.
4. Measurements that were established reflected only a fraction of the total failures and tended to drive functional conflicts and inappropriate behavior.

Given these potential obstacles, the service order improvement team concluded that several elements were critical to the initiative's success. First, a formal quality improvement process following W. Edwards Deming's plan-do-check-act (PDCA) cycle needed to be developed and utilized. Without the organizational mechanisms in place to prioritize improvement opportunities, identify root causes, and implement changes, the service order initiative would again falter.

Second, process data and cost-of-poor-quality metrics would be critical for making decisions on the key "leverage points" to address. The goal was to identify those opportunities that provided the best return on investment in terms of lower failure costs and improved customer satisfaction. Process and cost-of-poor-quality data would provide the means to identify defects in the system and to quantify their relative impact, allowing the team to focus on the "vital few" problems that accounted for the greatest loss in customer satisfaction and productivity.

Third, a "collaborate and integrate" approach was needed to identify, influence, and incorporate other company initiatives. The team members did not want the quality improvement process to be seen as another program distinct from the company's other initiatives such as business process reengineering. Instead, each of the initiatives needed to be coordinated and integrated to leverage the company's improvement efforts.

Finally, the team realized that rushing to develop performance measures before understanding the processes would be fatal. Team members believed that quick fix quality improvements initiatives that ignored real process improvements would eventually lead to an organizational "death spiral" shown in Figure 1.3. In contrast to "quick fix" cost cutting or downsizing, long-term improvements in customer satisfaction and profitability required a complete reevaluation of the way business is performed. The resulting action plan for the service order bold goal consisted of six steps.

1. Identifying customers of the product or service, assessing their requirements, estimating which quality requirements were not being met, and translating customer requirements into detailed descriptions of the product or service.
2. Assessing current work processes by flow charting existing processes, identifying current measurements at points of failure, and identifying opportunities with a high degree of perceived financial or customer impact. This was accomplished through the identification of process activities that did not directly contribute to the deliverable product or service. Process-oriented cost-of-poor-quality assessments were used to quantify the cross-functional costs arising from these nonvalue-added activities.
3. Determining the root causes of high-impact improvement projects.
4. Implementing a project team structure to drive root-cause elimination, focus improvement efforts, and support and distribute best practices.
5. Establishing business unit process coordinators to facilitate, integrate and drive local projects, and to leverage corporate efforts.
6. Establishing performance measures to assess the improvement efforts. These measures reflected root-cause issues and were primarily nonfinancial in nature. The cost of poor quality was reestimated periodically to provide an overall scorecard of quality progress.

Figure 1.4 summarizes the role of the cost of poor quality analysis in the service order bold goal's TQM effort. The service order

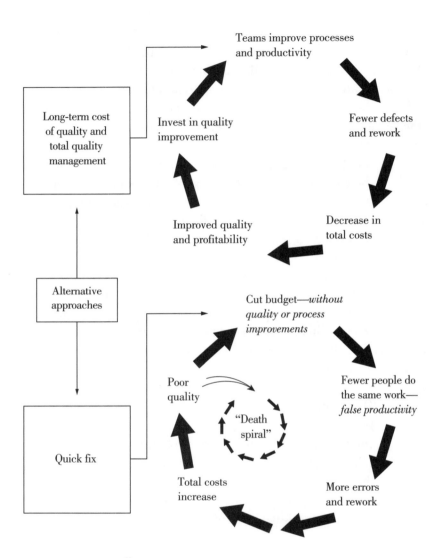

The Pacific Bell Cost-of-Quality Handbook, © 1992.

Figure 1.3 Cost of poor quality: long-term improvement perspective versus the vicious circle of "quick fix" cost cutting.

improvement initiative clearly illustrates a number of elements that were found in companies that successfully use cost of poor quality for management decision making and problem solving: (1) the technique was explicitly used to support a broader business or quality initiative, (2) the cost-of-poor-quality information was seen as only one of many weapons available in the team's improvement arsenal, and (3) an effective quality improvement process using a variety of problem-solving tools was established to identify and eliminate the identified root causes. Without these supporting mechanisms and the explicit link to broader corporate objectives, Pacific Bell would undoubtedly have seen cost-of-poor-quality measurement as inadequate for decision making and problem solving, just as it is in the many companies that fail to put the necessary supporting mechanisms in place.

5. *Using the cost of poor quality to develop targeted performance measures.* While estimates of poor-quality costs are useful for identifying improvement opportunities and providing high-level periodic scorecards of progress, they often lack credibility when used to measure an individual's or department's performance. Consequently, successful companies typically link the cost-of-poor-quality to the measurement of quantifiable goals using either project-based or root-cause measurement methods.

Project-based measurement: Many companies tie performance measurement to the achievement of specific quality improvement project goals. At the Materials and Controls Group of Texas Instruments, for example, divisional managers and representatives from marketing, engineering, manufacturing, production control, quality, and finance meet during the annual financial planning cycle to establish key cost-of-poor-quality improvement projects for the coming year. The highest payback improvement projects are identified and responsibility assigned. Anticipated savings from the improvement projects are then incorporated into product line profit forecasts. Project savings are subsequently tracked and compared to the forecasts to evaluate the performance of the project teams.

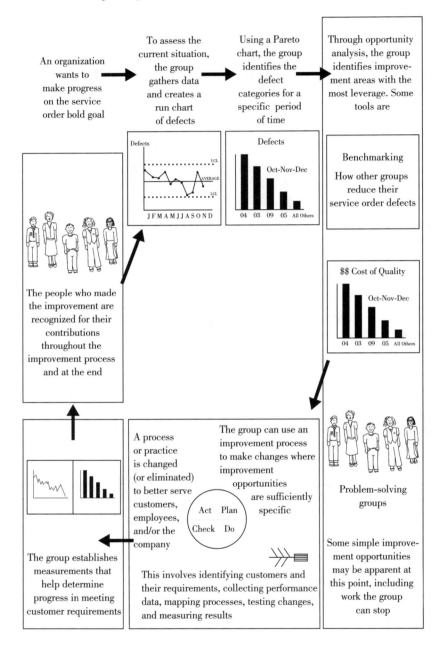

Figure 1.4 The cost of poor quality is an element within the Pacific Bell TQM system.

As shown in Table 1.1, the results from the individual improvement projects are summarized at the group level to provide an overall indicator of the organization's progress. In this way, managers work to achieve quantifiable goals that they helped to establish, thereby avoiding the credibility gap that typically arises when estimated poor quality cost figures are used for performance evaluation.

Root-cause measurement: A second technique is to measure performance using nonfinancial metrics that are associated with the root causes of poor quality costs. With this method, reported poor-quality costs are first used to identify the largest opportunities for improvement. Analyses are then performed to determine the root causes of these costs. Based on the analyses of the financial impact of the root causes of poor quality, performance targets for the elimination of the root causes are set. For example, a root-cause analysis might show that the leading cause of rework is paint defects. Performance is then evaluated based on the percentage of units with paint defects. Periodic cost-of-poor-quality assessments are subsequently conducted to determine whether the reductions in defects translated into lower costs, an issue that is discussed in more detail in Chapter 2.

The root-cause method of performance measurement offers two advantages. First, the measures are credible to managers since they are based on actual defect counts. Second, the nonfinancial measures can provide short-term, often real-time, feedback on performance, whereas financial measures are typically reported with some lag.

A health care products company uses a variation of the root-cause method to provide daily cost-of-poor-quality reports to employees. The major sources of failure costs in each function are identified and a standard cost per incident assigned. Daily counts of the number of incidents are multiplied by the associated standard costs to calculate failure costs for the day. The following morning, the previous day's failure costs are posted on a trend chart, allowing managers and employees rapid feedback on their performance.

The defense group of a major American manufacturer uses a similar method to measure supplier performance.[36] The use of a

Table 1.1 Texas Instruments Material and Controls Group, Motor Controls PCC cost-of-quality project savings.

199X Cost Reductions ($K)

Cost of Quality Projects	First Quarter	Second Quarter	Third Quarter	Fourth Quarter	Year 199X	Variance from Annual Plan
Yield Improvement	26	61	55	54	196	150
Upgrade Assembly	20	24	32	44	120	53
Redesign Molded Part	16	20	24	53	113	(55)
Nondestruct Testing	10	11	14	17	52	13
Laser Coding	9	10	9	10	38	30
Flash Reduction	8	9	11	10	38	22
Stat Process Control	93	119	128	127	467	(90)
Total	**182**	**254**	**273**	**315**	**1024**	**123**

Adapted from Christopher D. Ittner and Robert S. Kaplan, Texas Instruments: Cost of Quality (A), case 9-189-029, Boston: Harvard Business School, 1988.

cost-based approach for rating supplier performance grew out of a study that revealed that more than 50 percent of the 100,000-plus production receipts during the previous year had paperwork or hardware discrepancies or did not meet delivery schedules. The defense group's management was extremely concerned about the soaring administrative costs related to supplier-related nonconformances costs, which were conservatively estimated at $5 million to $10 million annually. The obvious need for quality and delivery improvement prompted management to sponsor the development of a system to identify and fix responsibility for quality and delivery problems. The resulting supplier performance rating system serves to motivate both company buyers and suppliers to improve quality and delivery performance, recognize and reward supplier excellence, and reduce excess costs.

The supplier performance rating system measures the added administrative costs incurred to resolve supplier hardware, paperwork, and delivery deficiencies. As shown in Table 1.2, each type of nonconformance "event" is assigned a standard cost based on industrial engineering studies of the hours required to solve the problem. For each event, the number of occurrences during the

Table 1.2 Nonconformance cost standards

Nonconformance Event	Standard Hours to Correct	(Hrs. x $50)
Documentation	3	$ 150.00
Material Review Board	12	600.00
Return to Supplier	6	300.00
Rework	15	750.00
Under Shipment	7	350.00
Over Shipment	2	100.00
Late Delivery	10	500.00

Source: Lawrence P. Carr and Christopher D. Ittner, "Measuring the Cost of Ownership," *Journal of Cost Management;* Fall 1992: 42–45.

previous quarter is multiplied by the associated standard cost to obtain the total cost of nonconformance. A supplier rating index is then calculated using the following formula.

$$\text{Supplier rating index} = \frac{\text{Nonconforming costs} + \text{Purchase price}}{\text{Purchase price}}$$

The purchase price is the total cost of invoiced goods purchased from that supplier during the rating period.

Table 1.3 provides an example of the method used to calculate the supplier rating index. The output from the supplier rating system assists in identifying which suppliers need help in meeting quality and delivery standards. The index also serves as a bid multiplier during the source selection process to determine the "true" cost of purchasing from a given supplier. A comparison of two potential suppliers for the same product illustrates the use of the bid multiplier. Based solely on quoted price, supplier A is the low cost vendor. After factoring in past quality and delivery performance using the supplier rating index, however, supplier B represents the better overall value.

Table 1.3   Supplier rating index example of calculation

Purchase Cost: $250,000

Nonconformance Costs:
Return to supplier (2 units @ $300 each): $600
Under shipment (5 shipments @ $350 each): $1750
Late delivery (3 shipments @ $500 each): $1500

Total Nonconformance Costs: $3850

$$\text{Supplier rating index} = \frac{(\$3850 + \$250{,}000)}{\$250{,}000} = 1.015$$

Source: Lawrence P. Carr and Christopher D. Ittner, "Measuring the Cost of Ownership," *Journal of Cost Management;* Fall 1992: 42–45.

	Supplier A	**Supplier B**
Quoted price per unit	$100	$105
× supplier rating index	1.1	1.0
Total cost per unit	$110	$105

General Mills provides another example of how poor quality costs have been integrated into the supplier performance measurement and rating process. As a part of its total quality process, the General Mills approach to supplier performance review and rating is described as follows:[37]

Total Quality
At General Mills, Inc. (GMI) quality equates to championship products and championship execution. It flows naturally from our commitment to be the fastest and most cost effective in our industry at meeting our customers' requirements... a relatively simple statement to make... but we all know how challenging this assignment is. GMI has always ranked high in product quality within our industry, but now quality has become an obsession—a healthy one and one our troops are really behind. We want to by unequivocally #1 in product quality. We're asking today not only to enlist [the support of our suppliers] for our quality efforts, but to commit to [the quality goals of our suppliers] as well. Total Quality is a two-way street.

Total Cost Approach
We are committed to total cost regarding raw materials—total cost includes the cost of materials as well as the value of quality and service. Total costs will determine [the suppliers with whom] we place our business.

Identify the Best Suppliers
We must do a better job of identifying the best suppliers from a total cost standpoint. Our ability to quantify this will be based on a supplier performance system we have installed—a computer based program which provides an objective profile of all suppliers in the area of quality, on time performance and the [cost of poor quality].

Continuous Improvement
We are dedicated to work with suppliers to achieve continuous improvement— where we are not improving, we must both seriously re-evaluate the continuation of the business relationship.

Reward System
Simple plan here—more business for the best total cost suppliers.

Conclusion

The competitive challenges of foreign competition and increasing customer expectations are causing top management to look at the quality process as a source of competitive advantage. For an estimated 70 percent of the companies in this country, however, the quality process has failed to produce results that support the strategic or financial initiatives of top management. In contrast, a few successful companies have used quality improvement as the cornerstone of their competitive strategies and accomplishments in the marketplace.

Our study of quality management approaches and best practices of more than 30 industry leaders demonstrates that successful companies manage their quality processes differently. In these companies, quality management practices have evolved beyond more established approaches in two important respects: (1) the companies have developed an enterprise-wide view of the quality process that involves every department and function of the business in the accomplishment of the strategic and financial initiatives of top management, and (2) this enterprise-wide approach focuses traditional quality tools and techniques on the elimination of nonvalue-added activities and waste as the primary means to improve financial performance.

The chapters to follow discuss the crucial concepts and practices we observed at the case study sites. Chapter 2 presents a framework for understanding the cause-and-effect relationships among strategic quality planning, quality improvement, productivity, profitability, customer satisfaction, and competitiveness. The chapter concludes with an analysis of the critical management decisions that are required to transform quality improvement into a competitive weapon in the marketplace.

Chapter 3 presents a framework for strategic quality planning. Examples and illustrations from a variety of companies are presented including a chronology of strategic quality planning at the H.J. Heinz Company. Chapter 4 explores the modern application of cost-of-poor-quality concepts as a means to identify and quantify nonvalue-added activities and waste; the use of the cost of poor quality as a catalyst for organizational change and as a performance measure; and the application of the cost of poor quality as a tool to manage various aspects of the improvement process. The updated cost-of-poor-quality concepts provide the foundation for us to review the quality-based cost management approach and describe how the quality process can become an integral method for improving financial performance as well as customer satisfaction.

Chapters 5 and 6 present detailed case studies on the H.J. Heinz Company and the Westinghouse Electric Corporation. The case studies focus on how two world-class companies are achieving their business and financial objectives using the quality process. The case studies present an overview of the competitive environment and the management process employed by each company to implement quality-based cost management. Chapter 7 presents the lessons learned from our study and highlights the crucial issues and best practices for improving financial performance using quality improvement methods.

The quality-based cost management approach is developed based on a synthesis of the unique approaches and practices used by over 30 successful companies. A detailed presentation of quality-based cost management techniques and considerations is presented as a practical and effective guide for companies to lower costs, increase profits, and improve cash flow. Chapter 8 presents a cost-of-poor-quality assessment methodology that blends activity-based costing with quality improvement concepts to identify and quantify the nonvalue-added costs caused by poor quality. Chapter 9 covers the cost-driver analysis methodology for determining the financial impact of potential improvement projects and setting improvement project priorities on the basis of payback and financial performance. Chapter 10 presents an approach for (1) selecting the improvement projects that make the greatest contribution to improving profitability, competitiveness, and customer satisfaction, (2) preparing the improvement project plan, (3) monitoring and measuring the progress of the improvement teams, and (4) reporting to top management on the progress and overall effectiveness of the quality improvement effort.

Notes

1. David A. Garvin, *Managing Quality* (New York: The Free Press, 1988), 26.
2. Garvin, *Managing Quality*, p. 222.
3. Garvin, *Managing Quality*, p. 46.
4. Robert H. Schaffer and Harvey A. Thomson, "Successful Change Programs Begin with Results," *Harvard Business Review* (January–February 1992): 80.
5. ASQC Quality Costs Committee, *Principles of Quality Costs, 2d ed.* edited by Jack Campanella (Milwaukee: ASQC Quality Press, 1990), 55–56.
6. Gilbert Fuchsberg, "Quality Programs Show Shoddy Results," *Wall Street Journal* (May 14, 1992): B1.
7. Schaffer and Thomson, "Successful Change Programs Begin with Results," 81.
8. A. Blanton Godfrey, "Strategic Quality Management Part I," *Quality* (March 1990): 17.
9. Jay Mathews and Peter Katel, "The Cost of Quality," *Newsweek* (September 7, 1992): 49.
10. Schaffer and Thomson, "Successful Change Programs Begin with Results," 82–85.
11. Michael Beer, Russell A. Eisenstat, and Bert Spector, "Why Change Programs Don't Produce Change," *Harvard Business Review* (November–December 1990): 158.
12. Godfrey, "Strategic Quality Management Part I," 18–19.
13. Garvin, *Managing Quality*, p. 37.
14. Garvin, *Managing Quality*, p. 27.

15. Joseph M. Juran, *Juran on Leadership for Quality* (New York: The Free Press 1989), 50.

16. ASQC Quality Costs Committee, *Principles of Quality Costs*, 2d ed., p. 6.

17. Joseph M. Juran, *Quality Control Handbook*, 1st ed. (New York: McGraw-Hill, 1952).

18. A. V. Feigenbaum, "The Challenge of Total Quality Control," *Industrial Quality Control* (May 1957): 17, 22–23.

19. W. J. Masser, "The Quality Manager and Quality Costs," *Industrial Quality Control* (October 1957): 5–8.

20. Much of the analysis in this section is based on the work of Christopher D. Ittner, *The Economics and Measurement of Quality Costs: An Empirical Investigation* (doctoral thesis, Harvard University Graduate School of Business, June 1992).

21. J. J. Plunkett and B. G. Dale, "Quality-Related Costing: Findings from an Industry-Based Research Study," *Engineering Management International* 4 (1988): 247–257.

22. ASQC Quality Costs Committee, *Quality Costs: Ideas and Applications, Volume 2*, ed. Jack Campanella (Milwaukee: ASQC Quality Press, 1989), 245.

23. Christopher D. Ittner, "An Examination of the Indirect Productivity Gains from Quality Improvement," *Production and Operations Management* (forthcoming).

24. W. Edwards Deming, *Quality, Productivity, and Competitive Position* (Cambridge, Mass.: MIT Center for Advanced Engineering, 1982).

25. H. James Harrington, *Poor-Quality Cost* (Milwaukee: ASQC Quality Press, 1987), 112.

26. Robert N. Mefford, "The Productivity Nexus of New Inventory and Quality Control Techniques," *Engineering Costs and Production Economics* 17 (1989): 21–28.

27. Surveys were mailed to the members of the Illinois Manufacturers' Association. The survey results were tabulated from the 79 responses that were returned out of 1,690 questionnaires mailed, a response rate of 4.6 percent. Each response provided information about the sophistication of the company's

quality improvement process. The respondents were ranked according to the reported level of sophistication of the quality process, and the companies with the highest rankings were contacted. Two manufacturing companies agreed to participate in a detailed cost-of-poor-quality assessment. The same team of consultants conducted a detailed cost-of-poor-quality assessment at each site. The results of the detailed cost-of-poor-quality assessments were averaged to obtain the follow-up research results.

28. Hawley Atkinson, "Justifying a Quality Initiative to Top Management," technical paper, Society of Manufacturing Engineers, Detroit, Mich., 1990.

29. "1987 ASQC/Gallup Survey," *Quality Progress* (December 1987): 13–17.

30. ASQC Quality Costs Committee, *Principles of Quality Costs*, 2d ed., 9–10.

31. Technical Assistance Research Programs (TARP), *Consumer Complaint Handling in America: Final Report*, Washington, D.C.: U.S. Department of Commerce, 1979.

32. C-17 Program reports to the U.S. Air Force, 1993.

33. Notes from Lawrence P. Carr, Wellesley, Mass.: Babson College, 1991.

34. Ronald Henkoff, "Cost Cutting: How To Do It Right," *Fortune* (April 9, 1990): 46.

35. Portions of the discussion are based on the following Pacific Bell publications: *Total Quality at Pacific Bell: How Pacific Bell Employees and Suppliers Are Working Together to Serve Our Customers*, 1993, and *The Pacific Bell Cost-of-Quality Handbook*, 1992.

36. Lawrence P. Carr and Christopher D. Ittner, "Measuring the Cost of Ownership," *Journal of Cost Management* (forthcoming 1994): 42–45.

37. Supplier Performance System, General Mills, Inc., 1991.

2 Quality Becomes a Competitive Weapon ___

Executive Summary

A key finding of our study is the importance of understanding the cause-and-effect relationships among strategy, quality, productivity, profitability, and competitiveness. The success of the case study companies is based on taking the necessary actions to develop an understanding of the logical cause-and-effect framework that connects business strategy to improved financial and operational results. Transforming business and quality strategies into competitive gain occurs through a series of four critical steps.

1. The quality process embraces the strategic vision and goals of top management, aligning the objectives and priorities of the quality process and the business.
2. Improvement projects are selected on the basis of improving profitability and customer satisfaction by eliminating the high payback root causes of poor quality and the related nonvalue-added activities and waste.
3. Productivity gains from higher quality are trapped and held by making the organizational alterations necessary to eliminate nonvalue-added activities and processes.
4. Profitability gains from higher productivity are trapped and held by redeploying resources from nonvalue-added activities into value-added activities.

Competitive pressures will no longer permit companies to rely on a vague sense that higher quality will somehow increase competitiveness or market share. Successful companies invest the time and effort necessary to understand the logical cause-and-effect framework between quality improvement and corporate performance, thereby managing quality as a competitive weapon.

QUALITY BECOMES A COMPETITIVE WEAPON

The lack of a clear understanding of the cause-and-effect relationship between quality improvement and corporate performance is the primary reason that common misconceptions about quality's benefit continue to exist. Most misconceptions are based on a shallow appreciation of facts or some common knowledge of quality's costs and benefits, often supported by obscure or irrelevant examples.

Common Misconceptions About Quality, Productivity, and Costs

Misconceptions about the linkages between quality and organizational performance have a negative impact on the quality process and need to be challenged and eliminated if an effective quality process is to be built. Four common misconceptions about quality, productivity, and costs are discussed here.

Misconception 1: You Can't Have Higher Quality and Lower Costs
A Rolex watch costs more than a Timex watch just as a Rolls Royce automobile costs more than a Ford Taurus automobile. In these examples, higher quality, as embedded in the product's specifications, does cost more. The more exaggerated the comparison, the greater the cost difference. There is no misconception about the fact that quality and cost vary dramatically as the products that are compared possess different features and functions, and satisfy different customer requirements.

The misconception that is most damaging occurs when a company does not understand the impact that not conforming to a product's specifications has on the cost structure of the entire business. The visible evidènce of nonconformance is the excess assets and inventory required to support operating inefficiencies, the extra people required to fix the mistakes and errors, and the additional expenses consumed by rework, scrap, and rejects in every aspect of the business. The penalty for not recognizing the relationship between higher quality (that is, higher conformance) and lower cost is a decline in competitiveness that costs a business sales, jobs, and profitability. Businesses that do not understand this higher conformance–lower cost relationship are missing a significant opportunity to lower costs and increase financial performance through quality improvement.

The lack of understanding is so widespread that most companies badly underestimate the true costs of poor quality, often by as much as 300 percent to 500 percent. Since most companies are unable to quantify the full financial impact of poor quality, the notion that quality and cost are not complementary will continue to persist until a structured approach is developed to initiate improvement projects using financial criteria in addition to nonfinancial selection factors.

Figure 2.1 illustrates how the removal of errors and defects in one company resulted in both higher quality and lower costs. The example focuses on the connection between higher quality and lower costs using a gauge control project that targeted the elimination of two by-products of poor quality: (1) inferior products and (2) excessive costs. The connection between higher quality and lower cost was first established by conducting an assessment to identify the direct and indirect financial consequences of poor quality. This was followed by an analysis to determine the causes of the identified poor quality costs. The analysis showed that the major root cause was gauging problems. By focusing an improvement team on eliminating the errors and defects caused by faulty and inaccurate gauging, the company was able to increase quality and lower costs. Management assigned a sales department representative to arrange for the sale of the additional, usable shafts that became available when the number of defective shafts decreased. As Figure 2.1 shows, increasing the number of usable shafts produced from a given quantity of raw material, machine time, burden, and labor resources provided the means for

Manufacturer of high-tolerance steel alloy shafts initiated a quality improvement project to upgrade gage control to (1) ensure operators knew proper techniques for using gages and (2) properly calibrate all gages.

Gauge Control Improvement Project

Production Batch Averages	Before	After
Number of shafts produced	400	400
Average number of shafts rejected in final inspection	26.4	4.4
Average number of returned shafts	18	0
Percentage of acceptable shafts	88.7%	98.9%
Total number of acceptable shafts	356	396
Batch Costs		
Total labor, materials, machine time, and burden	$24,480	$24,480
Financial Impact		
Total cost per acceptable shaft	$69.00	$61.88
Selling price per acceptable shaft	$106.15	$106.15
Total sales	$37,661.54	$41,992.40
Gross profit	$13,181.54	$17,512.40

Impact on quality: Unacceptable shaft percentage drops 90% to 1.1%
Impact on cost: Cost per acceptable shaft drops 10% to $61.88
Cost-of-poor-quality reduction increases gross profits by $4,330.86

Figure 2.1 Quality improvement generates higher quality and lower costs.

the company to transform the higher shaft quality and lower production costs into greater sales and profitability.

Misconception 2: Customer Satisfaction Is Not Related to Value

If two companies are selling identical products in the marketplace, the largest market share will go to the company that is the most price competitive and offers its customers the superior value. The logic is simple: The less a company charges for an equivalent product, the greater the value to its customers. Unaware of the changes in customer expectations that occurred during the 1980s, companies often dismiss the notion that customer satisfaction can be, or should be, related to equivalent or higher quality at a lower price.

The misconception that customer satisfaction and value are unrelated is perpetuated by managers who are committed to outdated competitive strategies from 1960s and 1970s which assume that either availability or reliability provides the basis for satisfying customers. Following World War II, consumer demand was high and companies were able to succeed by simply having a product available for consumers to purchase. As more manufacturers entered the market and the availability of products increased, competitors began to compete on the basis of price. As consumers became better educated in the 1970s, the basis of competition shifted toward greater reliability, a trend that began as consumers learned that more reliable products were less expensive in the long run and, accordingly, were willing to pay a premium for a product with greater reliability.

Companies that have been successful using a low price or a reliability strategy have shown strong resistance to changing or adapting to the next shift in consumer expectations. Consumer experiences with foreign products such as automobiles, consumer electronics, radial tires, motorcycles, and televisions taught them it is possible to buy products that possess the combination of high reliability and competitive pricing. This experience changed the consumer's perception of high quality from superior reliability to superior value—the combination of both higher reliability and lower price.

For companies under the misconception that the customer's perception of higher quality is not related to price, a value-based strategy appears to be counterintuitive. Even in the face of declining market share and lower profits, companies experience great difficulty in adapting their management style and corporate culture to a marketplace where customer satisfaction is a function of both reliability and price. Many companies have not realized that competing on the basis of superior value began to emerge as the dominant strategy of successful companies in the late 1970s.

Westinghouse, for example, recognized the tremendous potential of competing on the basis of superior value by monitoring its foreign competition. In the early 1980s Westinghouse changed its corporate strategy to competing on the basis of superior value as a way to gain market share by offering customers products with the desired features and functions at a competitive price. The top management of Westinghouse realized that the only way to succeed against its global competitors was to provide products and services that offer its customer a value that is equal or superior to anything offered by the competitors.

The misconception that customer satisfaction is not related to value continues even though surveys of consumers' perceptions have documented the trend toward defining a quality product as "one that provides performance or conformance at an acceptable price or cost."[1] A study by *Consumer Reports,* for example, compared quality ratings with price and showed that high "market shares were consistently associated with brands like General Electric and Whirlpool, which scored high on value, rather than with brands that ranked high on quality or price alone."[2] For companies trying to sell products to customers who have routinely come to expect superior value, the only viable alternative is managing the quality process to achieve lower costs while maintaining, or even increasing, existing standards for conformance to specifications based on customer requirements.

Misconception #3: Schedule Adherence and On-Time Delivery Are Not Related to Quality

The only impediments to making scheduled deliveries are all of the things that go wrong: the unplanned schedule changes due to defective parts, the quality-related problems at bottleneck operations that disrupt production, the inferior materials from the supplier that won't run properly, the error in the secondary operation that has to be reworked before final assembly, the tools that are now out of specification due to the latest engineering change orders.

The manufacturer of steel alloy shafts provides an example of how on-time delivery is affected by quality. The increase in the company's ability to satisfy schedule commitments is a result of the quality improvements illustrated in Figure 2.2. The lower reject rates discussed earlier made the production process more reliable and consistent. Since production scheduling is driven by customer orders, a more reliable and consistent process gives the company the capability to schedule delivery more accurately. The backlog of orders due to missed delivery dropped from 21 percent to 4 percent in a 45-day period. The first key to improving the company's delivery performance was freeing up the capacity that was previously dedicated to producing nonconforming products in order to catch up on the backlog of missed orders. The second was a much more reliable and consistent production process that dramatically reduced missed delivery dates for new orders received by the company.

The consumer durables group of an American manufacturer provides a similar example of the impact of poor quality on schedule adherence. An examination of the causes of schedule delays found that 41 percent of the unplanned schedule changes in one plant were due to internal or supplier quality deficiencies. The effect of these unplanned schedule changes was missed delivery schedules and lower productivity. A study in another unit of the company found that a 10 percent reduction in scrap at a key bottleneck process (reducing scrap from only 0.60 percent of output to 0.54 percent) increased schedule realization by 2.5 percent. These

Gauge Control Improvement Project

	Before	After
Percentage acceptable shafts	88.7%	98.9%
Productive hours per shift	151	170
Acceptable shafts per hour	2.1	2.3
Increase in acceptable shaft throughput per shift	—	40
Missed order backlog as a percent of total orders	21%	4%

Figure 2.2 Quality improvements drive higher schedule attainment.

gains were achieved by reducing the amount of time that the assembly line was idled as the bottleneck process was shut down to identify and eliminate quality problems.

Figure 2.3 shows how reductions in defects improve on-time delivery in an electronics manufacturing plant. Over a five-year period, the plant went from a defect rate of 8,700 parts per million and a 59 percent on-time delivery to a defect rate of 1,500 parts per million and an on-time delivery rate of 94 percent, with the improvement in schedule realization largely attributable to the gains in quality.

As these examples show, higher quality and improved on-time delivery performance are complementary. Yet many companies have not recognized that one of the major effects of higher quality is more

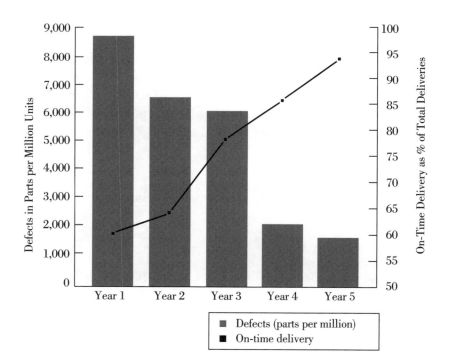

Figure 2.3 Reducing defect rates improves on-time delivery performance.

responsive delivery capability. Competitive strategies and market conditions of the 1960s and 1970s placed a premium on delivery, which was often attained by sacrificing quality. Even though today's winning strategies and market conditions have changed, it is still common to see managers reacting to delivery pressures by sacrificing quality. These managers do not realize that the ability to make schedule is dependent on quality, and that by sacrificing quality the company is losing the customers it works so hard to keep. The lack of understanding about the cause-and-effect relationships between quality and schedule perpetuates this misconception.

Misconception 4: Quality Is the Responsibility of the Shop Floor

Many of the quality tools and techniques developed over the last 40 years have targeted the shop floor. As a result, a large percentage of experienced quality professionals have a manufacturing or shop floor orientation. Transferring shop floor experience to nonmanufacturing departments and functions has been difficult. While the underlying concepts are the same, the differences in terminology and functional personality have proven to be formidable barriers. Sales, marketing, engineering, finance, administration, data processing, purchasing, and other nonmanufacturing functions and departments have typically ignored, or been ignored by, the quality process. The net effect is a misconception built up over time that quality is a shop floor or manufacturing concern.

This misconception is now being challenged as service organizations receive recognition for the quality they provide to their customers. When the Malcolm Baldrige National Quality Award was won by Federal Express and the Ritz-Carlton, the appreciation of how important quality can be in nonmanufacturing environments increased. Manufacturing companies are now starting to look more closely at their white-collar or nonmanufacturing areas to find ways to involve the entire organization in improving quality.

Comprehensive assessments of the cost of poor quality show that the nonmanufacturing areas of the company present significant opportunities for cost improvement. Figure 2.4 shows the results of a cost of poor quality assessment by Thermo-King, a Westinghouse company that was a runner-up in the Malcolm Baldrige National Quality Award competition. This assessment confirms, along with other cost-of-poor-quality assessments, that nonmanufacturing operations often account for the majority of true poor quality costs.[3]

Thermo-King has found that a multiplier effect exists between the easy-to-measure, commonly reported poor-quality costs and the true cost of poor quality, which includes the impact of poor quality in white-collar and indirect functions. Thermo-King reports that its "experience indicates that a multiplier effect of at least three or four is directly related to such hidden effects of quality failure."[4] The hidden effects include the excess costs driven by white-collar

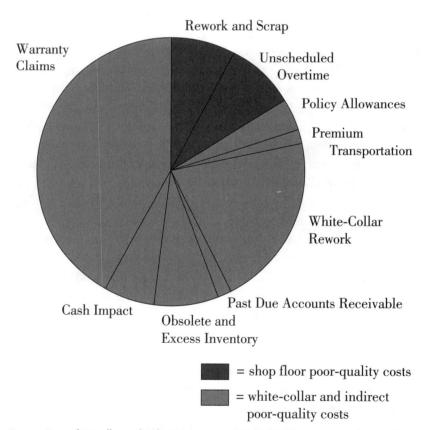

Figure 2.4 White-collar and indirect costs exceed shop floor poor-quality costs by 300 percent to 500 percent.

productivity losses and indirect effects such as excess and obsolete inventory, wait time and downtime due to quality problems, and lost sales that are routinely omitted by most poor-quality cost reports.

Cost of poor quality assessments often exclude white-collar and indirect costs because the information needed to identify or quantify these costs is not readily available. Since indirect failure cost information is usually not available in the existing financial or operating systems, companies such as Thermo-King use a variety of data-gathering tools to collect the required information. Table 2.1 shows a sample of the cost-of-poor-quality elements that Thermo-King identifies and quantifies in the controller's department.

Even though more companies are beginning to measure the indirect and white-collar costs of poor quality, the total number doing so remains relatively small. The misconception that quality is the concern of the shop floor will persist until there is a significant increase in the number of companies that understand and use cost-of-poor-quality tools and techniques in indirect and white-collar areas of the business. The wider availability and application of practical and effective cost-of-poor-quality tools and techniques will speed recognition of the importance of white-collar quality, and help to dispel the misconception that quality is the responsibility of the shop floor.

Establishing a Logical Cause-and-Effect Framework

The misconceptions about quality improvement that plague many companies are rooted in a lack of understanding about the complex relationships of quality, productivity, and profitability. The foundation for using quality as a competitive weapon is developing a logical cause-and-effect framework that provides everyone involved with an understanding of how the quality process delivers meaningful results. Without exception, the successful companies in the study base quality-related decisions on a clear understanding of the cause-and-effect relationships between the goals they want to accomplish and the steps required to achieve those goals.

Truck and Trailer Division—Quality Failure Cost Worksheet
Controller's Department
Week ending _____

I have spent the following time during the week on quality failure costs.

Cost Department	Hours	Financial Planning and Controller	Hours
Cost database corrections	_____	Revise financial forecast	_____
Process salvage reports	_____	Correct billing problems	_____
Process debit memos	_____	Correct account numbers	_____
Physical inventory maintenance	_____	Correct sales product codes	_____
Correct billing problems	_____	Supplier payment problems	_____
Correct account numbers	_____	Expense report problems	_____
Correct sales product codes	_____	Engineering change notices	_____
Engineering change notices	_____	New product planning changes	_____
New product planning changes	_____	Equipment is down	_____
Equipment is down	_____	Time spent on warranty claims	_____
Time spent on warranty claims	_____	Correcting statements due to errors	_____
Correcting statements due to errors	_____	Time spent on allowances and deducts	_____
Telephone calls due to errors	_____	Telephone calls due to errors	_____
Correspondence due to errors	_____	Correspondence due to errors	_____
Other	_____	Other	_____

Table 2.1 Sample of cost-of-poor-quality elements.

Figure 2.5 illustrates the steps that link the business strategy, quality improvement project selection, productivity, and profitability. These steps represent critical points in managing the overall cause-and-effect framework that transforms quality into a competitive weapon. The first critical step is developing a quality process that embraces the strategic vision and business goals of top management. This step is crucial for aligning the priorities and objectives of the business and the quality process. The experiences of the companies participating in the study indicate that the quality process can focus on the requirements of the business in two ways.

1. In the short term, the quality process makes the business more competitive by providing higher quality, lower costs, improved asset utilization, and increased sales.
2. In the long term, the quality process plays a role in building a sustainable competitive advantage in the marketplace by providing increased customer satisfaction and profitability.

Upper management must blend the short-term and long-term customer and business requirements, thereby providing a balanced business vision that is capable of satisfying a diverse set of interests and expectations. The quality process needs to reflect the broader business vision to answer the questions of how, when, why, and where the quality improvement process will contribute to the accomplishment of overall business goals and objectives.

Figure 2.6 shows a conceptual framework linking the strategic vision, project selection, productivity, and profitability. The framework begins with top management addressing the threats and opportunities in the marketplace and providing strategic direction and priorities for the business. Implementing quality as a source of competitive advantage requires that upper management share the strategic vision with operating managers, thereby providing a reference

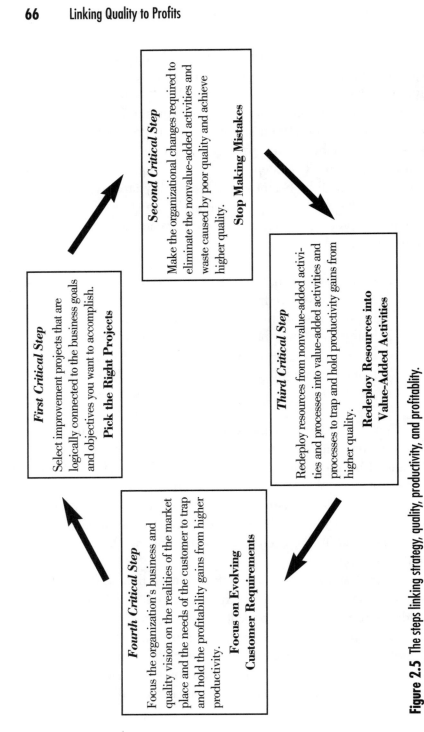

Figure 2.5 The steps linking strategy, quality, productivity, and profitablity.

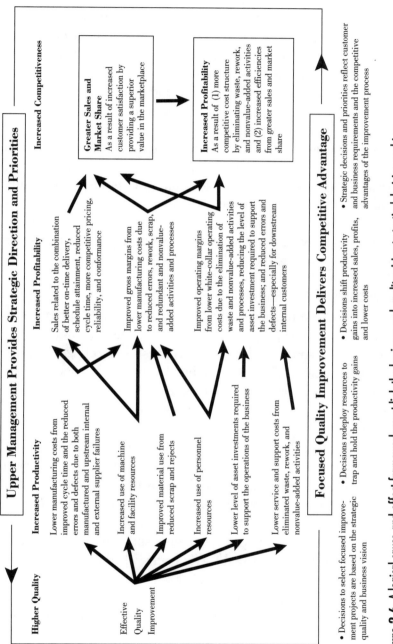

Figure 2.6 A logical cause-and-effect framework must link the business and quality vision to tactical decision making.

point for operating managers to refer to when making the tactical decisions required to implement the strategic quality plan.

If top management's business mission and strategy effectively address the threats and opportunities of the marketplace, managing in accordance with the quality vision will result in increased competitiveness. If the strategic planning and quality implementation processes are consistently updated, the business can achieve a sustainable competitive advantage in the marketplace. However, if upper management relies on strategies that are outdated or do not reflect the evolving customer requirements in the current marketplace, any competitive advantages from effective quality management will be dissipated. Understanding the relationships among quality, productivity, profitability, and competitiveness is crucial to achieving meaningful business results and establishing the business worth of the quality process.

Linking Quality to Productivity

In establishing a framework that connects quality improvement to the goals of the company, the second critical step (following development of the strategic plan and objectives) is selecting, planning, and implementing the vital few improvement projects that can create a genuine competitive difference. The initial success from the gauging project discussed earlier was due to

- Selecting an improvement project that made a genuine competitive difference. In this particular instance, the project was selected on the basis of improving quality and delivery performance to avoid losing a major customer as well as increase sales revenues from other customers.
- Implementing an operator training and gage calibration project plan that provided for (1) better schedule attainment by reducing cycle time, (2) higher sales due to greater output of acceptable product from the same level of raw material and labor, and (3) greater productivity resulting from reduced waste and nonvalue-added costs per unit of acceptable output sold to customers.

- Planning the sequence of management actions needed to connect the higher quality from the gaging project to improved financial and operational performance.

Figure 2.7 illustrates the flow from effective quality improvement projects to higher quality, leading ultimately to increased productivity. The flow begins with the strategy of top management being reflected in the quality process through the selection, planning, and implementation of vital projects. The resulting higher quality leads to permanent changes in the operating environment that increase productivity by allowing (1) the production of more acceptable products with the same level of resources or (2) production of the current level of acceptable output with fewer resources.

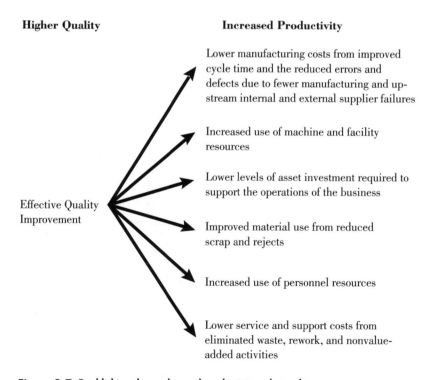

Figure 2.7 Establishing the quality and productivity relationship.

Trapping and Holding the Gains

The third critical step is making the decisions necessary to trap and hold the productivity gain on a permanent basis. The successful implementation of the gauging improvement project relied on more than just the training of operators and calibration of the instruments. Those two activities only began the chain of events that translated quality improvement into higher quality and increased productivity.

If the improvement plan had not recognized that the company's manufacturing standards had a built-in factor for allowable rework, there would have been little incentive to be more productive. The incentives were changed from meeting the standard to exceeding the standard. Productivity was no longer measured against a target that accepted 90 percent acceptable as being good enough. The new measure of how good it can be was based on continually increasing the amount of salable output from a given level of input resources. In order to improve on the upstream and downstream output, it became clear that management had to address changes in culture, accounting measures, compensation, and operating philosophy if the productivity gains from higher quality were to be realized and sustained in the long term.

The need to make organizational changes to capitalize on quality improvements is illustrated in Figure 2.8. The company in question had achieved a 20-percent reduction in the number of units that needed to be reworked but had realized almost no reduction in rework costs. The reason was that the company, like many American manufacturers, included a fixed number of rework personnel in its direct labor standards and considered these workers a cost of doing business. Consequently there was no incentive for line managers to reduce rework head count below the number set in the standard. As a result, the efforts of the quality improvement team to reduce rework had no impact on productivity. The rework reduction projects created an opportunity to eliminate nonvalue-added activities but, because the company did not take advantage of this opportunity, the firm was unable to trap and hold the potential productivity gain from higher quality.

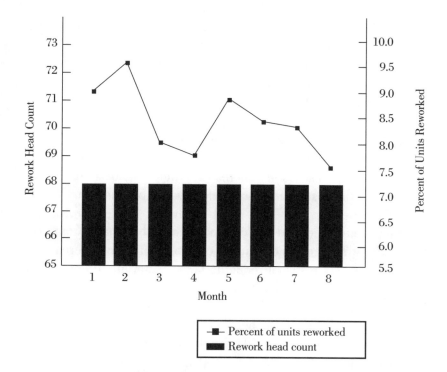

Figure 2.8 The potential productivity gain from higher quality was lost when the company did not eliminate nonvalue-added activities.

Management cannot assume the organization will adapt and make the necessary changes. In the short run, management must be the architect of change through project selection, planning, and implementation. Over the longer run, management must take the steps to institutionalize the improvement through a series of sustaining, organizational alterations such as revised policies, procedures, compensation programs, and incentive practices. Figure 2.8 demonstrates what happens when there is no clear connection between the actions taken and the ultimate results that a company wants to accomplish. If the ultimate goal was reducing rework *and* lowering labor costs to be more profitable, then the project was not a success. If a company selects and implements projects with no goal in mind other than increasing the number of project teams deployed, then almost any results will be satisfactory. If, on the other hand, a company selects and implements projects with specific financial and nonfinancial goals in mind, both the projects selected and the management actions taken must be logically connected to the ultimate results the company wants to achieve.

Higher Productivity Drives Increased Profitability

Higher productivity can increase profitability in a number of different ways. Most visibly, increased efficiency boosts profits by eliminating the cost of inferior or poor quality products that would otherwise be borne by the good products. For example, the gauging project dropped the cost per acceptable shafts from $69 to $61.88, a 10 percent decline in cost per shaft. The decrease in cost was a direct result of reducing labor, material, and overhead expenditures associated with the production of rejected shafts. The cost reduction of $7.12 per shaft represents an increase in gross profits of nearly 20 percent. The increased productivity translates into greater profits for the company; the sale of an additional 40 shafts created $4,300 in additional profits to the company. Alternatively, the productivity gains could have been translated into lower prices, leading to higher market share by providing customers with increased value.

Income Statement Effects. Figure 2.9 shows the connection from effective quality improvement and increased productivity to higher profitability, which is achieved through lower costs and increased sales. In the case of the high alloy shaft manufacturer, the improvement in gross margins was due to the reduction in manufacturing costs from increased machine, material, and personnel utilization through eliminating waste, rework, defects, and rejects. Improved gross margins were the beginning of a series of financial benefits that cascaded through the income statement and balance sheet as higher quality drove productivity and profitability improvements.

The income statement effect of improved profitability was due to (1) reduced costs and expenses and (2) increased revenues. In addition to manufacturing costs, the shaft manufacturer lowered

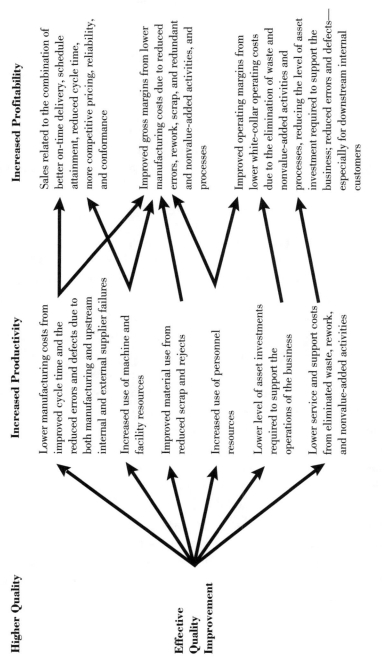

Higher Quality

**Effective
Quality
Improvement**

Increased Productivity

Lower manufacturing costs from improved cycle time and the reduced errors and defects due to both manufacturing and upstream internal and external supplier failures

Increased use of machine and facility resources

Improved material use from reduced scrap and rejects

Increased use of personnel resources

Lower level of asset investments required to support the operations of the business

Lower service and support costs from eliminated waste, rework, and nonvalue-added activities

Increased Profitability

Sales related to the combination of better on-time delivery, schedule attainment, reduced cycle time, more competitive pricing, reliability, and conformance

Improved gross margins from lower manufacturing costs due to reduced errors, rework, scrap, and redundant and nonvalue-added activities, and processes

Improved operating margins from lower white-collar operating costs due to the elimination of waste and nonvalue-added activities and processes, reducing the level of asset investment required to support the business; reduced errors and defects—especially for downstream internal customers

Figure 2.9 Higher quality drives increased productivity and profitability.

white-collar costs by reducing or eliminating nonvalue-added activities such as time wasted on resolving customer complaints, expediting material due to defective product, conducting defective product reviews, handling returned goods, accounting for the returns and credits related to defective raw material and finished product, and redoing production schedules to meet revised delivery dates for quality-related schedule slips.

Reductions in inventory and buffer stock lowered the costs related to material handling, storage, and inventory loss due to obsolescence and theft. Overall plant efficiency increased due to less congestion in the plant. Improved material, labor, and facility use increased cash availability which was used to reduce the interest costs for working capital borrowings.

While the shaft manufacturer offered competitive pricing prior to the quality improvements, the initial increase in revenue came from satisfied current customers who experienced the higher product and delivery reliability. As manufacturing, white-collar, and indirect costs decreased, the shaft manufacturer decided to pass a portion of the cost savings to selected customers in the form of a price reduction. Combined with the increased product and delivery reliability, the effect of the price reduction was a rapid increase in sales which created higher capacity utilization. Improved use of the existing facilities contributed further to profits as the revenue increases were achieved without additional investments.

Balance Sheet Effects. Cash flow improved rapidly as the raw material and work in process inventory requirements fell. The manufacturer reduced and later eliminated the need for buffer stock to protect the operation against quality problems, which improved cash flow and lowered the level of assets required by the business. Accounts receivable collection problems due to poor quality were eliminated. Cash flow was improved further as the current level of fixed assets proved adequate to support increased revenues.

A significant cycle time reduction in the support areas of the company was achieved through the elimination of nonvalue-added activities and processes. The previous cycle time, measured from order receipt to order shipment, was seven weeks. Of this cycle, nearly four weeks was consumed by order entry, purchasing, inventory receipt, and production scheduling. This was reduced to just over one week through the following improvements in the white-collar, support elements of the business.

- Raw material suppliers were culled down to the three who were capable of consistently making delivery schedule.
- The company's backlog of orders and the resulting material requirements were shared and discussed with raw material suppliers to give them visibility to future raw material requirements.
- Raw material buyers upgraded their procurement practices and supplier selection to reflect the needs for schedule attainment, competitive pricing, and consistent material quality.
- Production scheduling was automated with a "window" set so that no orders would be accepted with less than a 10-day order-to-receipt requirement. This gave the company better control over the rush orders that previously disrupted the entire inventory, scheduling, and manufacturing process. Capacity on second shift was dedicated to rush orders, allowing the company to maintain the production flow of scheduled orders while handling rush orders on a timely basis.
- Master blueprints were archived and made available electronically to ensure that primary and secondary operations always had the authorized, up-to-date blueprint from which to schedule machines, plan setups, and schedule personnel.
- Nonvalue-added activities and processes, such as delaying the secondary operations until the master blueprint was returned from the primary operations or using an out-of-date master blueprint for machine setups and manufacturing, were eliminated. The availability of electronic master blueprints provided the capability to produce products in both the primary and secondary operations, which cut the cycle time even further, lowered inventory, and reduced rework due to smaller batch sizes and improved throughput.

Achieving Sustained Competitive Advantage

The fourth critical step is making the decisions necessary to increase competitiveness and achieve the strategic goals of top management. Efforts to create competitive advantage face the same challenges as trapping and holding the productivity gains from higher quality. Although increased productivity improves profits in the short term, the ability to enhance long-term profitability depends on the steps made by top management to understand and satisfy ever-changing customer requirements. The final step in the process of transforming quality improvement into increased competitiveness is shown in Figure 2.10.

As the consumer electronics manufacturer rework example showed, a reduction in defects does not naturally or automatically work its way to the bottom line. Leaving the same number of personnel in the rework department was a failure of management to (1) do the proper planning to identify and understand all the changes that would be required to increase productivity and profitability through higher quality and (2) take the appropriate actions to redeploy now redundant assets into value-added operations.

Analog Devices, a semiconductor manufacturer, provides a powerful example of the need to take the appropriate actions necessary to translate quality gains into competitive success.[5] Over a three-year period, Analog increased its yields by 100 percent and reduced outgoing defects from 500 parts per million to 50 parts per million. Despite the tremendous strides made by Analog in improving quality, its stock price fell from $24 in 1987 to $8 in 1990. Some of this decline was due to market, industry, and competitive factors. But an important reason for the decline was the failure of Analog to take advantage of the extra flexibility, capability, capacity, and opportunities that the increase in quality had created. Analog failed to increase the sales volume of existing products or to develop, redesign, or market new products to take advantage of the opportunities that manufacturing had created. Lacking these steps, Analog was unable to translate improved quality into higher profits or market value.

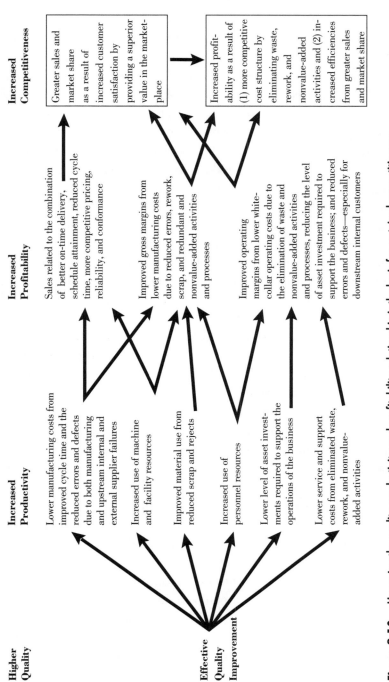

Figure 2.10 Managing the quality, productivity, and profitability relationship is the basis for sustained competitiveness.

In the case of the high alloy shaft manufacturer, the sales department participated as a member of the quality improvement project. Sales management was aware that additional shafts would be available, and the necessary actions were taken to sell the increased output. If management had not been involved and had not understood what actions were required to capitalize on the productivity gain, the company would likely have increased inventory rather than sales.

As these examples illustrate, companies must first understand the relationship of quality, productivity, and competitive position in their business, and must then take the appropriate actions to ensure the benefits are actually realized. A consumer durable goods company illustrates how one firm has realigned its quality improvement process based on an improved understanding the cause-and-effect relationships between quality and profitability. In response to rising warranty costs, the company initiated an improvement project to identify and eliminate the root causes of product failures in the field.

Field failures were found to fall into two categories: dead on arrival (DOA) and time dependent. The DOA category related to the warranty claims and expenses for units that failed within the first month of operation. The time-dependent category refers to warranty claims for units that fail between the second and twelfth month of operation. Internal studies determined that DOA category costs were primarily due to manufacturing problems, while the time-dependent failures were generally due to engineering and design problems that affected reliability.

The company had historically concentrated its inspection efforts on detecting manufacturing defects that caused DOA units. As Figure 2.11 shows, 98 percent of the available appraisal budget was spent on eliminating the DOA failures, which accounted for only 20 percent of total warranty costs. Time-dependent failures accounted for 80 percent of total warranty costs but received only 2 percent of the available budget. After examining the two sources of field failures and their related costs, an improvement project was initiated to set up a reliability testing center that would concentrate on detecting and eliminating the causes of time-dependent failures.

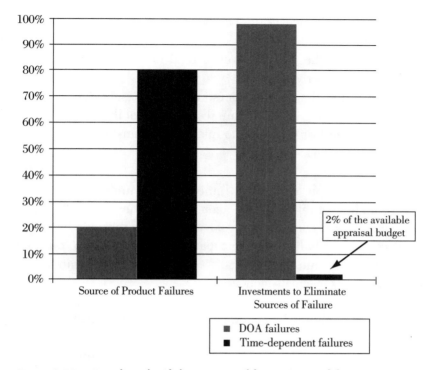

Figure 2.11 Time-dependent failures accounted for 80 percent of the warranty costs but received only 2 percent of the available appraisal budget.

The reliability center subjects a random sample of units to heavy load testing. By isolating reliability problems in the center rather than waiting a year or more for warranty claims to indicate that a problem exists, the company has been able to take action on problems much sooner. The early detection of reliability problems offers immediate increases in productivity by preventing engineering and design failures from being manufactured in the first place, reducing the shipment of defective units to customers and cutting back on resources dedicated to correcting the field failures.

The $200,000 investment in annual operating costs for the reliability testing center has had an estimated payback of $4,312,000 per year, based on the ability of the center to

- Prevent catastrophic field failures in which defective units jump to 5 percent of units produced. Such catastrophes had occurred twice in the past years as a result of new design failures.

- Reduce the current level of field failure incidence by 15 percent per year.
- Reduce the level of personnel and assets dedicated to maintaining a field failure response capability.
- Prevent lost sales due to quality problems and a tarnished reputation.

This example shows the importance of understanding the cause-and-effect relationships among strategy, quality, productivity, profitability, and competitiveness. By identifying the underlying root causes of field failures, the company has been able to translate higher quality into lower costs, fewer customer complaints, and increased customer satisfaction.

Conclusion: Quality Is Free—After Management Has Done Its Job

The experiences of companies like the shaft manufacturer, General Electric, Thermo-King, the consumer electronics manufacturer, Analog Devices, and the consumer durables manufacturer are evidence of the significant financial gain that improved quality can provide. But the financial gain only occurs after management has built a foundation by (1) understanding the cause-and-effect relationships between the strategy, quality, productivity, profitability, and operating performance and (2) developing a culture where the decisions necessary to implement changes can be made. After management has put these two ingredients into place, companies can begin to implement effective quality improvement programs with a reasonable expectation of improved financial and operational performance.

The remainder of this book discusses how to gather the information needed for an effective management decision-making process and how to develop the logical cause-and-effect framework. More specifically, the complementary facets of strategic quality planning and quality-based cost management are presented to allow managers to develop the information they need to manage their own unique situations effectively.

Notes

1. David A. Garvin, *Managing Quality* (New York: The Free Press, 1988), 45.
2. Garvin, *Managing Quality,* 46.
3. Warranty claims at Thermo-King are primarily due to non-manufacturing, engineering-related design problems rather than manufacturing defects.
4. ASQC Quality Costs Committee, "Quality Cost and Profit Performance" in *Quality Costs: Ideas and Applications, Volume 1,* ed. Andrew F. Grimm (Milwaukee: ASQC Quality Press, 1987), 215–222.
5. Amin H. Amershi and Srikant M. Dakar, *Incomplete Contracts, Production Expertise, and Incentive Effects of Modern Manufacturing Practices* (working paper, Stanford University, 1992), 10.

3 Strategic Quality Planning_____

> *Managing the quality dimension of an organization is not generally different from any other aspect of management. It involves the formulation of strategies, setting goals and objectives, developing action plans, implementing plans, and using control systems for monitoring feedback and taking corrective actions. If quality is viewed only as a control system, it will never be substantially improved. Quality is not just a control system; quality is a management function.*
>
> —1983 White House Conference on Productivity

Executive Summary

As top management begins to understand the competitive potential of quality improvement, its strategic importance increases rapidly as companies look to the quality process as a source of competitive gain and advantage in the marketplace. It has become readily apparent, however, that the typical approach and orientation to quality assurance lack the vision to satisfy top management's strategic requirements. The failure of quality assurance to meet management's requirements has been particularly troublesome in one area—improving financial performance.

When existing cost-of-poor-quality approaches fail to provide the connection between quality and profits, many companies concentrate their efforts on improving nonfinancial measures of quality, such as the number of teams or the percentage of people trained, in the hope that better financial results will automatically follow. Unfortunately, many of these companies have found that simply focusing on nonfinancial measures of quality, in isolation from the overall strategic thrusts of the business, does not produce the desired payback.

Successful companies now realize that the control system approach used in most quality improvement initiatives and cost-of-poor-quality applications is too narrow to meet the requirements of top management. The control system approach must be expanded into a much broader management initiative that embraces the overall strategic vision, establishes long-term goals, and recognizes the importance of accomplishing both financial and nonfinancial objectives. This enterprise-wide approach to managing the quality process adds the missing financial dimension and, in conjunction with nonfinancial considerations, is powerful enough to accomplish the ultimate quality objectives: to improve customer satisfaction and increase profitability.

Strategic quality planning provides companies with the structure to develop financial and nonfinancial goals that integrate quality planning with the business and financial planning processes that are already in place. Combined with the tools and techniques of quality improvement, successful companies now have the capability to link quality with improved financial performance. This chapter examines how the companies participating in our study developed a strategic planning capability that added a financial dimension to the quality process.

STRATEGIC QUALITY PLANNING

American managers have awakened to the value of quality improvement, finally realizing that the loss of profitability and market share is often due to poor quality. This awakening has occurred over a period of time and is the result of a wide variety of forces and events in the market. The most powerful of these forces has been the success of Japanese manufacturers in markets that have traditionally been the domain of American companies. The Japanese have used the superior reliability and price competitiveness of their products to gain large shares of industries that had previously been dominated by American manufacturers, such as semiconductors, machine tools, radial tires, automobiles, and motorcycles.

The loss of market share, profitability, and reputation to Japanese competition has provided the incentive for top managers to take an interest in quality. As companies have learned how to manage the connection between quality improvement and profitability, the importance of quality in a competitive strategy increases. The achievement of world-class results by companies like Xerox, Westinghouse, Hewlett-Packard, H.J. Heinz, Harley-Davidson, and others demonstrates that quality can work for American companies as well.

The companies that participated in the study have all struggled with the same problems and false starts that are a part of implementing a quality process for the first time. The lack of hands-on experience makes it difficult for companies to find a starting point. The difference for the successful companies in our sample was realizing that the quality process has to be managed in the same way that any function is managed—planning, setting goals, building action plans, and implementing.

These companies managed the quality process by first establishing a quality mission that reflects the needs of the business, understanding the internal and external business environment, and developing action plans to guide the quality implementation. In managing the quality process, participating companies have followed a similar evolutionary path to creating the strategic quality plan: (1) top management accepted the need to improve quality, and (2) a strategic quality planning process that initially mirrored the business planning process was developed. As the companies gained experience with quality improvement, more advanced and refined aspects of the quality process were incorporated to provide a powerful strategic quality planning process that could effectively support the evolving strategic imperatives of the business.

Top Management Recognizes the Need to Improve Quality

Acceptance of the need for higher quality encouraged top management to establish a quality improvement strategy and make a commitment to compete based on quality improvement. For each case study company, recognition of the need to improve quality occurred within a unique set of circumstances. At H.J. Heinz Company, for example, top management recognized that improving quality would increase the effectiveness of competitive strategies that were already in place. In the case of Westinghouse Power Generation (PGBU), quality improvement provided the means to survive in the face of emerging competitive threats. At the USCO of Xerox Corporation top management recognized the need to improve quality in response to a challenge from headquarters to improve profitability and increase sales.

The Heinz commitment to the quality improvement process came in September 1986 when a group of executives gathered to evaluate additional strategic options and alternatives. The company was looking for ways to leverage the successful Low Cost Operator I and II strategic initiatives as a means to maintain its profitability and competitiveness. Frank Adamson, now manager of quality analysis at World Headquarters, presented the group with a new perspective on cost management—the cost of poor quality: the cost of not doing things right the first time. J. Wray Connolly, a senior vice president responsible for identifying major opportunities in the manufacturing area, subsequently recognized the concept's potential for providing Heinz with a fresh perspective on methods to both control costs and quality. TQM started to gain momentum when top management grasped the impact of poor quality and its related costs on the company.

In the case of PGBU, top management elevated quality improvement to a strategic imperative in 1988. The business unit faced serious competitive threats on three fronts: (1) the product portfolio was out of balance with the market, (2) its reputation for quality was, at best, average, and (3) competition was intensifying, especially as subsidized European competitors entered the U.S.

market. Top management concluded that total quality offered the means to achieve business success by improving customer satisfaction and increasing cash flow through the elimination of waste.[1]

At USCO the initial motivation came from the group's president, who challenged his senior staff to improve profitability in the face of increased pressure for improved financial performance from corporate headquarters. While the senior USCO managers were fully aware of the quality campaign taking place elsewhere in Xerox, they wondered how applicable some of the quality ideas would be in a marketing organization. It was the chief financial officer who recognized the competitive potential of quality and funded the investment required to get the process started.

While the events leading up to the recognition of the need for improved quality were unique to every situation, the response by successful companies was consistent: Top management made an initial commitment to the quality process and authorized the investment needed to develop a strategic quality plan. Resources were then allocated to explore ways in which the quality process could satisfy the strategic requirements of top management, leading to the development of a strategic quality planning process.

The Evolution of Strategic Quality Planning Process

Early in the quality initiative, strategic quality planning approaches tended to concentrate on (1) understanding the tools and approaches of quality improvement and (2) determining specific steps that need to be taken for the quality process to contribute to the overall success of the business. Subsequently, successful companies realized that quality is a dimension of the business that needs to be managed strategically, just like any other function, to achieve a competitive advantage. As a result of this orientation, companies are now formulating strategies, establishing goals and objectives, preparing action plans, implementing action plans, and building management systems to measure quality progress, provide feedback, and take corrective actions as required.

The Heinz business planning approach, for example, emphasizes goal-setting and performance measurement to produce superior financial performance. The strategic quality planning process was patterned after this business planning approach, with the addition of elements specific to the quality process. An early priority in the Heinz strategic quality planning process was identifying high payback opportunities to focus the quality process on achieving greater competitive advantage through lower costs. Figure 3.1 highlights seven key elements of the original strategic quality planning approach, which dates back to the mid-1980s. The Heinz strategic quality planning approach was driven off the business mission and established a series of high level quality goals and performance measures to link day-to-day quality activities with the achievement of business objectives.

1. The quality charter reflects the corporate mission statement and the Heinz commitment to achieving business objectives through quality improvement.

> We at Heinz are committed to providing our customers, whether external or internal, with products and services that fully satisfy their requirements. This commitment shall be achieved through the mobilization and involvement of everyone in the corporation in a relentless and continual search for improvement to make every aspect of our work right the first time—all with the objective of securing for our company a meaningful and permanent competitive advantage, and for our shareholders an above average return on their investment. [emphasis added]

2. Anthony O'Reilly, chairman, CEO, and president of Heinz, established two long-term TQM goals: a reduction of at least 50 percent in the (1) cost of poor quality and (2) customer complaints within four years. These two quality goals are consistent with the broader business priorities and align the objectives of the quality process with the objectives of the business. By establishing these two long-term goals, Heinz has made the quality process measurable and

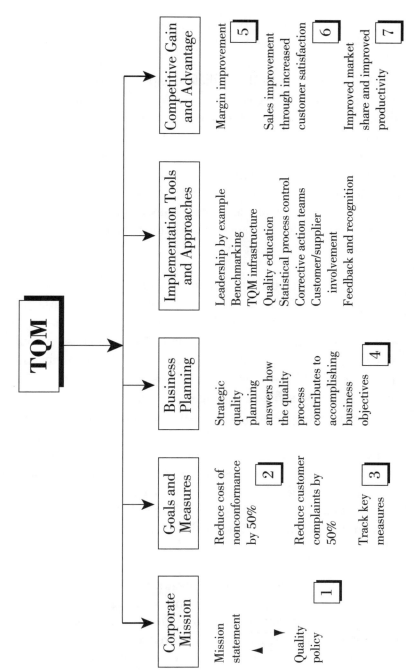

Figure 3.1 The strategic quality planning process at Heinz links day-to-day quality activities with business objectives.

has created the capability to track overall quality improvement progress.

3. The progress of the affiliate companies in achieving these two long-term quality goals is reported to top management every six months. Reporting within each affiliate is done monthly and consolidated into a semiannual report for top management. A key element in the deployment of the quality process throughout the worldwide Heinz organization is linking senior management compensation to the achievement of the two long-term quality goals. As much as 30 percent of the bonus compensation for senior managers is directly tied to meeting targets for reductions in the cost of poor quality and customer complaints.

4. Each of the affiliate companies is responsible for strategic quality planning, which is a component of the business plan. Strategic quality planning is conducted by operational personnel who set the quality strategy as a part of the business planning process. This ensures that implementation of TQM occurs where it is most valuable—in the day-to-day operations. Operations personnel are responsible for managing the quality process, conducting the cost-of-poor-quality assessments, performing root-cause analysis, selecting improvement projects, and implementing solutions. Because of the emphasis that is placed on managing and deploying the quality process using operating personnel, there is only one full-time TQM coordinator at each affiliate company. The TQM coordinator serves as a resource that operations personnel can call on for assistance with training, results tracking, and education.

5. Early on, improvement projects were selected on the basis of eliminating the cost of poor quality and customer complaints. Every project has stated objectives, time frames, and supporting performance measures that focus on reducing poor quality costs and customer complaints. By setting challenging goals and holding the operating personnel responsible for results, Heinz has been

able to deploy the quality process throughout the entire organization to achieve increased customer satisfaction (through the elimination of complaints) and sustained profitability (through the elimination of poor-quality costs). The net result is the creation of a quality improvement culture that goes after substantial, cross-functional issues that are vital to creating competitive advantage, rather than targeting many small projects that are well intentioned but not particularly meaningful to the corporation as a whole.

6. Heinz has broadened the conventional concept of poor quality costs to include lost sales and lost market share. For example, if an affiliate company is losing market share on a brand, the loss of revenue is classified as a cost of poor quality. An improvement team is assigned to analyze the problem of lost market share and determine through root-cause analysis what went wrong. For example, an improvement team was deployed when the Ore-Ida brand of Tater Tots experienced a drop in market share. The team discovered that an increase in production line speed made the Tater Tots mushy, which contributed to the slowdown in sales. The solution was to slow the speed of the production line to improve taste, resulting in a jump in sales of 8.8 percent.[2]

7. Productivity is increased through the elimination of waste, scrap, rework, and redundant and nonvalue-added activities. Heinz learned early in the TQM process that unless resources are effectively redeployed into value-added efforts, quality improvements cannot be converted into lower costs, higher sales, or increased customer satisfaction.

The strategic plan provides a cause-and-effect framework to guide decisions relating to the quality improvement process. Strategic quality planning helps to assess what works and what doesn't work, knowledge that is critical for answering a variety of increasingly difficult quality management questions.

- Which projects have the greatest payoff?
- How long does it take to realize benefits?

- How should resources be allocated?

- How should improvement priorities be set?

- How do projects contribute to the accomplishment of quality and business goals?

- What barriers will the improvement teams encounter?

- What organizational changes are needed to support quality improvement?

If the connection between the improvement projects and goals is logical, then the quality process can be managed to deliver improved financial performance. If the connection is fuzzy, illogical, or unclear, then the chances of success are no better than random luck. Figure 3.2 illustrates the connection between the overall Heinz quality objective and the two long-term Heinz quality goals that drive project selection. The key tracking measures for each project are used to monitor and measure the performance of the improvement teams, give management visibility into the improvement process, and provide the information needed to take corrective actions that yield success.

The cost of poor quality has provided Heinz with a perspective for managing costs. Top management has used this perspective to its competitive advantage, generating a bottom-line improvement of more than $250 million. This improvement is the result of a cost management approach that extends the use of quality tools and techniques, such as problem solving and empowerment, to solve problems that cross functional boundaries and challenge people to look at the business in new ways.

The Heinz TQM process is now entering its seventh year. As the quality implementation has grown in scope and breadth throughout the operating companies, the strategic quality planning process has become more refined. The strategic quality

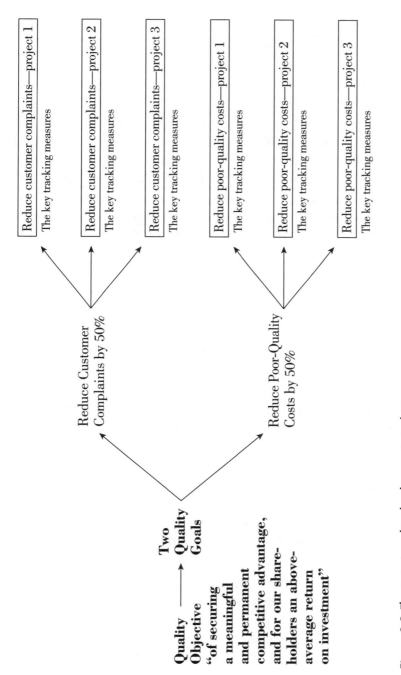

Figure 3.2 The strategic quality plan drives project selection.

planning process has evolved from the approach described previously to now include the

• *Addition of customer satisfiers and satisfaction measures.* Heinz started with a focus on customer dissatisfiers because the information was readily available from customer complaints and suggestions. The addition of customer satisfiers gives Heinz a better understanding of what product and service features and functions customers find most important and influential in the purchasing decision. With its trade customers, Heinz now measures a number of key customer satisfiers such as on-time delivery, order fill rates, invoicing errors, returned goods, and customer deductions. Performance in product and service markets is tracked through the documentation and investigation of consumer complaints, consumer satisfaction surveys, and consumer focus groups. The purpose is to measure progress in satisfying consumers, as well as to identify features and functions that are important at the consumer level.

• *Integration of the strategic quality planning process into the business planning process.* Like other companies, Heinz originally prepared the strategic quality plan independently from the business planning process. Preparing a separate strategic quality plan allows companies to gain specific quality planning experience. As operating managers become more experienced with the application of quality concepts, successful companies integrate the preparation of the quality and business plans. While it remains important for strategic quality planning to answer the question of how the quality process contributes to accomplishment of business goals and objectives, successful companies find it difficult to tell where business planning stops and strategic quality planning begins.

• *Development of key performance measures that further integrate business and quality processes.* The strategic quality planning process is now linked to customer satisfaction and marketplace performance through a series of key performance measures. Key performance measures have been established at two levels, the first being the common denominator measures agreed on by the affiliates, and the second reflecting a more detailed view of internal performance and processes tailored to an affiliate's unique situation. Examples of common performance measures that address the business performance of affiliate companies include operating income divided by a measure of business effectiveness (operating income/net profits after tax, unit sales, and market share by major product line); consumer contacts (consumer complaint and consumer compliment frequency); customer service (on-time deliveries, order fill rates, and invoicing errors); innovation judged by the percent of sales from new products; and plant efficiency (productivity, process capability, accident incident rate, absenteeism, and yield and inventory levels). Examples of second-level performance measures used at the affiliate level include cost reduction, capital and asset utilization, cycle-time reduction, machine effectiveness, materials and energy usage, and waste management. Each affiliate also monitors critical product and service performance characteristics that drive customer satisfaction.

Since the key performance indicators are bottom-line oriented and closely related to the costs and/or revenues for the firm, Heinz uses these performance measures as a prime measure of the effectiveness of affiliate management. The key performance indicators represent a corporate scorecard that will truly reflect whether time, energy, and ingenuity are translating into continued improvement and increased competitiveness and an assurance of future prosperity.

Like Heinz, many of the case study companies began strategic quality planning by adopting a process that was similar to their established planning approaches, with several important exceptions. First, the strategic quality planning process emphasized quality and related management concepts. New ideas and perspectives included problem solving pushed down to the lowest levels within the organization, empowered employees with the authority to make bounded and limited changes, cross-functional improvement teams tackling problems that were vital to the success of the business, and structured problem-solving processes where decisions based on fact replace decision processes based on intuition or guesswork.

The second exception was the use of the cost of poor quality to provide management with a new perspective on improving financial performance by eliminating the excessive costs of nonvalue-added activities and waste caused by poor quality. Combined with an updated approach to conducting root-cause analysis, the combination of strategic quality planning and cost-of-poor-quality measurement provided management with the information needed to use quality tools and techniques to manage costs.

As Figure 3.3 illustrates, the quality planning process consists of four steps linking strategic goals to the implementation of day-to-day improvement activities. From a management perspective, these linkages are vital to ensuring that day-to-day decisions are guided by the long-term strategy and long-term goals. It doesn't matter whether the scene is the purchasing department, shop floor, top floor, or a sales meeting—the hundreds or thousands of decisions that are made every day must be made with a common goal and strategy in mind. This begins by establishing the quality mission and building a shared sense of purpose about the company and what it is trying to accomplish.

Step 1: Establishing the Quality Mission

The quality mission tells everyone involved why the quality process exists and what the quality process is intended to accomplish. The quality mission is the official expression of what is expected from the quality process. Setting this expectation provides the foundation for building the culture and performance expectations for the quality process. It is essential that the quality mission reflect the business mission and provide the vision, values, and goals so that people can understand how the quality process contributes to the accomplishment of the broader business mission.

Companies use different approaches to establish the quality vision and values, but the desired result is the same: to focus the quality process on the accomplishment of business goals and objectives. An example is provided by the Westinghouse Productivity and Quality Center (PQC), the corporate quality orga-

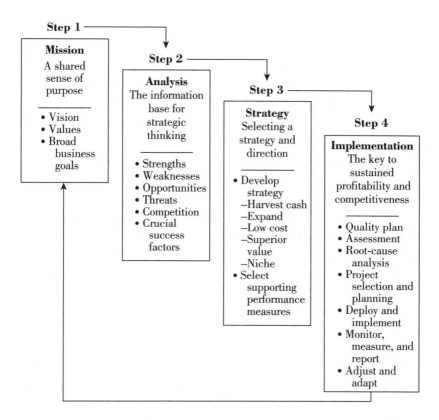

Adapted from *Dynamic Planning for the High Technology Business—Guidebook,*
International High Technology Practice, KPMG Peat Marwick, 1991.

Figure 3.3
Strategic quality planning guides implementation of the quality process.

nization of Westinghouse. The PQC was created by Westinghouse
as a means to improve the competitiveness of operating units by
providing total quality tools and techniques. The mission statement
of the PQC clearly states that quality improvement is a means for
accomplishing business goals: "Contribute to corporate value
growth by being a catalyst and resource for Westinghouse units to
enhance operating performance through continuous Total Quality
improvement."

This mission statement answers the following important fundamental questions.

- Why should Westinghouse invest in quality improvement? As a means to enhance operating performance.
- Why is the PQC in existence? To contribute to corporate value growth.
- How will this happen? By enhancing operating performance through continuous total quality improvement.

There isn't any doubt about why Westinghouse has invested in the PQC, nor is there any doubt about the expectations that top management has set for the PQC. The strategic thrust of the PQC, as stated in the 1992 strategic quality plan, is straightforward: "Strategically, PQC will place heavy emphasis on achieving solid business results using Total Quality tools and methods. The next few years are the time to *step up to the payoff* for our previous TQ efforts."

The PQC has been called on by Westinghouse top management, as has every other operating unit, to improve financial performance and increase cash flow as a part of the overall solution to the competitive and financial pressures facing Westinghouse. Improving cash flow, for example, is one of the specific goals in the PQC strategic quality plan.

When asked how it is contributing to the success of Westinghouse, the PQC response is two-fold: (1) by providing services on a revenue generating basis to Westinghouse and outside companies, PQC provides a valuable resource while remaining self-reliant and free of any corporate subsidies, and (2) Westinghouse operating units are more profitable and cash flow positive as a result of using the services of the PQC. At the present time, Westinghouse estimates that its quality process has generated over $1.1 billion in additional cash flow, primarily by reducing inventories and eliminating facilities due to improved productivity.

The Heinz quality charter, described earlier, reflects the commitment to contributing to the achievement of business mission and goals. No mystery, no excuses. The Heinz TQM motto sums up the philosophy and perspective of successful quality processes quite well: *TQM means business.*

Xerox USCO, Heinz, Westinghouse, and others have established their own unique quality missions, yet each unique mission statement addresses two crucial issues.

1. Presenting the purpose or vision of the quality process, which is an expression of how quality improvement will contribute to the accomplishment of the broader business mission or purpose
2. Setting broad goals for the quality process that are aligned with the goals of the business

These two issues can be clearly seen in the Xerox quality mission shown in Figure 3.4.[3]

Establishing a quality mission requires a clear understanding of the business vision. Aligning business and quality visions and goals is essential if the quality process is to become a source of competitive advantage to the business. To help guide the development of the quality mission, the following guidelines and checklists are provided.[4]

Mission Statement Guide

The objective of a quality mission is to communicate the purpose of the quality improvement process. The mission statement provides the employees, management, customers, and owners with an understanding of the quality process, its goals and direction, and its role in achieving overall business goals.

The quality mission statement answers these questions: Where is the quality process going? What do we expect the quality process to become? What is its purpose? What are our corporate values? What are our most important long-term goals?

Mission Statement Questionnaire

Part 1: The Vision

The quality vision provides the picture of what the quality process is trying to become. The following questions should guide the development of the quality vision.

- *Where have the business and the quality process come from?*
- *What do you want the foundation of the business and the quality process to be?*
- *What do you want the business and quality process to offer customers, owners, employees, managers, suppliers, and community?*
- *What business need(s) does the quality process satisfy?*
- *What would the business be lacking if the quality process no longer existed?*
- *What would you want the customers, owners, employees, managers, suppliers, and community to say about the quality process?*

Based on the questions above, draft a vision statement that describes the purpose of the quality process's existence.

Part 2: The Values
Develop the value statements that support the vision statement. Values are the concepts or characteristics of the company that are desirable, that influence the selection of alternatives, and, ultimately, end up in actions.[5]

- *What values guide the day-to-day behavior of the quality process?*
- *What are the values toward your customers? Employees? Managers? Suppliers? Community?*

Based on the values that are important to the business and the quality process, write a statement describing the values that are most important in achieving the quality vision.

Part 3: The Goals
Long-term goals make the mission statement measurable and tangible. The goals provide the link between the quality vision and the strategies established to accomplish the vision.

- *What are the two or three most important long-term goals for the business?*
- *What are the two or three most important long-term goals the quality process can accomplish that contribute directly to achievement of the important long-term goals of the business?*

Xerox Quality Mission

- The fundamental principle of the quality strategy is meeting customer requirements.
- The definition of quality is meeting the customer's requirements all of the time.
- The process starts with a vision at the top. Senior management drives the process. However, employee involvement is absolutely key. It is the people who do the work and they know how to do it best. Training and sharing of information are critical to the Leadership Through Quality implementation.
- Quality is a strategic tool used to improve competitiveness and organizational effectiveness. The focus is on the processes as well as products.
- Quality is a long-term process requiring continuous improvement and patience.
- Leadership Through Quality is a fully integrated business process.

Excerpted from Xerox training literature.

Figure 3.4 The Xerox quality mission guides the quality process and aligns the quality process with business goals.

Motorola provides employees with a card to carry when performing their daily duties. This card, shown in Figure 3.5, serves to remind each employee of the quality mission, beliefs, goals, and initiatives in just a few words. Side 1 of the Motorola reminder card gives the mission statement, and side 2 describes the beliefs, goals, and key competitive initiatives Motorola uses to accomplish its mission. Like Motorola, all of the successful companies that participated in the study use the mission statement to convey the message that the quality process is a key ingredient in the success of the business.

Side 1

OUR FUNDAMENTAL OBJECTIVE
(Everybody's Overriding Responsibility)

Total Customer Satisfaction

MOTOROLA

Side 2

Key beliefs—*how we will always act*
•Constant respect for people
•Uncompromising integrity

Key goals—*what we must accomplish*
•Best in class
 –People
 –Marketing
 –Technology
 –Product
 –Manufacturing
 –Service
•Increased global market share
•Superior financial results

Key initiatives—*how we will do it*
•Six-sigma quality
•Total cycle time reduction
•Product, manufacturing, and
 environmental leadership
•Profit improvement
•Empowerment for all, in a
 participative, cooperative, and
 creative workplace

Figure 3.5 The Motorola reminder card describes the objective, key beliefs, key goals, and key initiatives for business success.

Step 2: Analyzing the Current Situation

The next step in the strategic quality planning process is to analyze and understand the environment and circumstances surrounding the business and quality process. The current situation analysis should be an unbiased appraisal of competitive pressures, company strengths and weaknesses, market opportunities, competitive threats, and critical success factors. Understanding the current situation is critical if those responsible for managing the quality process are to make informed decisions and avoid fatal mistakes.

Westinghouse's PQC provides a good example of why an understanding of the current situation is so essential. In 1989, the operating profit from the seven divisions of Westinghouse was $994,000,000, approximately 8 percent of sales. In 1990 and 1991, operating profits were $1,447,000,000 and $973,000,000, respectively. Offsetting the operating profits, however, was a major provision that reduced operating income over the two-year period by nearly $2.7 billion. In 1991, Westinghouse reported an operating loss of $867,000,000. In just a matter of three years, net income swung from a profit of $922 million to a loss of $1.1 billion—a change of over $2 billion.

The great majority of the $2 billion swing was due to losses and provisions for the financial services business unit. In February 1991 the board of directors of Westinghouse approved the downsizing of the financial services business to reduce the exposure to under-performing and high-risk assets. The decision was based on the continuing deterioration of the U.S. economy and weaknesses in the markets served by the financial services business unit, notably real estate and highly leveraged corporate transactions. The changing and uncertain business conditions in those markets made it prudent, in management's view, to alter the strategy of the financial services business unit.

Not surprisingly, the environment in which the PQC provides its services to Westinghouse business units has changed dramatically over these three years. The PQC has shifted its strategies toward accelerating the return from investments in quality. The following quote is taken from the situation analysis done by the PQC as a part of its quality planning process: "The Corporation's financial situation will continue to drive the demand for Total Quality process solutions over much of the three-year planning period. Westinghouse units will increasing perceive TQ improvement as a means for cash generation and profit improvement."

The most critical issue that the PQC has identified in its analysis of the key issues and opportunities currently facing Westinghouse is "achieving even greater 'payoff' from Total Quality initiatives throughout the Corporation. Total Quality has passed the startup stage at Westinghouse. As Chairman Paul Lego has pointed out, it is time to move aggressively into the payoff."

The situation analysis and identification of key issues have focused the efforts of the PQC in response to a dramatic shift in the external environment. The collapse of real estate values and the over-leveraging by American companies in the 1980s represent threats to the survival of Westinghouse. The PQC has responded to these threats with a renewed focus on cash generation and the elimination of poor quality costs.

Just as the PQC has responded to dramatic change in the external business environment, every quality process must be responsive to changes in the competitive situation facing the corporation. By understanding market dynamics and anticipating future customer requirements, the quality process becomes an integral part of the organization's success.

Assessing the External Environment
The following questions and considerations are provided to help guide the analysis of the external environment.

External Analysis Considerations. To ensure that the quality plan realistically reflects the external environment, the external analysis should examine the important threats and opportunities relevant to both the business and quality planning process. The objective is to identify the key industry and company success factors, along with the most significant threats, opportunities, and strategic choices facing the business and the quality process. The external analysis involves an assessment of the industry, competitive environment, markets, customers, and competitors. Typical considerations in conducting the external analysis are as follows:

Customers
- What are their primary motivations to purchase your product or service?
- What is their buying behavior and process?
- What are the buying influencers and the buying motivators?

The market environment
- Are there any demand opportunities that have not been filled or handled unsatisfactorily?
- Are there any key customer groups not yet penetrated?
- Are there ways to segment the market according to feature, function, price, or other relevant segmentation factor?
- How large is each segment?
- Growth potential?
- Future requirements?
- Who are the most profitable industry participants?

The economic environment
- What are the significant macroeconomic factors that influence the industry?
- Your company?
- Are there any important regulatory issues facing the industry?
- Are there any important demographic trends that must be addressed?

The industry
- What is its size?
- Stage in the product life cycle?

- Competitive structure?
- Cost structure?
- Barriers to entry?
- Barriers to exit?
- Industry trends?

Competitors
- What are their strengths?
- Weaknesses?
- What are the key success factors for the strongest industry participants?
- Behavior in the market?
- Corporate culture?
- Management style?
- Level of profitability?
- Share of the market?
- Share of key market segments?
- Strategy for competing in the market?

Summarize the information from your external analysis and discuss the most significant opportunities presenting themselves to your company.

- What are the most favorable opportunities in light of the external data analysis?
- What are the critical risks your company faces?
- How can the quality process directly contribute to taking advantage of these opportunities?

Discuss the most crucial short-range and long-range threats facing the business.

- How can the quality process contribute directly to neutralizing or reducing the threats to the business?

Discuss the common success factors of the successful industry participants.

- How can the quality process directly contribute to enhancing or improving the critical success factors of the company?

Finally, summarize the action steps to be taken for implementing key finding resulting from the external analysis.

Assessing the Internal Environment

The following set of questions and considerations is provided to help guide the analysis of the internal environment.

Internal Analysis Considerations. The objectives of the internal analysis are to perform an honest and realistic examination of your company's resources to arrive at a consensus of strengths and weaknesses. Typical areas of analysis are financial resources, marketing and product development resources, human resources, technical and engineering resources, manufacturing resources, and other resource areas important to the company. The following are considerations in conducting the internal analysis.

Financial resources
- What are the key operating ratios in the industry?
- How does the company compare to industry standards with respect to the income statement and the balance sheet?
- What operating and financial trends are present?
- What are the financial strengths and weaknesses?
- What are the strengths and weaknesses of the revenue stream?
- Which product lines are most profitable? Least profitable?
- How stable is cash flow?
- What are the capital requirements?
- What are the internal and external financing capabilities?

Human resources
- What are the strengths and weaknesses of the management team?
- Quality process?
- Where are there gaps?
- What additional expertise is needed?
- What are the strengths, limitations and weaknesses of the employees of the business?
- Are additional resources needed?
- How does the organization encourage the growth and development of its people?
- What steps does the business take to hire and retain talented people?

Internal strengths and weaknesses need to be identified and discussed for any of the following areas that are relevant to the operation of your business.

- Marketing
- Operations
- Distribution
- Cash management
- Cost management
- Capital availability
- Information systems
- Product quality
- Service quality
- Customer loyalty
- Creativity in marketing, engineering, design, or other key areas
- Productivity
- Service
- Other

These areas need to be assessed with respect to strengths, weaknesses, capabilities, historical performance,and present status.

Summarize the information from your internal analysis and describe your company's primary strengths. Describe the primary strengths of the quality process.

- How can the quality process enhance the company's strengths?

Describe your company's primary weaknesses and describe the primary weaknesses of the quality process.

- How can the quality process minimize the company's weaknesses?

Summarize the key success factors that have been important to your company and the quality process.

- What can the quality process do to enhance the success factors that have contributed to the company's success in the past?

Summarize the action steps to be taken for implementing key finding resulting from the internal analysis.

The answers to the internal and external environmental assessment play a major role in determining the quality strategy that a company pursues. The environmental assessment reveals the strengths and weaknesses of the organization, with the quality strategy selected on the basis of achieving broader business goals and objectives by maximizing strengths and minimizing weaknesses.

Step 3: Selecting a Strategy

A strategy represents a business's commitment to a direction and a set of priorities that offer the organization its best chance for success. To be effective, participants in the quality process must first understand the overall business strategy and then determine how quality improvement best supports this strategy.

As described previously, Westinghouse faces a very difficult situation due to losses in its financial services business unit. In response to the cash flow crisis that these losses have created, the PQC now concentrates on cash flow generation. PQC uses a phased approach to implement the cash flow generation strategy.

1. When the PQC first becomes involved with a business unit, the initial phase is to reduce costs by eliminating the costs of poor quality. The short-term result is an increase in cash generation, profits, and customer satisfaction through lower costs and more competitive pricing.

2. The second phase of the strategy for generating cash is reducing the level of asset investment required to support the business by increasing the productivity of both people and facilities. Being able to produce more products using the same level of resources allows operating units to generate additional cash by reducing asset investments.

3. The third phase of the strategy is revenue generation. By improving features and functions in relation to price, the increased customer satisfaction produces a higher of level of sales. Given a lower cost and asset investment structure, the end result is the creation of a sustained level of profitability and cash generation.

The strategy of the Heinz TQM effort also reflects the mission of the business and the realities of the current situation. For example, Heinz's Star-Kist unit has always faced tough competition and has used its TQM process with great success in meeting its challenges. In the marketplace, this unit's dedication to improving quality and customer satisfaction has paid off handsomely. Coupled with its highest quality and lowest cost strategy, Star-Kist's dolphin-safe tuna strategy has earned the brand an even more dominant market position. The company's environmental leadership has raised consumer awareness of the Star-Kist label and helped its market share exceed 40 percent, a historic high. The national rollout of Star-Kist chunk white tuna in spring water elevated the company's market share for albacore tuna to 36 percent.

Star-Kist's competitors haven't fared as well. The loss of market share and resulting decline in per unit profitability caused the competition to rethink their strategies for competing against Star-Kist products. The answer was to sell out to ownership groups that could operate at a lower cost. Beginning in 1988, changes in ownership of Star-Kist's two major competitors created significant disruptions in a previously steady marketplace. In 1988, the Van Camp brand, Chicken of the Sea, was sold to P. T. Mantrust of Indonesia. In 1989, Bumble Bee was sold to Unicord of Thailand. As production has moved to Indonesia and Thailand, Star-Kist now must compete with two different companies that have obvious labor cost advantages.

If anything, the level of price competition will intensify as the new foreign owners attempt to capitalize on their lower labor costs. The response by Star-Kist has been to continue focusing the quality process on cost improvement through fish procurement and operations strategies. As described by Andrew Barrett, president of Star-Kist Seafood Company in the 1991 *Annual Quality Report to Employees.*[6]

> *Star-Kist is in the "quick fix" stage of our journey from strictly low cost operator to true total quality management. Each and every one of us must diligently implement TQM to rise above the competitive turbulence. . . . Our short-term goals are clear and attainable, but dependent upon each one of us holding true to our vision for the future: accepting the responsibility for continued improvement at Star-Kist. For the long term we must perpetuate and nurture the spirit of our mission, our TQM initiative and our revitalized attitude, for it is the driving force for the future at Star-Kist.*

Star-Kist is relying on TQM to compete against its new foreign competitors, just as it has previously depended on TQM to compete against domestic competitors. The strategy of using TQM to increase quality, lower costs, and improve customer satisfaction remains unchanged. The new competitive threat has merely reinforced the basics that have made Star-Kist so successful in the past. The emphasis going forward is to concentrate on identifying, selecting, and implementing the "vital few" projects that contribute the most to achieving increased customer satisfaction, reduced costs, greater market share, and improved margins.

Setting a strategic direction involves considerations of the business mission and goals, competitive threats and opportunities, and organizational strengths and weaknesses. The following two basic strategies surfaced repeatedly when we examined the approaches taken by successful companies.

1. Competing on the basis of offering the customer superior value in the marketplace relative to competition. Recognizing value as a crucial customer requirement marks a significant shift in developing competitive strategies. Many companies believe that low price or high quality alone are no longer sufficient to earn a company meaningful market share or sales.

2. Adding a financial dimension to the quality process by using quality tools and techniques to lower costs. The counterbalance to more competitive pricing in the marketplace must be more effective cost management in all phases of the business. If not, lower profitability will result as value-based competitors continue to exert pressure on prices. In order to maintain a satisfactory level of profitability and still provide customers with superior value, successful companies use higher conformance quality to reduce the costs of operations and offset the competitive pressures that force prices lower.

Our observations indicate that the strategic importance of quality increases significantly as the level of competition intensifies. The companies that benefit the most are those in industries where pricing and costs are critical success factors. Companies that benefit the least are those in industries that are (1) not driven by price or cost, (2) companies in market niches that are not intensively competitive, or (3) companies in industries where competition is regulated or limited.

Examples of industries that are relatively insensitive to price or cost are video games and wonder drugs. The success of a video game manufacturer is much more dependent on being first-to-market with the next good idea. For the video game manufacturer, margins are so large that cost inefficiencies may be of little consequence. For companies with regulated or limited competition, such as those companies protected by patent laws, the pressure to manage costs effectively is reduced. In these types of competitive environments, the payback from implementing effective strategic quality planning may not justify the efforts. What has proven to be a competitive nightmare for some companies, however, is the loss of insulation from competitive pressure or dramatic shifts in the market. Forced to compete in an open market, many telephone companies, utilities, and defense contractors are at a significant disadvantage. The recent price competition that has erupted in the market for cigarettes, for example, suggests that the industry structure may be entering a period of rapid change.

For those companies that can benefit from effective quality management, the quality mission and strategy must drive the improvement project selection if quality is to become an effective element in the competitive strategy. Figure 3.5 shows how strategic direction and knowledge of cause-and-effect relationships lead to the selection of projects that contribute to competitive success. Selecting improvement project is a more critical task than most companies realize, because the selection of the wrong improvement projects almost guarantees failure. Undertaking the wrong improvement project has the same negative effect as making the wrong decision regarding capital investments, product development, product marketing, or financing. Improvement projects must be selected on the basis of their ability to contribute to the achievement of the organization's financial and nonfinancial goals.

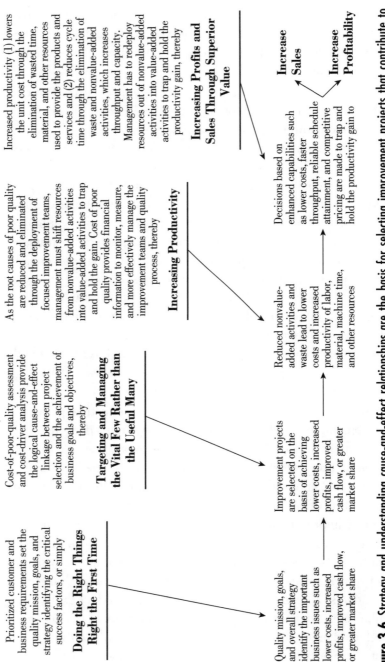

Figure 3.6 Strategy and understanding cause-and-effect relationships are the basis for selecting improvement projects that contribute to increased competitiveness.

Without the information needed to select the high payback, high impact projects, companies frequently pursue a mixture of well-intentioned but nonvital, possibly trivial, improvement projects. The fatal flaw is that no matter how successfully these projects are implemented, they contribute very little to the overall competitiveness of the organization.

The key to selecting improvement projects that can make a genuine difference is understanding the business strategy. A company needs to consider a variety of options and factors in setting a strategic direction. Guidelines for selecting a strategic quality direction are presented here.

Strategic Direction Considerations. List considerations for the quality process to ensure the quality plan realistically reflects the strategy, priorities, goals, and objectives of the business. The consideration of strategic direction is done to identify and evaluate strategic quality alternatives and to develop criteria to evaluate the alternatives.

The following are considerations in developing criteria to evaluate strategic quality alternatives.

Qualitative criteria
- Consistent with the business mission, goals, and culture
- Builds a sustainable competitive advantage
- Considers external threats and opportunities
- Leverages internal strengths and minimizes weaknesses
- Addresses potential competitive responses
- Reasonably achievable
- Consistent with intuition and experience

Quantitative criteria
- Sales volume
- Profit contribution
- Return on investment enhancement
- Market share improvement
- Product line profitability

- Overall operating profitability improvement
- Reduction in required levels of asset investments
- Other quantitative factors (experience curve or multiple factor analysis)

Three strategic options are open for using the quality process to a competitive advantage: (1) supporting the business strategy, (2) developing quality-related strategic options, and (3) establishing competitive barriers.

Supporting basic business strategies
- Maintain market share
- Expand product offerings
- Integrate forward or backward in the industry value chain
- Diversify into different markets or products
- Specialize
- Harvest cash from a particular market or product line

Developing quality-related strategic options
- Become low-cost producer by eliminating poor quality and its related costs
- Set the industry standard for customer satisfaction by sharply reducing customer complaints, increasing customer satisfaction levels, and offering competitive pricing
- Establish a superior value strategy by increasing conformance to requirements, and by lowering product price through reduced operating costs or asset investment levels

Establishing competitive barriers
- Reputation or image barriers based on the perceived price-to-features/functions ratio in the marketplace
- Product barriers based on reliability and flexibility
- Competitive barriers based on superior business, product, or service processes

The strategic alternatives analysis should be screened against (1) the business and quality mission, (2) the company's ability to leverage strengths and minimize weaknesses, and (3) the capability to take advantage of market opportunities and neutralize competitive threats. Alternatives that pass through these initial filters should be judged against the implementation criteria of practicality, cost, time to implement, and general level of difficulty.

The third level in assessing which strategic alternatives is asking the question, "Does this really make sense?" If you cannot support an alternative because it goes against your intuition and common sense, then stop and gather more facts or data. Analyze the alternative to better understand why it doesn't seem right. Experience can be a valuable tool but it can also be a barrier to new ideas. New alternatives sometimes seem counterintuitive. While your initial reaction may not be favorable, take the time to *objectively* evaluate and understand a new or different alternative before you reject it.

Before the final selection of the quality process's strategic direction is made, a number of steps should be taken to ensure that all relevant information and ramifications have been considered.

- List the qualitative and quantitative criteria used to evaluate strategic alternatives. The use of consistent criteria helps maintain objectivity in the evaluation process.
- Summarize the results of brainstorming on strategic alternatives. List all the alternatives identified regardless of how unusual or different. Remember, the final selection will be made from this listing of alternatives so develop a wide variety of alternatives. Use combinations of alternatives where appropriate.
- Summarize the results of evaluating the strategic alternatives. Score the alternatives according to the quantitative and qualitative criteria developed earlier. Also consider how an alternative can be used to create competitive barriers and sustainable competitive advantages.

- Select the most promising alternatives for further consideration and evaluation against the implementation criteria.
- For the alternative selected as the strategic direction for the quality process, summarize the goals and objectives for achieving the strategy. Goals and objectives for achieving the strategy should be set for both the near term and long term. Provide the key milestones or targets to determine if the strategy is working and progressing fast enough to accomplish the long-term goals on schedule. By monitoring the progress of each improvement project team, management can judge the success of the improvement process in achieving the quality strategy.

The strategic quality planning checklist that follows highlights important planning considerations every organizations should keep in mind. This is followed by a checklist of common planning failures to help companies avoid the many "sand traps" that other companies have fallen into.

Checklist for Strategic Quality Planning

	Yes	No
Is top management involved in leading and participating in the quality planning process?		
Are you building a consensus on a common direction?		
Have you developed and communicated an enterprise-wide quality vision?		
Are you emphasizing strategies and action plans as the heart of the process?		

Yes   No

Are you identifying and focusing on the
most important strategic issues?

Are you addressing alternatives for each of
the important strategic issues?

Are you planning to use ongoing feedback
to confirm or reconsider goals and strategies?

Are you striving to integrate a strategic
mind-set into the quality culture?

Are you establishing time lines and responsibilities for implementation throughout the
process?

Checklist of Common Quality Planning Failures

Yes   No

There is a lack of involvement of top management and key operating personnel.

There are unrealistic expectations or schedules.

The decision makers and influencers in the
organization are involved in a productive
manner.

Too many people are involved, and the
process is bogged down.

<u>Yes</u>   <u>No</u>

Sufficient resources of people, time, or money haven't been committed.

The long-term vision and goals of strategic planning have been confused with short-term objectives and tactics of operational planning.

Strategic planning has not been linked with operational planning.

Goals have not been linked with strategic plans and action plans.

There is a lack of follow-up to ensure that the quality process yields results.

The critical business issues haven't been identified or made the focus of the planning process.

The process has been stuck in the analysis stage and is not moving toward results.

Priorities haven't been established and resources haven't been allocated.

Those responsible for or affected by the quality plan have not bought in.

The process has been made a one-time effort and has not evolved into an ongoing process that builds on the experiences of the company and the quality process.

Conclusion

Top managers of companies are recognizing the need to improve quality as a means to lower costs, increase customer satisfaction, improve market share, and enhance competitiveness. The strategic impact of quality is becoming a primary concern as more companies view quality improvement as a competitive opportunity. The role of the quality process is changing as quality takes on greater and greater strategic importance. Strategic quality planning and its implementation now require the integration of business and financial perspectives with the traditional quality assurance techniques to meet the needs of the business and its customers.

Understanding the strategic direction and priorities set by top management is a prerequisite for effective quality management. Managers responsible for implementing the quality process can answer the question of how quality contributes to the success of the business after they (1) establish the quality mission, (2) analyze and understand the current competitive situation, and (3) select a quality strategy that reflects the needs of the business.

The experiences of Westinghouse, Heinz, and others illustrate the key role that quality can play in the success of a business. These experiences also illustrate that

- Strategic quality planning is evolutionary. Early efforts concentrate on understanding what works and what doesn't, building a culture within which quality improvements can be sustained, and establishing a solid foundation of quality skills through education and training. As experience and understanding grows, refinements to the basic planning process are introduced.
- Quality strategy, priorities, and objectives change with the internal and external environment. Changes in technology, competitors, customer expectations, and the economic outlook are just a few of the major influences that cause changes in the strategic quality plan. The quality strategy evolves by adapting to changes in the environment.

- It is likely that much of the information required to develop the strategic quality plan is already available. Planning efforts in other functional areas of the business require much of the same information. The time and effort required to prepare the quality plan can be shortened considerably by using the information already gathered by others.

The effort required to establish the quality mission, evaluate the environment, and select an appropriate quality strategy that reflects the business goals and objectives must be done to avoid one of the most crucial errors companies make in both business and quality planning: *Setting goals without a strategy and implementing strategies without a goal.*

Using the format that follows, try this simple test. Think about your organization and the most important goals and strategies. It doesn't matter if you are the CEO and look at the entire business, you are in your first job out of school, or somewhere in between. Once you have the goals and strategies in mind, write them down.

Goals **(Where You Wish to Be)**	**Strategies** **(How You Will Get There)**
1.	1.
2.	2.
3.	3.
4.	4.
5.	5.

Now, for each of the goals you listed, draw a line to the strategy that accomplishes that goal. For each strategy, draw a line to the goal that represents the achievement of that strategy. Any goal or strategy not linked together represents a point where goals and strategies are disconnected.

These disconnects are major gaps in the planning process of the organization, and usually occur because of changes in management methods, pressures on pricing or costs, market adjustments, or the inability of a business to balance short-term and long-term goals. The articles and surveys described in chapter 1 provide evidence of major gaps in the quality planning process judging by the high percentage of companies that fail to achieve meaningful results using quality improvement.

Goals without strategies are generally unattainable, regardless of the goal's importance. A strategy specifies logical steps, establishes priorities, and attracts resources that are required to achieve the goal. Trying to accomplish a goal without a supporting strategy is like driving around Phoenix with a road map of Chicago. The flip side of the problem is a strategy without a goal. The strategies will produce results but it is unlikely the results will be what the company wanted.

Chapter 4 presents an overview of the approach successful companies are using to implement strategies that focus on improving the financial performance dimension of quality improvement. The use of the cost of poor quality as a change management and performance measurement tool is discussed, as well as applying the cost of poor quality for project selection, measurement, and reporting on various aspects of the improvement process.

Notes

1. Frank Bakos, speech to the Westinghouse Total Quality Symposium, Pittsburgh, Penn., October 1992.
2. Garrett DeYoung, "Does Quality Pay?" *CFO Magazine* (September 1990): 31.
3. Lawrence P. Carr, *Xerox Corporation,* (Babson College teaching case, 1992).
4. Adapted from International High Technology Practice KPMG, *Dynamic Planning for the High Technology Business— Guidebook* (Seattle: KPMG Peat Marwick, 1991).
5. Kenneth R. Andrews, *The Concept of Corporate Strategy* (Homewood, Ill.: Dow Jones-Irwin, 1971), 113.
6. Andrew Barrett, *1991 Annual Quality Report* (Newport, Ky.: Star-Kist Seafood Company, 1991).

4 Quality-Based Cost Management: A Framework_____

Executive Summary

This chapter presents the use of quality tools and techniques to manage costs, a process we term quality-based cost management. The framework presented in the following pages is a synthesis of approaches developed by market and industry leaders to increase financial performance and customer satisfaction through quality improvement. Quality-based cost management is not a cut-and-slash cost reduction program posing as a quality initiative. On the contrary, quality-based cost management focuses quality improvement tools and techniques on increasing customer satisfaction *and* profitability by targeting the high payback opportunities for quality improvement.

This chapter explores (1) the use of modern cost-of-poor-quality applications as a means to consistently identify and quantify the nonvalue-added activities and waste driven by poor quality, (2) the use of cost-of-poor-quality measurement as a change management tool, and (3) the importance of using financial and nonfinancial performance measures to manage the improvement process on a day-to-day basis. The chapter concludes with an overview of quality-based cost management that highlights the cost-of-poor-quality assessment, cost-driver analysis, project selection, monitoring and measuring improvement progress, and reporting to management.

QUALITY-BASED COST MANAGEMENT: A FRAMEWORK

Companies are looking for new ways to compete more effectively in response to ever increasing foreign and domestic competition, changing customer expectations that now measure superior quality in terms of superior value, and continuing pressure on profit margins. Although the tools and techniques of quality improvement provide a strong foundation for problem solving, building and deploying teams, and analyzing processes, they often lack the means to prioritize quality efforts to meet strategic challenges or communicate the need for change.

Blending the strategic imperatives for cost management and profitability—the *voice of the business*—with the requirements of the customer—the *voice of the customer*—is difficult. The requirements of the business and the customer sometimes appear to be in conflict. Yet, to be successful, companies must come to the realization that both the customer and the business must be heard and represented in the day-to-day quality process. Even with a solid quality foundation in place, many companies possess little or no experience in aligning the quality process with the strategic challenges.

Each company brings its own unique perspective to balancing the voice of the customer with the voice of the business. Westinghouse views the balance between the requirements of the customer and the business as a natural part of its corporation-wide total quality process.

> From the perspective of total quality, everything starts with customers and their perception of value. Customer satisfaction requires us to provide a value-to-price ratio which is equal or superior to world-class competition.
>
> At the same time, total quality performance requires us to do this with an above average value-to-cost ratio to achieve superior financial performance.
>
> These market realities and financial imperatives establish requirements—for products and services, as well as for the processes by which we supply them. They are the bedrock from which total quality standards must be generated.
>
> This approach requires competing primarily on the basis of comparative value. Competitive cost and price are important but are not the driving competitive factors.

While each company has its own unique strategy for achieving competitive advantage through quality improvement, the emphasis on both profitability and customer satisfaction was consistently observed in the case study companies. Baxter Healthcare and USCO of Xerox, two companies recognized for effectively using quality improvement to gain competitive advantage, are representative of companies that use cost-of-poor-quality measurement to focus the quality process on increasing both customer satisfaction and profitability.

Baxter Healthcare[1]

The Quality Leadership Process (QLP) provides a method for understanding what quality is costing the company. Further, it provides a method of prioritizing the elements that comprise our costs of quality. Appropriate corrective actions can then be taken to reduce unnecessary costs.

Cost of [poor] quality is more than just a measurement, though. When understood and used properly, the cost of [poor] quality can generate momentum and help set priorities for reducing or eliminating problem areas.

Measuring in terms of dollars attaches new significance to quality, and gives tangible value to quality concepts. Cost of [poor] quality relates quality to profitability—the bottom line.

USCO[2]

Cost of [poor] quality is a financial measurement—a measurement that gives us the tools to identify and prioritize opportunities to conform to our customer requirements in the most cost effective way. Understanding and applying the cost of [poor] quality will aid us in achieving our four common goals of:

• Customer Satisfaction—By reducing the number of errors we make and simplifying our approach to meeting customer requirements, we will improve our external customers' perception of and satisfaction with Xerox.

• Human Resource Management—By eliminating rework and other unnecessary activities associated with nonconformance costs, we should improve employee job satisfaction and productivity.

• Business Results—Cost of [poor] quality actions lead to improved return on assets by capturing lost opportunities (more revenue) and reducing nonconformance costs (lower expenses and asset levels).

> • *Leadership Through Quality—Cost of [poor] quality application, in addition to itself being a major quality tool and objective, will result in our using other quality tools. Using the Quality Improvement and Problem Solving Processes as well as Competitive Benchmarking will enable us to pursue cost of [poor] quality opportunities in a logical and efficient way.*
>
> *We at USCO will seek out cost-of-[poor]-quality opportunities in every function, and every partnership and at all levels of our business.*

Top management at both Baxter Healthcare and Xerox recognizes the strategic importance of using the quality process to enhance financial performance. Cost-of-poor-quality measurement provides the means to bridge the quality process with the emphasis on profitability. Using the cost of poor quality, top managers at the two companies promote the quality process as a competitive thrust that is completely consistent with their financial orientations. As stated by Karl Bays, then Baxter Healthcare's chairman of the board, "Winning corporations have shown time and time again that the issue of quality is perfectly manageable. They have also taken it not as a fad but as a priority... a crucial criterion for competitive success."[3]

The cost of poor quality facilitates a broader and more robust quality process that addresses both the voice of the business and the voice of the customer. Used in a positive way, cost-of-poor-quality measurement and analysis promotes buy-in to the quality process, and lays the groundwork for the corrective actions needed to increase both profits and customer satisfaction.

Quality-Based Cost Management as a Cultural Change Agent, Performance Measure, and Facilitator for Cross-Functional Problem Solving

Cost-of-poor-quality measurement is one of the key elements of a quality-based cost management process that emphasizes the entire business, providing a means to focus the quality improvement process on increasing customer satisfaction and profitability. From the top floor to the shop floor, a common foundation is established for making decisions on the basis of facts and a genuine understanding of cause-and-effect relationships between quality and profitability.

Quality-based cost management can help companies manage change and facilitate cross-functional problem solving by coordinating and communicating the need for quality improvement throughout the organization. As a performance measure, quality-based cost management provides the means to deploy a financially oriented quality strategy across the entire organization and then to evaluate the progress of the organization in achieving the strategy.

As a Cultural Change Agent

Adoption of cost-of-poor-quality measurement at the case study companies typically coincided with the start of a major quality initiative, usually triggered by increased foreign competition or other competitive pressures. For companies accustomed to fire fighting and reactive, inspection-oriented responses to problems, the new quality initiatives represent significant shifts in philosophy. The director of quality in one case study company describes this shift in philosophy:

> Quality must become a vital part of running the business and be given top priority in every area of the business. This takes a culture change that permeates the entire organization. The culture change results in everyone in the organization recognizing the importance of quality, understanding quality, and accepting the responsibility for its improvement. Achievement of the culture change sets the stage for a step change in quality performance. The cultural change affecting the perception of quality requires people to break a number of old habits and adopt new ones . . .
>
> Changing these old habits and the conventional ways of thinking about quality is the real thrust of a quality improvement effort. It is such a dramatic change that the successful organization will undergo a culture revolution.

The magnitude of these changes becomes clear when the ingredients of the new quality-oriented organizations are compared to traditional manufacturing environments. Where traditional manufacturing environments tend to treat quality control and process improvement as staff responsibilities and to rely on extensive inspection to sort good product from bad, the new quality improvement philosophy emphasizes continuous improvement, quality the first time, and problem-solving skills at all levels of the organization. Where the traditional manufacturing environment relies on top-down procedures characterized by clear functional responsibilities and the notion that management knows more than workers about what should be done and how to do it, the new quality philosophies call for a reduction in organizational barriers and an atmosphere of teamwork in which all employees, including production workers, are seen as full and equal contributors. Moreover, where traditional manufacturing systems emphasize production volume and sales targets over quality, the new quality approaches require quality considerations to play a central role in every manager's objectives.

In the majority of case study sites, the measurement of the cost of poor quality provided a means to promote these changes by signaling the need for quality improvement to financially oriented managers. As behavioral scientists have frequently noted, employees require strong indicators that the current state is unacceptable before accepting the need for change.[4] One of the first steps in change management is, therefore, creating some sense of urgency around the changes that are being advocated. By positioning these changes in terms of strategic imperatives that are compelling to members of the organization, their relationship to company health and survival can be more readily recognized.[5] For companies that measure performance in terms of financial results, the measurement of the cost of poor quality provides a tool for creating the necessary sense of urgency by linking the quality improvement philosophies to the historical core value of the organization—the bottom line.

The experience of Texas Instruments (TI) illustrates the role the cost of poor quality can play in promoting cultural change.[6] TI produces a variety of electronic products ranging from semiconductors to automation systems for manufacturers. During the

1970s, TI had emphasized strong financial controls and a quality philosophy that, while never formally stated, expected a certain amount of defective product to be returned by the customer. By the early 1980s, however, intensified foreign competition and studies questioning the quality of semiconductors produced by American manufacturers forced TI management to recognize that the company's long-term competitive success required a greatly expanded commitment to quality.

The resulting total quality thrust was based on the following principles.

1. Quality and reliability (Q&R) is management's responsibility.
2. Q&R is a responsibility of all organizations.
3. Managers' performance on Q&R will be a key criterion in performance evaluation.
4. Managers' commitment to Q&R will not be measured—only outcomes.
5. The only acceptable goal for Q&R is a level that surpasses TI's best worldwide competitors at any time.

As part of the total quality thrust, corporate management directed the divisions to implement a quality measurement system to supplement the firm's extensive system of financial indicators. For years, TI had evaluated the profit and loss performance of each business with a series of financial indices published each month in the *Blue Book*. In 1981, the company began a *Quality Blue Book* incorporating a variety of quality measures such as product reliability, defect rates, and customer satisfaction. The *Blue Book* format was deliberately chosen to communicate to managers that quality performance was now to be judged on the same level as financial performance.

Like its financial counterpart, the *Quality Blue Book* contains three pages of indices presenting actuals versus goals, previous period comparisons, and three-month forecasts. In contrast to the highly structured financial *Blue Book*, the indices in the *Quality*

Blue Book are generally determined by the responsible profit center manager, allowing managers to tailor the report to reflect the key indicators in each business.

The cost of quality is the one measure required in every *Quality Blue Book*. The cost-of-quality measure is designed to highlight the cost of doing things wrong. Explained TI's president in a statement to the company's employees:

> Some people think quality costs money, because they see the costs of quality in terms of new testing equipment, added inspectors, and so on. But these are the costs of doing it wrong the first time. If we design a product right the first time, and build it right the first time, we save all the costs of redesign, rework, scrap, retesting, maintenance, repair, warranty work, and so on.
>
> Consider how much of your time is spent in doing something over again. How much of your assets are tied up in rework, retesting, repair, and making scrap? How much material is wasted at TI? If we could eliminate these costs by doing it right the first time, we would have true people and asset effectiveness, and improved profitability, without having to add a dollar to billings.

As this quote suggests, the cost-of-quality measure ties the total quality thrust into the company's established profit improvement programs, thereby emphasizing the benefits of quality improvement in terms consistent with the company's strong financial orientation. Noted a division general manager, "Motivating senior management isn't a problem. They already know that quality is critical. The cost of quality is most helpful for the middle managers to see the consequences of quality on overall income."

A controller at another division commented:

> The cost of quality ties quality progress into what we are here for—to be a profitable world class manufacturer constantly improving quality. The cost of poor quality numbers have shocked the [profit center] managers. We initially showed them cost of quality figures of 10 percent: 10 percent of sales value, and an even greater percentage of profits, down the hole. It is now down to a less shocking 4 to 5 percent. Managers are saying that they haven't found all of the costs but the trend is right. Even today's lower percentage is not making

them comfortable. A cultural change was needed from the old to the new. We now recognize that budgeting for bad quality is ridiculous.

The TI experience is representative of the role cost-of-poor-quality measurement played in promoting organizational change in the research sites. The power of cost of poor quality to shape organizational perceptions in the case study companies has revolved around two factors. The first is the ability to link the need for change to the financial concerns that dominate discussions in these firms. The following quote summarizes the sentiments that were heard frequently during the course of the best practices study: "We had to dramatically change the quality attitude. This couldn't be a completely cold change. We had to show that quality improved profitability."

A quality manager at another firm added

> *It's important at the outset of a cultural change to establish an imperative. Cost of quality has been that imperative. It's been a two by four that smacked people between the eyes—"Holy cow, we're spending this much on poor quality?!" At the outset, cost of quality was a way to communicate to survivors. It came on the heels of a dramatic downsizing. It was like having your heels on the edge of the abyss. In a sense, cost of quality served to give a tight focus. The big crisis in the change scenario was not for sweetness, goodness, and light but for survival. Cost of quality didn't leave people feeling good but was an imperative. It pointed out a crisis, a way of communicating it, a way of pointing out the foolishness that was going on.*

The second factor is the credible signal sent through the adoption of an accounting-based quality report. As one manager noted, "People have seen programs come and go. In first approaching total quality, it was seen as the same thing—'I wonder how long it will last?' We needed to convince them the quality system was here to stay. Credibility came from having the accounting function generating the quality cost report."

Stated another, "We thought it was important to get accounting to take responsibility for the cost-of-quality report. We were trying to institutionalize quality awareness. Accounting always tracked the important things so we thought it was important for them to track the cost of quality." As these quotes suggest, accounting systems have traditionally reflected what is important in these firms. By implementing cost-of-poor-quality reporting with the participation of the accounting function, top management provides a strong signal that quality is not a "program of the month" that will disappear within a short period of time.

As a Performance Measure

As an enterprise-wide performance measure, the cost of poor quality communicates the strategy and intent of upper management and establishes the quality improvement process as a top priority. By designing performance measures that encourage commitment to upper management's strategy, it is far more likely that employees will respond in a manner consistent with the strategic requirements of the business.

The wrong performance measures create barriers between an organization's strategies and the decisions made in response to different cultural and reward systems (Figure 4.1). For example, if a buyer's compensation is based on how little is paid for purchases from suppliers, it is highly unlikely that the buyer will ever be committed to using supplier quality ratings in the source selection process. It really doesn't matter if supplier ratings that incorporate multiple criteria are beneficial, people do what they are paid to do. If a company pays people to do the wrong things, people do the wrong things.

If a company competes on the basis of the quality and cost, how does keeping track of measures, such as the number of teams, increase quality or lower costs? It doesn't. The only way to focus the quality improvement effort on higher quality *and* lower cost is to develop performance measures that encourage employees to identify, prioritize, select, and implement improvement projects that provide higher quality *and* lower cost. The most common strategy for deploying quality teams can be summed up by the phrase "more is better than less." The underlying logic is that by broadly

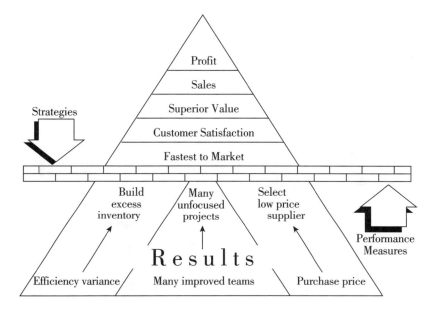

Figure 4.1 The wrong performance measures create barriers between strategies and achievement of business objectives.

deploying teams, the benefits will be broad. Many companies have found, however, that implementing numerous local improvement projects without focusing on overall objectives can be counterproductive. Xerox, for example, trained most of its manufacturing employees in cycle time reduction. The employees started numerous local cycle time reduction projects but achieved little reduction in overall cycle time. What Xerox later realized was that local, department-specific improvements did not necessarily translate into the global, enterprise-wide breakthrough in cycle time that Xerox needed to stay ahead of the competition.

Similarly, the Productivity and Quality Center at Westinghouse trained over 2500 quality circle leaders by the early 1980s and those leaders started over 3000 projects, involving nearly one-fifth of the Westinghouse employees. There were a number of significant successes achieved through the quality circles, but the successes had a local and somewhat isolated influence. The result was

Figure 4.2 The correct performance measures link strategy and organizational actions.

pockets of excellence but not the system-wide improvement that Westinghouse wanted and needed to remain competitive. The quality circle approach was superseded by the deployment of multifunctional quality improvement teams to tackle more significant issues.

As shown in Figure 4.2, the right performance measures accomplish two critical tasks.

1. They communicate the strategic intent of management to the organization.
2. They communicate the achievement of strategic objectives to management.

A typical process for using the cost of poor quality to deploy a business strategy and assess the achievement of business objectives is described as follows:

1. As one element of the business and quality strategy, upper management sets a goal for reducing the cost of poor quality within a specific period.
2. Quality improvement priorities are set and projects selected based on expected reductions in poor quality costs.
3. Upper management deploys the strategy by holding lower levels of management accountable for achieving cost of poor quality reductions of a specified amount within a given time period. Resources are allocated to support the improvement teams. Actions such as requiring that managers periodically report on their performance in achieving cost-of-poor-quality reductions and tying a portion of compensation signals top management's commitment down through the organization. The strategy is deployed when day-to-day actions are directed toward the achievement of meaningful strategic results.
4. Quality improvement teams are rated based on how well they achieve their targets for lowering poor-quality costs. An exceptional team receives a bonus for outstanding achievement, providing a valuable signal of management's commitment to cost-of-poor-quality reduction.

As a Facilitator for Cross-Functional Problem Solving

The breakthrough gains that create competitive advantages come from implementing solutions that benefit the entire organization. Companies have discovered that the real key to increasing the competitiveness of the entire business is concentrating on solving issues and problems that cross functional boundaries. However, most companies have found it difficult to overcome organizational barriers and achieve cross-functional cooperation and coordination.

Companies typically encounter two problems when attempting cross-functional problem solving. The first is gaining top management's support. Educating top management is essential because only management possesses the authority and resources needed to initiate cross-functional cooperation. One way to gain top management's support is to provide an accurate estimate of the negative financial impact of poor quality. This gives managers reliable information to weigh the potential benefits from cross-functional problem solving against the anticipated costs.

The second problem is the resistance that departments have to cooperating with one another. Cost-of-poor-quality measurement and analysis provide the information needed to identify and highlight the cost of problems that cross-functional lines. Communicating the competitive and financial impact of poor quality to everyone in the company provides a powerful message regarding the need for cross-functional cooperation and participation. By appointing and monitoring cross-functional cost-of-poor-quality reduction teams, a mechanism exists to coordinate problem-solving efforts across the entire business. Horizontal or cross-functional cost-of-poor-quality problem-solving efforts, sanctioned and supported by upper management, offer the means to move beyond the limitations imposed by departmental or localized problem solving.

Quality-Based Cost Management: Adding a Financial Dimension to the Quality Process

Our examination of best practices found that many companies have developed structured approaches for using the quality process to manage costs. Figure 4.3 provides an overview of the major elements of quality-based cost management, each of which is discussed in detail in later chapters.[7] Broadly speaking, the quality-based cost management approach contains the following major elements:

1. *Cost-of-poor-quality assessment.* The cost-of-poor-quality assessment quantifies the financial impact of poor quality on the organization. The results from the assessment are then used to target specific areas for further investigation based on their potential financial payback.
2. *Cost-driver analysis.* A cost-driver analysis is performed for each of the areas targeted in the assessment. The

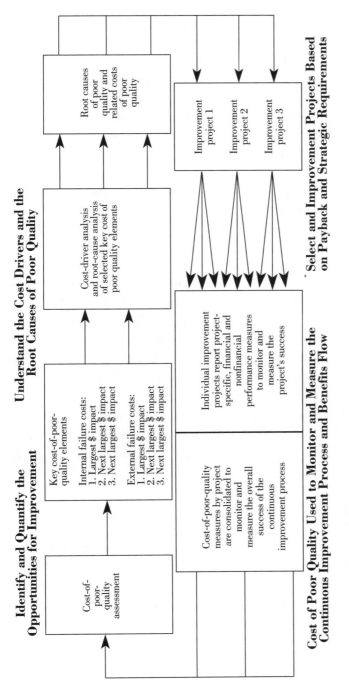

Figure 4.3 An overview of the quality-based cost management process.

Adapted from Hawley Atkinson, Gregory Hohner, Barry Mundt, Richard B. Troxel, and William Winchell, *Current Trends in the Cost of Quality: Linking the Cost of Quality and Continuous Improvement* (Montvale, N.J.: Institute of Management Accountants, 1991), 87.

objectives of the cost-driver analysis are (1) to identify the cause-and-effect relationships between the targeted cost element and its underlying root cause(s) and (2) to estimate the net financial payback from eliminating the root cause(s).

3. *Project selection and implementation.* Improvement projects are selected based on both the potential payback identified in the cost-driver analysis and the strategic imperatives established by the company in its quality plan. Formal project plans provide the game plan for the selected projects, documenting the project's purpose and its link to organizational success, identifying project participants and required resources, and setting realistic goals and time frames.

4. *Monitoring and measuring progress.* Monitoring and measuring improvement project success is based on the financial and nonfinancial goals established in the project plans. Individual project team results are then rolled up to report progress to higher levels in the organization. The combined project-specific reductions in poor-quality costs are subtracted from the baseline calculated during the initial cost-of-poor-quality assessment to develop an estimate of the current cost of poor quality, thereby providing a barometer of the quality program's success in improving financial performance.

The following example illustrates how one company used quality-based cost management to add a financial dimension to its quality process. Like many of the firms in our study, the company's quality journey was triggered by declining market share and eroding profit margins. In response, a cost-of-poor-quality assessment was performed to quantify the impact of poor quality and its related costs. Focusing only on internal and external failure costs in indirect and white-collar areas as well as the direct labor functions, the study showed the cost of poor quality to be 26 percent of sales.

Internal failure costs accounted for 79 percent of this figure while external failures accounted for 21 percent.

Figure 4.4 displays the largest cost-of-poor-quality elements uncovered by the assessment. As is typical in these studies, the assessment revealed that the six largest poor-quality cost elements accounted for 72 percent of the total. More important, three of these elements—uncontrolled inventory loss, returned goods, and penalties paid to customers for failing to meet delivery commitments—were identified only because white-collar functions were included in the assessment.

In just over four weeks, the company completed the assessment and selected the largest cost-of-poor-quality elements for the cost-driver analysis. Figure 4.5 depicts the completed cost-driver analysis for the delivery penalties, which was one of the cost elements targeted for further investigation. As the figure shows, the

---

- Key internal failure cost elements

	Total Failure Costs
100% inspection	23%
Uncontrolled inventory loss	17%
Scrap	13%
Operations corrective actions	5%

- Key external failure cost elements

	Total Failure Costs
Returned goods	9%
Penalties	5%

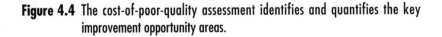

Figure 4.4 The cost-of-poor-quality assessment identifies and quantifies the key improvement opportunity areas.

Financial impact of the common root causes are determined after the cost drivers and root-cause percentages have been determined. Step 1: Allocate the key cost component across the activities and root causes. Step 2: Group common root causes to determine the financial impact.

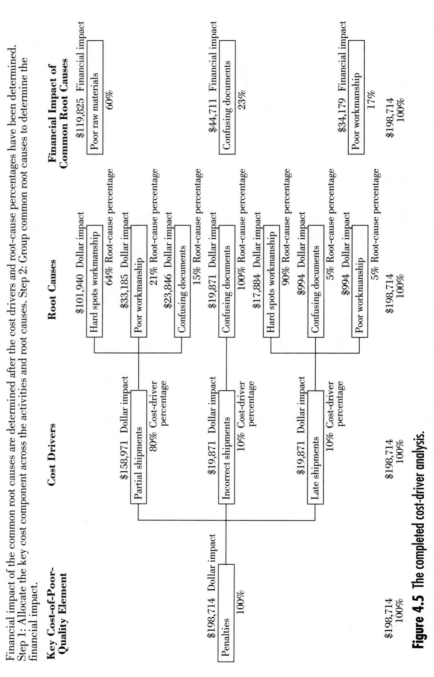

Figure 4.5 The completed cost-driver analysis.

initial investigation uncovered three cost drivers behind the delivery penalties: (1) partial shipments, (2) incorrect shipments, and (3) late shipments.

Further analysis of the cost drivers revealed a variety of underlying root causes of delivery penalties, the largest of which was hard spots in the raw material. Based on the information generated from the cost-driver analysis, the company established a team to revise the raw material specifications to eliminate the hard spots in raw material. Cost-driver analyses conducted for other key cost-of-poor-quality cost elements revealed that problems created by hard spots in raw material were widespread. The cost-benefit analysis for the project indicated the following financial benefit from the material specification project.

Cost to implement updated material specifications	$ 145,000

Financial benefits from eliminating hard spots

Income statement effects	
Reduced penalties	$ 119,830
Reduced uncontrolled material losses	368,940
Reduced direct labor costs	70,720
Reduced inspection costs	518,470
Reduced returned goods	78,960
Total income statement effects	1,156,920
Balance sheet effects	
Decreased inventory	$ 38,000
Decreased accounts receivable	168,560
Total balance sheet effects	206,560
Total benefits	$ 1,363,480
Estimated net financial benefits	$ 1,218,480

Using quality-based cost management, the company was able to focus on the source of the problem, not just the symptoms. Coupled with the financial information that is missing in many quality programs, this knowledge allowed the company to prioritize its improvement efforts and implement a cost-effective solution that improved both financial performance and customer satisfaction, providing a clear link between quality and profits.

Integrating Quality-Based Cost Management with Other Improvement Initiatives

While quality-based cost management is a powerful tool used by itself, companies in our study found that it can be even more powerful when used to leverage other improvement initiatives, such as process innovation, process-value analysis, and process reengineering, techniques collectively known as business process redesign. At the heart of each of these techniques is a common methodology that still requires companies to address many of the same challenges associated with effectively managing quality improvement initiatives.

Management Decision Points	*Management Challenges*
Identify and select critical process	Determine what is critical
Identify problem areas	Develop a consensus on the definition of nonvalue-added activities and waste
Gather specific data, determine the root causes, and document improvement opportunities	Prioritize areas for further investigation and determine the potential payback from a process improvement
Select redesign opportunities and prepare the project plan	Select improvement opportunities that can improve financial performance

Measure results   Determine if process
                                                   redesign improvement are
                                                   occurring fast enough to
                                                   achieve targets

Evaluate effectiveness   Determine the overall pay-
                                                   back from investing in
                                                   process redesign

Figure 4.6 maps out the stages of strategic quality planning and quality-based cost management into the elements of business process redesign.[8] As the figure clearly shows, the principles of quality-based cost management are just as applicable to process improvement and reengineering as they are to quality improvement. The underlying objective of providing useful information for improving financial performance remains unchanged. Companies have found that quality-based cost management can provide the information needed to identify points of leverage where new thinking on process design will provide the biggest benefit. By harnessing the power of quality-based cost management, companies have been able to magnify the financial results from business process redesign.

Conclusion—The Enterprise-Wide Approach

Top management's concept of how the quality process complements its competitive strategy and how it contributes to profitability must be expressed through the quality vision and long-term quality goals. The companies participating in the study of best practices have responded to this need by developing new approaches to align the priorities and objectives of the quality process with the priorities and objectives of the business.

Quality-based cost management extends the use of cost-of-poor quality information to all levels of the organization—from improvement team members to top management. The added capability to quantify and evaluate the improvement process lets companies link

Strategic Quality Planning

Critical business processes are selected for redesign based on their connection to the goals and objectives the business wants to achieve.

Quality-Based Cost Management

Step 1: Conduct Cost-of-Poor-Quality Assessment
Identify and quantify the costs of nonvalue-added activities and waste due to poor quality.

Step 2: Perform Cost Driver Analysis
Prioritize areas for further investigation based on cost of poor quality and determine the potential payback from potential improvement projects.

Step 3: Select Projects
Select the high-payback, high-leverage improvement opportunities.

Step 4: Measure Results
Analyze results of efforts to improve financial performance through business process redesign.

Step 5: Monitor Ongoing Performance and Report to Management
Monitor the improvement process and report the overall effectiveness and payback to management.

Business Process Redesign

I—Business Process Identification and Team Establishment

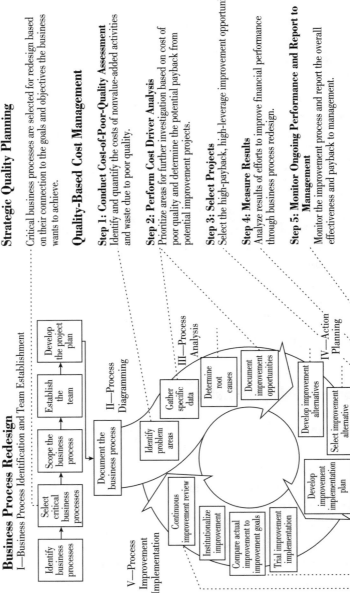

Figure 4.6 Quality-based cost management and process redesign.

the investment in quality to profits. Understanding the cause-and-effect relationships between quality and competitiveness lets companies estimate the effects of quality improvement on market share and profitability. By combining financial measurement with a cause-and-effect framework, companies are able to plan for and manage quality improvement in much the same way companies plan for and manage marketing, finance, production, sales, purchasing, or other functions of the business.

The end result is the availability of the information needed to build a common understanding about why quality works and the means to develop an effective approach for managing the quality process to deliver financial results.

The following two chapters present detailed case studies on the H.J. Heinz Company and the Westinghouse Electric Corporation. The studies focus on how two world-class companies achieve business and financial objectives using the quality process. The case studies present an overview of the competitive environment and pressures facing each company, and the process used by each company to implement quality-based cost management. Chapter 7 presents the lessons learned from our study of market and industry leaders and highlights the crucial issues and best practices for improving financial performance using quality improvement. Chapters 8 through 10 conclude the book by offering detailed discussions of the elements of quality-based cost management.

Notes

1. Baxter Travenol, *Cost of Quality: Laying the Cornerstone* (Deerfield, Ill.: Baxter Travenol Co., 1986), 3.
2. USMG Cost of Quality Team, *Cost of Quality: A Guide to Application* (Rochester, N.Y.: Xerox Corporation, 1987), v.
3. Baxter Travenol, *Cost of Quality: Laying the Cornerstone*, 20.
4. B. Hedberg and S. Jonsson, "Designing Semi-Confusing Information Systems for Organizations in Changing Environments," *Accounting, Organizations, and Society* (June 1978): 47–64.

5. Daniel A. Nadler, "Organizational Frame Bending: Types of Change in the Complex Organization," in *Corporate Transformation: Revitalizing Organizations for a Competitive World,* by R. H. Kilmann, T. J. Covin and Associates (San Francisco: Jossey-Bass, 1988), 66–83.

6. Christopher D. Ittner and Robert S. Kaplan, Texas Instruments: Cost of Quality (A) case 9-189-029 (Boston: Harvard Business School, 1988).

7. Material on the cost-of-poor-quality assessment and the cost-driver analysis was adapted from Hawley Atkinson, Gregory Hohner, Barry Mundt, Richard B. Troxel, and William Winchell, *Current Trends in Cost of Quality: Linking the Cost of Quality to Continuous Improvement* (Montvale, N.J.: National Association of Accountants, 1991), 65–81.

8. Business process redesign adapted from KPMG Peat Marwick, Federal Services Group, *Work Process Improvement Reference Guide* (Houston, Tex.: KPMG Peat Marwick, 1991). Portions of the reference guide and the process reengineering methodology were developed with the assistance of the Management Assistance Office of the NASA Johnson Space Center under contract NAS9-18239.

5 H.J. Heinz Company—A Case Study _____

Executive Summary

From its inception, Heinz top management positioned its TQM effort as an integral part of the way the business would be operated to accomplish business goals and objectives. Top management set the high-level, long-term goals to ensure that the priorities and objectives of the business and the quality process were aligned. A sense of common purpose and direction was instilled using the cost of poor quality, complaint reduction, and customer satisfaction as key performance measures for all levels of the organization. By establishing performance measures and implementing organizational changes that supported the achievement of the high-level performance goals, top management was able to communicate to everyone in the company that the success of TQM equaled success for the business.

H.J. HEINZ COMPANY—A CASE STUDY

When Henry Heinz founded his company in 1869 the first product was horseradish, packaged in clear glass bottles so that consumers could see the quality. Heinz entered the horseradish market at a time when the common practice for competitors was to use wood fibers and turnips to extend their product and then to disguise the adulteration using colored glass containers. The commitment to providing a quality product that started over 125 years ago has carried through to the present, with the H.J. Heinz Company now producing over 3,000 products for consumers in more than 200 countries and territories.

In the decade following 1981, Heinz increased its sales, operating margins, and earnings per share each year. Over the decade, earnings per share grew at an annual compounded rate of 14 percent, dividends increased at an annual compounded rate of nearly 17 percent, and the total return to shareholders, including price appreciation and reinvested dividends, was equivalent to 27 percent compounded annually—a world-class standard for performance in any industry.

This level of performance was achieved during a period when the processed food industry experienced sluggish growth and witnessed a number of bitter takeover battles. During the decade of the eighties, the industry was characterized by increased competition, higher energy costs, and escalating raw material costs. Heinz responded first with a competitive strategy entitled Low Cost Operator I, followed by Low Cost Operator II. The Low Cost Operator strategies were cost-reduction programs undertaken to improve gross margins and profitability.

Strategic Quality Planning

In the early stages of TQM, Heinz sought the assistance of Joseph M. Juran, Philip B. Crosby, and others whose teachings were incorporated into the Heinz quality culture. As described in chapter 3, the strategic quality planning process at Heinz emphasizes the improvement of financial performance as a part of its TQM process. Heinz uses the cost of poor quality, termed the cost of nonconformance, to provide the bridge from its earlier Low Cost Operator strategies to TQM. Because the focus on cost management did not change with the introduction of TQM, the shift from Low Cost Operator to TQM occurred quite naturally. Today the TQM initiative is viewed as an effort that is broader than the Low Cost Operator strategies by having the additional aspects of quality improvement but, at the same time, as also being quite consistent with the priorities of the past.

Analyzing the Current Situation

Heinz embraced TQM because senior management recognized the potential of TQM to complement the Low Cost Operator strategies. Instead of redefining its competitive strategy, Heinz simply asked how could TQM make the Low Cost Operator strategy more effective. The company's overall strategy did not change as a result of adopting TQM, and, accordingly, the existing assessment of strengths, weaknesses, threats, and opportunities was still applicable as Heinz implemented its quality initiative.

One impact of TQM was to refine the thinking about the types and frequency of data that were needed. As Heinz became more experienced with TQM, understanding the requirements of the internal and external customers became a higher priority. Efforts to satisfy the requirements of the internal customer, for example, showed that the needed information was not readily available, so the development of customer requirements information became a priority.

A process approach for gathering the required information was implemented. The process started with an examination of the requirements to be met, identified the inputs needed to satisfy the requirements, and then determined the source of the inputs. Heinz concentrated its efforts on gathering data that were useful for establishing and satisfying customer requirements and eliminating data collection that was unrelated. What Heinz ended up with was a smaller quantity of data that was much more useful for supporting the TQM process as well as meeting business objectives.

Selecting a Strategy

Since the overall strategy of being the low cost operator did not change, there was no strategic redirection. What did change was management's understanding of how quality affected costs and customer satisfaction. As the full impact of TQM on cost and customer satisfaction became known, management emphasized the implementation of focused TQM projects to reduce costs and eliminate customer complaints.

Understanding the cause-and-effect relationships between quality and competitiveness provided Heinz managers with the capability of identifying and selecting quality improvement projects that were consistent with the competitive strategy. The selection of focused quality improvement projects reflected the strategic imperative to compete on the basis of cost and quality. As the payback from focused quality improvements was demonstrated, management's commitment to TQM as a competitive strategy increased, providing momentum to improve quality further.

The Importance of Measurement at Heinz

Heinz emphasizes measurement throughout its quality process. The purpose of the measurement process is to define appropriate measures, establish standards, and display current and potential nonconformance problems in a manner that permits objective evaluation and corrective action.

Heinz's four distinct objectives of effective measurement are

1. To communicate openly that nonconformances exist in our work processes
2. To establish an atmosphere that allows for the honest reporting of errors
3. To ensure that all employees understand the purpose of measurement and the system used to provide for it
4. To help all departments understand their responsibilities for quality through the display of nonconformances

The measurement process at Heinz begins with the preparation of a departmental business mission statement that identifies the department's business purpose, major customers, major suppliers, and processes. The identification of the key processes to accomplish the business mission is done by each manager, supervisor, and employee of the department. Employee participation in the development of the process model is mandatory to ensure that the employees understand the key processes of the department. The process analysis approach emphasizes the following elements.

- Performance standards—identification of standards, personnel responsible for defining standards, and requirements to be satisfied
- Procedures—identification of procedures, personnel responsible for defining procedures, and requirements to be satisfied
- Inputs—identification of required inputs, suppliers of the inputs, and requirements to be satisfied by the inputs provided
- Outputs—identification of the outputs, identification of the customers, and requirements to be satisfied
- Facilities and equipment—identification of facilities and equipment required, personnel responsible for providing facilities and equipment, and the facilities and equipment requirements
- Training and knowledge—identification of training and knowledge required, personnel responsible for providing training, and requirements to be satisfied by the training and knowledge provided

Once the process analysis is completed, managers, supervisors, and employees are capable of identifying the measures of nonconformance for the functions analyzed. Display charts are used to record nonconformances and kept in plain view so personnel can see them easily. The employees responsible for the measurements post updates on a regular basis.

Heinz believes that there are two important benefits from a process analysis.

1. Everyone in the department gains a deeper understanding of how the business operates. Understanding the processes and the customer requirements is a necessary foundation of information for employees to meet the corporate goals to reduce cost of nonconformance and customer complaints. Concepts like the internal supplier and

the internal customer are much more understandable once the manager, supervisor, and employees have completed the process analysis.

2. One of the ways for nominating improvement projects to be carried out by the improvement teams, referred to as corrective action teams, or CATs at Heinz, is from the results of the key measurements taken by the department. Knowing the number of nonconformances that occur in a critical process is an example of how potential CAT projects are identified.

Measurement of nonconformances and understanding the processes involved are part of the effort put forth by Heinz to avoid a fatal error that plagues many quality processes: selecting the wrong projects. No matter how insightful the vision and strategy may be, implementing projects that are not vital to the accomplishment of the organization's objectives will result in delivering results that do not contribute to the accomplishment of strategic goals.

Implementing Quality-Based Cost Management: The Key to Sustained Profitability and Competitiveness

Top management commitment and involvement in the quality process has been and continues to be the principle determinant of TQM success at Heinz. The implementation of the Heinz quality process encountered the same problems and difficulties faced by any company. Top management commitment and support laid a solid foundation, however, allowing the organization to overcome the problems and difficulties that occurred. The Heinz track record of accomplishment is founded on good management practices, with the successful implementation of the quality process reflecting that management capability.

In contrast to companies that have been unable to produce meaningful results from the quality process, Heinz started the implementation of its quality initiative with two essential ingredients for success already in place: (1) real and measurable quality goals driven off business mission and goals and (2) a clear understanding, by everyone involved, of the contributions that the quality process can make to achieving the competitive strategy.

The quality vision and goals provide constancy of purpose and direction for the quality implementation. At any point in the implementation, individuals can reference the quality vision and quality goals to test activities and priorities. Testing activities and priorities against the vision and goals ensures that the current efforts are consistent with the organization's quality objectives.

Preparing the Quality Plan

The quality plan developed by the World Headquarters provides a good example of how Heinz and the affiliate companies implement the quality process. It is up to each affiliate company to prepare its own plan for assuring that the quality goals are achieved. The quality plan is the vehicle used to focus efforts and resources on accomplishing the twin quality goals of 50-percent reductions in the cost of nonconformance and customer complaints.

The quality plan for World Headquarters encompasses the following 10 elements.

1. Management commitment
2. TQM organization
3. Measurement
4. Cost of nonconformance
5. Quality awareness
6. Corrective action
7. Recognition/gratitude/celebration
8. Education
9. Goal-setting
10. Do it all over again

Linking the quality goals of the corporation to the goals of the affiliate companies is a crucial ingredient of the planning process. The World Headquarters quality plan describes how this is accomplished.

9. Goal-setting

Purpose: To turn pledges and commitment into action by encouraging individuals to establish and achieve goals that optimize overall corporate goals by clearly stating the requirements in terms of results and timing that will lead to our stated corporate goal of a 50 percent reduction in cost of nonconformance and a 50 percent reduction in consumer complaints by fiscal year 1994.

As a part of the goal-setting element of the quality plan, the weights that will be used in determining a manager's bonus are established based on the quality goals set by the manager. The weighting is sufficient to ensure that quality receives the attention it deserves, with the salaried performance appraisal form designating quality as the *first* major job responsibility. A portion of the quality goals must be accomplished through the manager's personal participation and cannot be delegated. In this way, managers who participate in the management incentive program serve as visible role models for the others involved in the quality initiative.

Possible TQM goals can include training or involvement in steering committees, quality improvement councils, and CATs. These goals are in addition to intermediate targets leading to the 50-percent reduction in cost of nonconformance. After completion of the quality education course, each manager and employee agrees to specific quality goals for the year.

Each quality improvement team develops specific goals for the CATs under its direction to achieve the overall, strategic quality goals set by the executive committee. Members of a quality improvement team (QIT) include the senior vice president, the reporting managers, and others at the discretion of the team. Accordingly, the goals set by the QIT are often cross functional and interdepartmental in nature. Goals reflect the need for cooperation and coordination across departmental and functional boundaries, activities that are generally difficult to accomplish in typical manufacturing environments. By elevating goal-setting and project selection to teams made up of functional and departmental managers, Heinz has been able to create a structure that is conducive to horizontal problem solving by coordinating the actions and interactions of multiple departments.

Heinz has effectively deployed cost of nonconformance as a performance measure by using the concept to link corporate goals, management compensation, and QIT activities. The focus on reducing cost of nonconformance occurs at all levels of the corporation, from individual employees to senior executives. This seemingly simple process has an extraordinarily powerful effect: Day-to-day activities of all people within the business are directed at accomplishing common organizational goals.

The ordinary decisions made during the course of every business day contribute to the accomplishment of the corporate goals. By linking the accomplishment of quality to the compensation of management, Heinz is paying people to do the right things. The disconnects between pay and performance that exist in so many quality processes have been minimized by Heinz.

The interweaving of cost of nonconformance into the various elements of the quality plan is the mechanism used by Heinz to assure that quality becomes a part of the day-to-day operating routine. The QIT structure closely parallels the existing organizational structure, thereby promoting the natural adoption of quality improvements into departmental operations. This framework ensures that the business processes of affected work groups are considered when planning for corrective actions.

Cost-of-Poor-Quality Assessment

Having developed a quality plan that addresses the goals of the organization, the next step is to identify improvement opportunities. The cost-of-nonconformance assessment is conducted by a CAT under the sponsorship of the quality improvement council. The purpose of the assessment is to define the components of the cost of nonconformance and then explain and demonstrate the proper use of cost of nonconformance techniques.

The objective of the assessment is to develop a system that reports the cost of nonconformance on a regular basis in a manner that is easily understood and readily usable by all levels of management. Cost-of-nonconformance reporting is used by management as a tool to control costs by achieving conformance to defined internal and external customer requirements. An equally important objective is to generate, promote, and target corrective action by quantifying for all personnel the financial impact of nonconformance to requirements.

Once the cost-of-poor-quality assessment is complete, the CAT that conducted the assessment is also responsible for defining and developing a measurement and corrective action tracking system. This system establishes the reporting to support the project-by-project improvement process at all levels of the organization, as well as providing management with the required status reports to encourage and control the improvement process.

The cost-of-poor-quality assessment begins with attendance of the cost-of-poor-quality corrective action team at a two-day workshop on identifying and calculating the cost of nonconformance. Although subsequent cost-of-poor-quality assessments become progressively more refined as experience increases, the emphasis is on keeping the assessment simple and efficient. One of the pitfalls described by Terry Gaab, manager of financial systems for Heinz Pet Products and Star-Kist Seafood Company, is the obsession with trying to get every detail of the cost of nonconformance. The use of sensible calculation techniques and a simple tracking mechanism is adequate. The point of the assessment, particularly in the first two or three years of the quality initiative, is to identify the easy improvement opportunities that have a high payback—which Heinz refers to as the "low-hanging fruit." By concentrating on harvesting the low-hanging fruit first, the early successes come much more quickly, allowing significant progress toward established goals and objectives.

Gaab was careful to point out that a complex and sophisticated accounting system approach often gets tangled up in minutia. Once that happens, the system becomes a diversion from the really important things, like deploying and supporting the efforts of CATs to eliminate poor quality and its related costs.

Mary Ann Bell from World Headquarters cited three key reasons for developing cost-of-nonconformance information.

1. *To gain management's attention.* The cost-of-poor-quality assessment expresses the need for quality improvement in a language that everyone can understand—dollars and cents. The assessment demonstrates that quality improvement is not expensive; failure to improve quality is.
2. *To help management prioritize improvement efforts.* The cost of nonconformance and the follow-up root-cause analysis indicate where corrective action efforts afford the greatest return. Experience has shown that a small percentage of the causes of poor quality account for a high percentage of the costs of poor quality or cost of nonconformance.
3. *To measure improvement.* The cost of nonconformance provides a system of measurement to monitor the effectiveness of the quality improvement process.

Identifying the Cost of Poor Quality
The following are the basic cost-of-poor-quality definitions used by Heinz.

Cost of Nonconformance. These are the costs incurred because things were not done right the first time. These nonconformance costs result from failures found both before and after the delivery of the product or service. Examples include

- Errors due to a lack of training, unclear procedures, or misunderstood requirements
- Absenteeism
- Scrapping or reworking of a product or service
- Unproductive meeting time
- Computer downtime
- Consulting fees if consultants were brought in to solve a problem
- Lost sales or lost profit opportunities

Price of Conformance. These are the costs incurred to make sure things are done right the first time. These costs are expended in an effort to prevent nonconformance from occurring. Examples include

- Training programs
- Auditing
- Proofreading
- Confirmations (that is, travel arrangements, meeting times)

Cost of Poor Quality. The sum of the cost of nonconformance and the cost of conformance is the cost of poor quality.

Error-Free Costs. Cost incurred from value-added activities that are required to support the basic functions of our business are considered error-free costs. These are needed to produce a product or service, if everything is done right the first time, according to specified requirements. Examples include the cost of

- Typing a letter or other document (not including proofreading or correction)
- Making a travel reservation
- Preparing a check request
- Transferring funds among bank accounts
- Selling a product or service
- Entering orders correctly the first time
- Writing a computer program correctly the first time
- Purchasing necessary goods and services
- Employee development

Three basic techniques are used to calculate the cost of nonconformance: (1) use of established accounts such as scrap and rework, (2) the review of staffing to identify employees whose sole job is to identify or correct defects, and (3) the distribution of labor and resources between error-free and quality-related activities. If no detailed time-keeping system exists, or the system does not provide enough detail to distinguish between error-free and quality-related activities, a survey is made of all employees.

Meetings are first held with all employees to review what constitutes cost of conformance and nonconformance to ensure that common definitions are used. The department manager prepares a list of the conformance and nonconformance costs either incurred by the department or associated with that department's activities. The job activities worksheet used to guide the analysis is shown in Figure 5.1.

After the department manager has completed the list of conformance and nonconformance items and individual employees have completed their job activity worksheets, another meeting is held with the department manager. The purpose of this meeting is to review the reasonableness of the identified conformance and nonconformance activities and identify any significant omissions. Fully burdened costs are used in the assessment. For example, if 20 percent of the department's salary costs are spent on cost-of-nonconformance items, 20 percent of the benefits are assumed to be related to the nonconformances as well.

The instructions for the cost-of-nonconformance analysis worksheet provide a reminder that

> *Existing accounting or other cost tracking systems may not capture all costs of quality, such as lost sales or profit opportunities, but existing systems should be used whenever possible. Creating a new accounting system is not the objective of the cost of nonconformance analysis. When estimates must be made, the methodology should be kept simple.*

It is the responsibility of the department that bears the costs of conformance and nonconformance to report these costs, *regardless of controllability or accountability.* In many instances, the reason for the nonconformance may be external. In order to obtain a true company-wide view of the total cost of conformance and the cost of nonconformance, however, all incurred costs must be reported. During the cost-of-nonconformance analysis, the representative will include, where applicable, the department manager's representation that certain reported costs are beyond the control of the department. The assessment form is shown in Figure 5.2.

Cost-of-Poor-Quality Analysis
Job Activities Worksheet

Job title_____

Incumbent_____

Instructions: Please identify below all job activities that represent either the cost of conformance (the time spent checking to ensure that no nonconformances exist in job inputs or outputs) or cost of nonconformance (the total time spent on correcting nonconformances). Indicate the approximate percentage of your time that is devoted to each. Please attach an additional page if necessary.

Description of Activity   **Time**

Cost of conformance:

1. _____   _____%
2. _____   _____%
3. _____   _____%
4. _____   _____%
5. _____   _____%

Cost of nonconformance:

1. _____   _____%
2. _____   _____%
3. _____   _____%
4. _____   _____%
5. _____   _____%

Figure 5.1 Heinz uses worksheets and listings to guide the cost-of-poor-quality assessment process.

Summary Cost-of-Quality Assessment Form

Department Name:

Department Number:

Description	Subaccount	Fiscal year 1994 Budget	Error-Free Cost	Price of Conformance		Price of Nonconformance	
				Controllable	Uncontrollable	Controllable	Uncontrollable
Salaries	120						
Overtime—salaries	160						
Physical exam expenses	177						
Payroll expenses—fixed	199						
Supplies and small tools	200						
Air shipments	393						
Telephone	400						
Freight	410						
Travel	429						
Travel-related expenses	430						
Employment expenses	450						
Employee moving expenses	460						
Professional fees consulting	548						
Professional fees	550						
Subscriptions	560						
Membership dues	570						
Partly deductible meals and entertainment	580						
Sundry expenses	600						
Rent	840						
Rent—machinery	850						
Grand total							
Total allocated							

Figure 5.2 The summary cost of quality assessment form follows the departmental budget format.

The inclusion of a department manager's representation that certain quality costs are beyond the control of the department is the mechanism that addresses a critical issue. Poor quality and poor-quality costs do not respect organizational boundaries, yet these same organizational boundaries often prevent companies from effectively solving problems. The formal recognition that poor-quality costs caused within one area of the company may surface in another area serves as a visible signal to the entire company that problems are often interdepartmental. This signal provides the justification for assembling interdepartmental CATs to solve problems that cross boundaries within the organization.

The individual cost-of-nonconformance elements are presented in a format similar to that used for departmental budgets. A form showing the budgeted subaccounts serves as the summary for the cost-of-nonconformance analysis of a department. The form is completed in two stages.

1. Budgeted amounts are broken into error-free costs, cost of conformance, and cost of nonconformance.
2. Significant costs incurred for conformance and nonconformance that are not the same as budgeted items are itemized below the budget information or on a separate sheet. Costs that are not controllable are noted either on the cost-of-conformance and nonconformance worksheet, a separate piece of paper, or the bottom of the summary worksheet.

A cost-of-conformance and nonconformance worksheet (Figure 5.3) is optional and is often used to summarize the information gathered from the activity worksheets and to quantify the cost of conformance and nonconformance.

Throughout the cost-of-poor-quality assessment, the CAT members responsible for conducting the assessment communicate the ground rules to everyone involved.

- The cost of nonconformance is not to be used for *individual* performance appraisal.

**Cost-of-Nonconformance Analysis
Cost-of-Conformance and Nonconformance Worksheet**

Completion of this form is optional. You may find it helpful in organizing your thoughts and in summarizing your work.

Department name _____

Subaccount number _____

Fiscal year 1994 budget amount _____

Error-free cost _____

Amount _____

Notes/explanation _____

Price of conformance _____

Amount _____

Notes/explanation _____

Cost of nonconformance _____

Amount _____

Notes/explanation _____

Figure 5.3 The optional worksheet summarizes assessment results.

- The cost of nonconformance is not to be used to compare departments.
- The analysis is based on the existing systems and surveys as much as possible. The intention is not to create a new accounting system.
- Participation of department heads is essential.

- The analysis should be kept simple. The cost of refining the information should be balanced against the value of the increased precision.
- The compilation will identify all of the costs of conformance and nonconformance incurred, regardless of fault.

Once the cost-of-poor-quality assessment is completed, the results are given to the QIT. The results of the assessment are used to identify and prioritize opportunities for future improvement. The QITs summarize the cost-of-poor-quality assessment information and report the results to the TQM steering committee. On a semiannual basis, the TQM steering committee reports the results of the cost-of-poor-quality assessment along with other quality improvement activities to the top management of Heinz.

Root-Cause Analysis

Projects can be nominated for root-cause analysis in a variety of ways.

- Nonconformances identified as a result of the key measurements taken by a department
- Nonconformances that represent a barrier to the achievement of a goal established for a department manager, general manager, director, or vice president
- Nonconformances that result in a suggestion from any departmental CAT member
- A recommendation to eliminate nonconformances submitted through the quality recommendation process
- A request from another affiliate company to eliminate nonconformances through participation in an interaffiliate project

The CAT approach is the cornerstone of the Heinz quality improvement process. A CAT is responsible for analyzing and solving problems assigned to them by the QIT or department managers. The vast majority of time spent by Heinz personnel on quality improvement is incurred by the CATs. The primary purpose of the teams is to bring together the proper mix of employees from the affected departments who are qualified to study an identified problem, isolate the root-cause, and eliminate the problem forever.

Each CAT uses the Crosby problem-solving approach, consisting of the following five corrective action steps.

1. Define the problem.
2. Fix the nonconformance.
3. Identify the root cause(s).
4. Implement corrective action.
5. Evaluate and follow up.

The start of the problem-solving process for every CAT is to meet the following requirements.

- The CAT members must mutually agree to the team's mission.
- Every CAT must measure the nonconformance it is working to eliminate.
- Every CAT must identify the savings (cost of nonconformance) and/or revenue enhancement associated with the specific nonconformance it is attacking.
- Every CAT must submit a brief corrective action status report every month to an individual on the QIT. This report is produced using a preprinted, one-page format. The QIT collects, reviews, and forwards the reports to the TQM development coordinator. The reports are used for publicity and recognition purposes as well as keeping the quality council and the TQM steering committee informed.

A CAT goes through three steps to identify the root cause(s) of a problem assigned by the QIT. The steps begin after the team agrees on a mission statement and calculates the cost of nonconformance, if it has not already been done.

The first step is to *define the situation*. The CAT completes a process worksheet to ensure that the team understands the inputs, outputs, suppliers, customers, procedures, and performance standards. Once completed, the team continues its analysis and identifies the consequences of the problem. Further analysis defines the problem by determining who, what, when, and where. The team relies on the tools and techniques of quality improvement as a part of the problem-solving process. More measurements are taken if required. Once the CAT has defined the situation, the problems are prioritized.

The second step is to *fix* the largest or most influential problems. The fix is a temporary cure to minimize or reduce the effects of poor quality. For example, if the team determines that the primary reason for low line efficiency is a maintenance failure, a short-term fix that adjusts for the maintenance failure is identified and implemented before conducting further root-cause analysis or investigation. The team determines the fix options, assigns a cost to each, estimates the option's payback, and then reaches a consensus about the best fix or fixes to put in place until the root-cause analysis is completed.

By implementing a fix, the nonconformances and related cost of nonconformance and customer complaints are immediately reduced. Even though this step is a short-term bandage, any fix implemented on a cost-benefit basis allows a CAT to generate quick payback from quality improvement. By not waiting until the root-cause analysis is complete, Heinz achieves an immediate reduction in the cost of nonconformance and customer complaints, its two corporate quality goals.

The third step is to *identify the root cause(s) of the problem.* Again, many of the quality improvement tools such as fishbone diagrams or statistical process control (SPC) are used by the CAT to analyze and understand the problem. The team concentrates on isolating the cause-and-effect relationships by repeatedly asking the question, "Why?"

Once the root cause(s) of the problem is identified, the CAT determines the nonconformance cost reduction or revenue enhancement potential associated with each root cause, identifies the costs to permanently eliminate the cause(s), estimates the benefits to the company, and then reaches a consensus on the recommended corrective actions. By judging potential improvement projects on the basis of net benefit (estimated cost of nonconformance reduction or revenue enhancement less the cost to implement), Heinz maintains its focus on reducing the cost of nonconformance and customer complaints by 50 percent over four years.

Project Selection and Planning. The improvement projects identified through the root-cause analysis are referred to as corrective actions. The corrective actions are prioritized on a variety of criteria, including (but not limited to) the net benefits of nonconformance reduction and the reduction of customer complaints. Corrective actions where the cost to implement exceeds the expected benefit are postponed until a more cost-effective solution becomes available. In such cases, the implemented fix may become a longer-term remedy and stay in place. Corrective actions that have implementation costs that are not feasible given capital budget constraints are postponed until funds can be made available. Corrective actions that require a long time horizon to complete or reap benefits are likely to be postponed in favor of corrective actions that have a quicker payback.

A critical element in the Heinz strategy for selecting corrective actions is to harvest the low-hanging fruit. It makes better economic sense to first select the improvement projects that generate both high payback and lower customer complaints. The impact of the improvement process on achieving the two quality goals will be much greater and accelerate the achievement of the key objective of the Heinz Quality Charter: all for the objective of securing for our company a meaningful and permanent competitive advantage, and for our shareholders an above average return on their investment.

Heinz has learned that the Pareto principle is also applicable to the root causes of poor quality: 20 percent of the root causes often account for 80 percent of the cost of nonconformance and customer complaints. By placing the emphasis on eliminating these root causes, quality makes a direct impact on the bottom line. The effort expended to identify the high payback root causes of poor quality allows Heinz to take a rifle shot approach to targeting quality improvement, rather than the less reliable shotgun approach.

The planning for corrective action implementation begins once the actions have been prioritized and selected. One of the first planning steps is involving customers and suppliers, both internal and external, who can influence the success of the corrective action implementation. The specific requirements, actions, changes, or modifications are determined and a schedule is established for implementation. Responsibilities and completion dates are clearly spelled out.

The Heinz emphasis on quality planning and CAT planning is based on valuable lessons learned from six years of experience. Heinz has discovered that one project focusing on a $7,000,000 reduction in the cost-of-nonconformance problem is easier to manage, staff, and support than 100 projects chasing $70,000 each. More importantly, large focused projects have a much higher success rate and payback than many smaller projects. The net result is a quality improvement culture that goes after substantial, meaningful issues that are vital to creating competitive advantage, rather than many smaller projects that are well intentioned but not particularly meaningful to the corporation as a whole.

Once the low-hanging fruit is harvested, the emphasis shifts to harvesting the fruit in the "higher branches." Heinz Pet Products and Star-Kist Seafood Company have been using quality as a focused cost management tool for nearly four years and there is now a sense that much of the low-hanging fruit has been harvested.

The means used to reach the higher branches and identify the high payback projects is an expanded poor-quality cost element listing that goes beyond the cost of nonconformance to identify other nonvalue-added activities and waste such as excess material handling and manual rekeying of information between computer systems. The cost-of-poor-quality listing presented in appendix B is representative of the approach used by Heinz through the first five years of its quality initiative.

Deploy and Implement

The same CAT that conducted the root-cause analysis may continue with the implementation of the corrective actions, or the implementation may be done by a different team. The choice of whether the CAT should implement the corrective actions depends on organizational considerations such as the qualifications or skills required for team members and the availability of experienced personnel.

A critical element in the implementation is communication from the CAT to the various departments or organizational units. The CAT teams include employees from the affected units are members of to ensure that each affected department or organizational unit is represented. This representation gives the team the skills, balance, and perspective needed to develop effective solutions and maintain effective internal communications.

In addition to providing a balanced perspective and a natural communication link, the development of a quality structure that parallels the organizational structure helps to ensure that the corrective actions are perceived to be operationally and organizationally appropriate. The corrective action is developed and implemented by the same personnel who are responsible for day-to-day operations. The teams' selected actions are seen as operational improvements, thereby dramatically increasing the probability the actions will be accepted on a long-term basis.

Monitor, Measure, and Report

Every CAT must submit a brief monthly CAT report to an individual on the QIT. This report is produced using a preprinted, one-page form. The QIT collects, reviews, and forwards the reports to the TQM development coordinator. The reports are used for publicity and recognition purposes and for keeping the quality council and the TQM steering committee informed.

At an earlier stage in the quality process, each of the members of every CAT must mutually agree on the CAT mission, measure the nonconformance it is working to eliminate, and identify the savings (cost of nonconformance) and/or revenue enhancement associated with the specific nonconformance of its charter. These requirements form the baseline from which the performance of each CAT can be monitored and measured.

The semiannual report to top management follows the same format. The semiannual report to the TQM steering committees of the various affiliates contains a section on the progress in reducing the cost of nonconformance and customer complaints, as well as a section on the vital few projects currently underway to achieve these goals. The importance placed on regularly monitoring and measuring the effectiveness of quality improvement process is one of the key elements in communicating top management's sustaining support and commitment to quality.

The reports by Heinz U.S.A. shown in Figure 5.4 were submitted through the respective TQM steering committees to top management, illustrating the mechanisms used to monitor the units' quality progress. The emphasis on measuring the effectiveness of quality at each of the affiliate companies lets senior management determine if the investment in quality is paying off. The reporting of team level results is a bottom-up approach in which the performance of each CAT is monitored and measured. The individual CAT results are then tallied to determine the results for the affiliate company. Finally, the results for each affiliate are summed to determine the overall results for Heinz.

By linking the day-to-day activities of the CATs to the accomplishment of corporate goals, Heinz has been able to ensure that all of the decisions and activities of each CAT move Heinz toward the achievement of corporate objectives. Through the quality process, Heinz has been able to harness the collective efforts and energies of its people by providing an environment where people are doing the right things for the right reasons. The final element of the quality-based cost management system is to make solutions and improvements available to the rest of the Heinz affiliates.

Adjust and Adapt

Element 10 of the World Headquarters quality plan is do it all over again, emphasizing that quality is a never-ending process. The

Cost of Nonconformance Information

Cost of nonconformance: $47 million*
Cost-of-nonconformance reduction achieved to date: $18 million; 39% reduction
*Does not include the sales division

Customer Complaint Information
Complaints per million units shipped have decreased by 48%

Key Projects: The Vital Few Cost-of-Nonconformance Reduction

Projects in Progress	Key Measures	Cost of Nonconformance
Ketchup PET bottle cost reduction	• Cost of bottle • Conversion costs	$3.3 million
Net contents project	• Reduction in standard deviation • Percent marginal underweight	$480 million

Key Projects: The Vital Few
Customer Satisfaction Improvement/Complaint Reduction
Projects in Progress
Baby food film and consistency
Pickle product specifications

Next Six-Month Focus
• Continued emphasis on reducing process and fill weight variability
• SPC education for newly acquired companies
• Use of applied benchmarking at manufacturing locations

Figure 5.4 Reporting progress—Heinz U.S.A.

objectives of element 10 are to (1) communicate to all employees that the quality improvement process is continuous and (2) emphasize that quality is a permanent management responsibility. The quality plan sets out the actions required to maintain the continuous improvement philosophy.

The quality improvement council meets to review the progress achieved for each of the 10 elements of the quality plan. Quality improvement council members are assigned responsibility for one of the quality plan elements each year. The quality improvement council member can be assigned responsibility for the same element the following year, or assigned a different element. Enhancements and recommendations to the quality plan are developed each year for each of the 10 elements. The members of the CATs and the QITs are selected at that time based on the skill and experience requirements of the quality plans, with approximately one-third to one-half of the team members replaced each year.

New team members are trained according to the recommendations of quality plan element 8: education. The new team reviews the activities from the previous cycle and formulates a new plan. Recognition of outgoing members and announcements of new members is carried out as part of the element 7: recognition, gratitude, and celebration. These actions refresh the quality process with new people, spread the lessons learned from previous initiatives, and leverage the organization's expanding knowledge base.

Conclusion

TQM at Heinz began when top management recognized the contribution improved quality could make to reducing costs, improving profits, and increasing competitiveness. The TQM successes are the result of several critical factors, beginning with top management's commitment, the blending of TQM into the existing competitive strategy, the selection of improvement projects that increase both customer satisfaction and financial performance, and the establishment of quality as everyone's primary job responsibility. By focusing quality tools and techniques on the achievement of business goals and objectives, Heinz has developed a TQM approach capable of meeting the organization's competitive challenges.

A summary of the results achieved in reaching the company's goals shows the contributions that TQM is making. For the company as a whole, the cost of nonconformance was reduced by $80 million in the first full year of quality-based cost management, well on track to accomplishing the goal of $250 million. By the end of the second year, Heinz U.S.A. had achieved a reduction in customer complaints of 43 percent. TQM has had a positive impact on the competitiveness of Heinz, and the expectation for the future is more of the same, only at an increasing rate.

Improving at an increasing rate will be accomplished as education continues to take hold and successful approaches are shared across the company. The TQM goals are expanding to include measures of internal and external customer satisfaction, which means working even closer with customers to define their requirements. As the customers of the future are given a broader, more proactive role in defining requirements through real-time data links, the challenge will be meeting customer requirements even more precisely.

6 Westinghouse Electric Corporation—A Case Study_____

Executive Summary

Westinghouse's total quality approach provides the broad framework that guides the company's various operating units in implementing total quality. The actual implementation is left up to the individual operating units, and each implementation is unique in the sense that it reflects the culture and environment of the unit. Today there are Westinghouse operating units in various stages of implementing total quality, ranging from a world-class Malcolm Baldrige National Quality Award winner to operating units that have just started the journey.

While each implementation reflects the unique culture and character of the operating unit, the underlying total quality framework provides a consistent set of imperatives, requirements, and measures that must always be addressed. This framework helps to ensure that Westinghouse and its operating units are "committed to a consistent management strategy of creating value—for stockholders, customers, and employees. In today's highly competitive, worldwide markets, the imperative for value creation is managing our operations to achieve total quality in everything we do."

Westinghouse views total quality as a survival strategy, and, as such, it has become a hard-nosed management model for running a business in a very competitive global economy. The PGBU provides an in-depth look at how one operating unit has implemented Westinghouse's total quality approach and, by integrating quality into its approach for managing the business, established itself as an industry leader. PGBU has used the cost of poor quality to add a financial dimension to its quality process and link day-to-day improvement activities with the accomplishment of business goals and objectives.

WESTINGHOUSE ELECTRIC CORPORATION—A CASE STUDY

Westinghouse Electric Corporation is a technology-based firm dedicated to achieving solid growth for shareholders, customers, and employees. A world leader in the electrical industry throughout its 106-year history, Westinghouse serves a variety of customers in seven market segments: broadcasting, electronic systems, the environment, financial services, office furniture, power systems, and a diverse industrial electrical distribution and transport temperature control market.

In the early 1970s, Westinghouse first encountered strong foreign competitors. By the mid-1970s, it was obvious that significant changes were occurring as Japanese and other foreign competitors built strong competitive positions in markets that were traditional strongholds of American manufacturers. Westinghouse chartered a team to determine strategies for combating foreign competition and find new ways to improve productivity and profitability. The team determined that the way to combat the growing threat of foreign competition was to focus on increased productivity, and it concluded that an entirely new management approach needed to be created and nurtured to successfully compete on a global basis.

In 1980 Westinghouse appointed a vice president of productivity and founded the Productivity Center. The mission of the Productivity Center was to develop and apply improvement methods, techniques, and technologies to help Westinghouse become more competitive in the global marketplace. Bob Kirby, chairman of Westinghouse at that time, provided the initial productivity seed fund to fund medium- to high-risk productivity projects that operating companies could not normally afford to support out of their own operating income. Over $60 million was invested. From 1980 to 1985, when U.S. productivity was growing at less than 3 percent per year, Westinghouse productivity grew at over twice that rate—even greater than the average productivity improvement of Japan.

Early on, the Productivity Center developed a variety of approaches to improve performance and helped operating units to apply these approaches. As the center became more established and gained experience in implementing productivity improvement techniques, it determined that the real driver of increased productivity was higher quality. In 1981 the Productivity Center became the Westinghouse Productivity and Quality Center.

Techniques and methods were soon developed to improve operational quality, but the gains were seen as "centers" or "pockets" of excellence, essentially piecemeal improvements. While the first two years of the quality initiative witnessed significant progress, the quality circles, which operated within single departments with self-chosen goals, started losing steam by 1983. What was needed was a broad, enterprise-wide initiative that could improve competitiveness in every aspect of the business, and in 1984 a high-level study team tackled the issue. The team's responsibility was to identify an approach to leverage the achievements of the pockets of excellence and transform the company into a tough, effective competitor in every aspect of its business. The result was a recommendation that Westinghouse adopt a total quality policy as the official keystone of the corporate competitive strategy. The Productivity and Quality Center proposed to develop the total quality approach. Top management agreed with the recommendation and total quality became the corporate-wide management model for the company.

Operating units with existing quality circle programs embraced the additional elements of the total quality concept, while organizations without existing quality circle programs began their total quality initiatives. A broad education program was started, with quality circles being replaced by multifunctional QITs responsible for pursuing assigned problems and process improvements. The total quality process continued to evolve and produced notable successes along the way: the Commercial Nuclear Fuel Division won the first Malcolm Baldrige National Quality Award in 1988; the Furniture Systems Division was a finalist in the 1989 Baldrige competition; and Thermo-King was a 1990 finalist for the Baldrige Award.

The financial results for the decade of the 1980s were equally notable in comparison to the 1970s: Profits and profit margins doubled; return on equity moved into the 18 to 21 percent range; return to shareholders was in the top 10 percent of the Fortune 500; and total return grew at an annual average rate of 25 percent a year. Former chairman Paul Lego noted that "Westinghouse had a super successful decade in the 1980s. And our emphasis on total quality had a lot to do with it." Westinghouse posted 29 straight quarters of improved shareholder earnings between 1983 and 1990. Of the thousands of publicly held corporations, few had a better record of creating value in the 1980s.

The 1990s have represented a period of difficult change for Westinghouse. As described in chapter 3, the losses of the financial services group have strained the cash resources of Westinghouse, causing the company to take dramatic steps. Top management is evaluating a variety of alternatives, both external and internal to the company, to build the foundation for long-term business success. Externally, the company is considering alternatives such as the sale of business units to raise cash and reposition itself for the future. Internally, one of the steps Westinghouse has already taken is renewing its emphasis on total quality as a competitive strategy for the 1990s and beyond.

The Westinghouse Total Quality Framework

The Westinghouse total quality framework is illustrated in Figure 6.1. The framework encompasses the following three key points.

> 1. The purpose of total quality is to positively impact all four of the key Westinghouse stakeholders: customers, stockholders, employees, and the public.

Requirements
- Customer satisfaction
- Stockholder value
- Employee satisfaction
- Public approval

Total Quality

Measurements
- Value/price ratio
- Value/cost ratio
- Error-free performance

Imperatives
- Customer orientation
- Human resource excellence
- Product/process leadership
- Management leadership

Figure 6.1 The Westinghouse total quality framework guides implementation.

2. The four imperatives of total quality process that must be addressed are customer orientation, product and process leadership, human resource excellence, and management leadership.
3. The measures to determine whether or not total quality is effective are the value-to-price ratio, value-to-cost ratio, and error-free performance.

Four imperatives are central to the Westinghouse total quality effort: customer orientation, human resource excellence, product and process leadership, and management leadership. While each operating unit within Westinghouse can implement total quality in its own unique way, each of the four imperatives for quality performance must be addressed.

Customer Orientation

"From the perspective of total quality, everything starts with the customers and their perception of value. Customer satisfaction requires us to provide a value-to-price ratio which is equal to or superior to world-class competition. At the same time, total quality performance requires us to do this with an above-average value-to-cost ratio, to achieve superior financial performance."

The customer-orientation imperative at Westinghouse is centered around two concepts.

1. Customer satisfaction is determined by the value-to-price ratio:

$$\frac{\text{Value}}{\text{Price}} = \frac{\text{Functions}}{\text{Price for functions}}$$

The company that has the edge in providing value to customer, that is, the highest value-to-price ratio, achieves market share leadership by offering customers more for their dollars.

2. Financial performance is determined by the value-to-cost ratio:

$$\frac{\text{Value}}{\text{Cost}} = \frac{\text{Functions}}{\text{Cost for functions}}$$

The company that can offer equivalent functions at the lowest costs will have superior financial performance. The only way a company can achieve superior financial performance and offer a competitive value-to-price ratio in the marketplace is through a cost structure that is superior to other companies.

The Westinghouse strategy is to achieve leadership in both the value-to-price and value-to-cost ratios and thereby become the leader in both customer satisfaction and financial performance. In support of this strategy, the PQC has developed a series of improvement tools to enhance an operating unit's competitive position by focusing on overall customer satisfaction.

For example, one of the improvement tools is the Value Edge Process, a technique for measuring customers' perceptions about the value of products and services offered by an operating unit and its competitors. The Value Edge Process assists in implementing a total quality strategy through

- A consensus process that identifies customer needs, wants, and expectations
- A diagnostic approach that quantifies the value-to-price ratio and the value-to-cost ratio
- A targeting process that identifies the changes needed in an operating unit's products, services, and delivery systems as well as its cost structure to achieve a competitive advantage

The Value Edge Process is one example of how Westinghouse addresses the reality that the company must compete in its selected markets primarily on the basis of comparative value. Recognizing that competitive cost and price are important success factors, Westinghouse consistently seeks to maximize market share and profits by increasing customer satisfaction through a superior value-to-price ratio while, at the same time, achieving a superior value-to-cost ratio.

Product and Process Leadership

Positioning the business to compete with a superior value-to-cost ratio requires that the business achieve product and process leadership. Products are all the things a business supplies its customers, including services, while processes include everything a business does to supply its customers with these products and services.

The product and process leadership focus effectively integrates all elements required to provide a product or service, such as work flow, people and organizational structures, information systems, and capital. Thoroughly understanding the customers' perceptions of value provides operating units with the information needed to set requirements for operational product and process performance to satisfy key strategic issues.

Human Resource Excellence

Employees are recognized as the most important resource for total quality. The key ingredients in achieving human resource excellence are

1. Participation. All employees participate in establishing and achieving total quality improvement goals.
2. Development. People are recognized as key strategic resources. Development opportunities are provided to ensure that each employee understands, supports, and contributes to achieving total quality.
3. Motivation. Employees are motivated to achieve total quality through trust, respect, and recognition.

Management Leadership

The most important element in the Westinghouse total quality improvement process is top management's leadership and commitment to the total quality culture. Top management commitment is mandatory for building the organizational base for a successful total quality process. Management has the responsibility to establish a culture in which individual and group actions reflect a total quality attitude; recognize total quality as a primary business objective in strategic business and financial planning; provide two-way communications that send a consistent message and reinforce the total quality process; and establish accountability measures for total quality that are reported, analyzed, and used effectively.

The Measures of Total Quality

Westinghouse places a high priority on measurement because it is only through measurement that continuous improvement can be gauged. By measuring deliverables, everyone can see whether the necessary progress is being made. Measures are considered to be a powerful driver of process improvement, allowing individuals or departments to judge if their efforts are moving them toward desired results of more efficient work processes and a customer focus.

The value-to-price ratio, value-to-cost ratio, and error-free performance criteria are used by Westinghouse business units to

- Quantify marketplace expectations about the value of its products, services, and delivery systems compared to its competitors
- Establish targets for changes in its resource allocations and costs consistent with the mission, strengths, weaknesses, and strategic direction

Using the cost of poor quality puts quality performance in terms of dollars, the same denominator as other business measures, and provides the means to identify opportunities that can improve the value-to-price and value-to-cost ratios while reducing the cost of errors. The total quality initiative uses the cost of poor quality to convey a message: It is the significant price each operating unit chooses to pay by not preventing errors and by not doing things right the first time. Emphasizing error-free performance reinforces the strategy of improving profitability by targeting and eliminating the root causes of poor quality and their related costs.

The Westinghouse Total Quality Improvement Process

The total quality improvement process is designed to blend the requirements, imperatives, and measures of the quality process with the strategic and financial objectives of the operating units. As shown in Figure 6.2, the process begins with an understanding of customer needs and ends with increasing customer satisfaction.

The improvement process must occur within an organizational culture developed and nourished by management: Every employee must be dedicated to the total quality vision, and management leadership in words and deeds must be evident throughout the entire process. The imperatives driving the adoption of the quality process, such as increasing competition or even survival, must be clearly communicated to every member of the organization. Management's priority is to create this awareness, build the

Figure 6.2 The Westinghouse total quality process begins with customer needs and ends with customer satisfaction.

understanding, and develop the ownership of the total quality improvement process needed to meet these challenges in order to achieve a competitive advantage in the marketplace.

An outcome of the awareness phase is a prioritized list of key issues and strategies needed to achieve the vision and goals of the quality process. Key issues represent major roadblocks to organizational success. Typical key issues that arise following a unit's analysis of its internal and external situation include: employee motivation and training, changing technology, information systems, planning procedures, or communications effectiveness.

Improvement opportunities are specifically identified during the annual planning process. The identification of opportunities and priorities begins with the goals and strategies of the operating unit. The operating unit focuses on the opportunities that can have the most effect on its overall business success. Once major opportunities have been established and approved, improvement targets are set for each opportunity. Typical opportunities include increasing internal and external customer satisfaction, improving on-time delivery, reducing the cost of poor quality, improving cash conversion efficiency, and lowering accounts receivable.

The real work of the improvement process gets done at the improvement team level. As noted by Westinghouse, "At this point, employee teams must get to work and perform improvement projects. Improvement only takes place in one way—project by project. This action element is where the planning culminates and actual total quality improvement occurs." Improvement opportunities are first divided into individual improvement projects and responsibilities assigned. Each project involves the development and analysis of alternative solutions, the selection and recommendation of the best solution to management, and the performance of the project. A multilevel, multidiscipline team structure provides the mechanism for extensive employee involvement and ownership.

Finally, the evaluation and renewal cycle measures the success of the projects and provides feedback to the entire organization. Changes and updates are continuously made to ensure that improvement continues, that project successes and learning experiences are shared, and that continuous renewal of commitment is occurring throughout the Westinghouse organization.

POWER GENERATION BUSINESS UNIT: AN IMPLEMENTATION CASE STUDY

While each implementation reflects the unique culture and character of the operating unit, the underlying total quality framework helps to ensure that Westinghouse and its operating units are

committed to a consistent management strategy of creating value—for stockholders, customers and employees. In today's highly competitive, worldwide markets, the imperative for value creation is managing our operations to achieve total quality in everything we do.

As shown in Figure 6.3, the PGBU has adapted the Westinghouse framework to develop a total quality process that is responsive to the unit's culture and competitive conditions. The goal of PGBU's total quality process is "to become the supplier of preference through total quality." In fact, top management has made total quality the center of its competitive strategy. As vice president and general manager Frank Bakos puts it, "total quality... harnesses, focuses and then intensifies all of the intellectual power in a business on developing and implementing winning strategies."[1]

Strategic Quality Planning

Although PGBU made significant improvements in quality during the early to mid-1980s, it was not until 1987 that quality became an integral component of the unit's competitive strategy. At that time, the business unit faced a major crisis. The organization's reputation was below that of its competitors and was reflected in poor product performance and customer dissatisfaction. PGBU had lost nearly 50 percent of its market share in servicing the units it manufactured. More worrisome, European companies were entering the U.S. market and ruthlessly driving down prices in an attempt to force competitors out of the market. PGBU's product portfolio did not reflect the demands in the marketplace, having little presence in growing markets such as combustion turbine engines and power projects. In markets where growth was flat or declining, the business unit had a major presence. Combating foreign competition and entering new markets required capital that was not available from the Westinghouse corporate office. Facing a difficult competitive situation, PGBU turned to quality improvement and waste reduction as a means to generate the necessary cash flow.

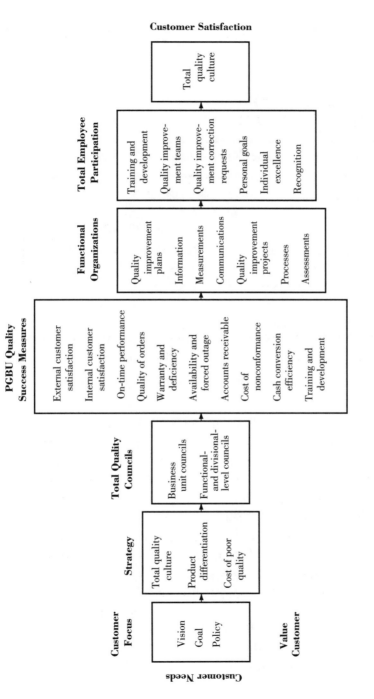

Figure 6.3 Customer-driven approach defines the vision, mission, strategy, and performance measures.

The business unit established the following vision, long-term goal, and quality policy to guide the resulting quality initiative.

PGBU Vision
To establish the Westinghouse Power Generation Business Unit as the world class quality Supplier of Preference to the power generation industry worldwide, and to instill the name of Westinghouse as the quality leader in the design, manufacture, and service of power generation facilities on a global basis.

We will become a totally customer needs-driven organization by achieving total quality excellence through customer satisfaction.

We will provide our employees the climate, the resources and the opportunity to develop their individual skills to their full potential; and we will conduct ourselves with openness and integrity to our customers, employees, suppliers, and communities.

PGBU Goal
To become the Supplier of Preference through total quality.

PGBU Quality Policy
To perform in complete accordance with customer and Westinghouse requirements.

The vision and goal clearly state the reason for the existence of the quality process—to achieve a culture that continually enhances its ability to satisfy customers by focusing on customers, understanding their needs, and providing superior value.

Selecting a Strategy and Direction
PGBU has defined three strategies to increase customer satisfaction, market share, and profitability through quality improvement.

1. Strategy—Pursue a total quality culture to continually enhance our ability to satisfy our customer.
   Objective—Achieve a total quality culture throughout PGBU.

2. Strategy—Use our total quality focus for differentiating our products and services and increasing our market share.
   Objective—Achieve product and service leadership.
3. Strategy—Increase our business unit's profitability and price competitiveness by improving every aspect of performance and reducing the cost of poor quality.
   Objective—Achieve world-class cycle time and cost-of-poor-quality levels.

The business unit has established a series of high-level, key performance metrics, called the 10 Quality Success Measures, to assess its progress in achieving overall PGBU goals and strategic objectives. The 10 Quality Success Measures are critical in two respects: (1) to quantify and make measurable the overall goal and strategic objectives and (2) to guide activities of the functional units in achieving the strategic objectives.

Figure 6.4 illustrates how PGBU connects its customer-driven vision, strategies, and objectives to the high-level performance measures. If the business unit can guide the functional units to perform according to expectations on the 10 key performance measures, then the strategic objectives will be satisfied. This, in turn, will lead to achievement of the overall goal: to become the supplier of preference to the industry. The PGBU structure linking the unit's vision, strategies, and performance measures builds the framework that integrates the overall goal with day-to-day quality priorities and objectives of the functional units.

The deployment of the business vision is an established process that has evolved with experience and is refreshed every year by resetting performance targets. Updating performance targets sets the expectations for the functional units and drives the development of quality plans that detail how the functional units will achieve their targets. Figure 6.5 shows how the business vision cascades down to the functional organizations.

Preparation of the quality plan begins with the total quality councils, which exist at each level of the organization. The quality

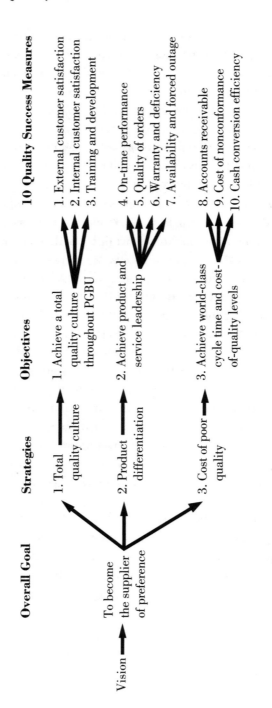

Figure 6.4 Performance measures guide quality improvement priorities of the functional units.

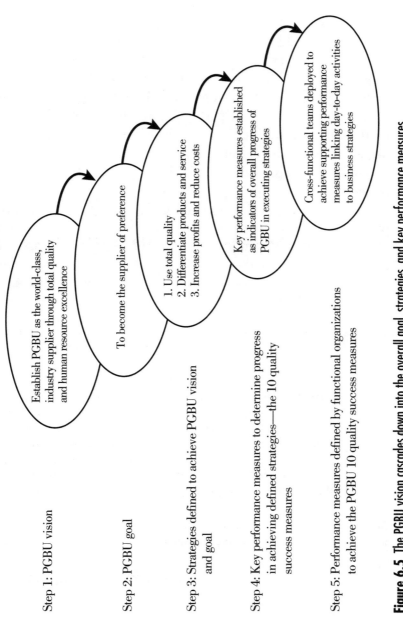

Step 1: PGBU vision

Establish PGBU as the world-class, industry supplier through total quality and human resource excellence

Step 2: PGBU goal

To become the supplier of preference

Step 3: Strategies defined to achieve PGBU vision and goal

1. Use total quality
2. Differentiate products and service
3. Increase profits and reduce costs

Step 4: Key performance measures to determine progress in achieving defined strategies—the 10 quality success measures

Key performance measures established as indicators of overall progress of PGBU in executing strategies

Step 5: Performance measures defined by functional organizations to achieve the PGBU 10 quality success measures

Cross-functional teams deployed to achieve supporting performance measures linking day-to-day activities to business strategies

Figure 6.5 The PGBU vision cascades down into the overall goal, strategies, and key performance measures.

councils coordinate initiatives to ensure the projects contribute to the goals and objectives set by the business unit total quality council. The responsibilities of the councils are to establish the long-term vision, goals, and objectives; provide the approach and direction for total quality; set policy and short-term goals; provide leadership, commitment, participation, and communication of total quality initiatives; define priorities, assignments, and needed resources for selected improvement projects; and conduct reviews, follow-up, evaluation, and recognition of improvement projects.

A unique aspect of the PGBU annual quality planning process is identifying two or three crucial business unit issues for special attention. Attention is focused on these crucial issues in the form of a Quality Planning Challenge. Figure 6.6 shows how the functional organizations responded to the 1992 Quality Planning Challenge to

- Select key quality initiatives emphasizing
  –Cycle-time and cost reductions
  –Support for strategic initiatives
  –Improve customer satisfaction
- Implement quality plans that utilize improvement strategies designed to drive the key quality initiatives
- Develop a measurable goal for each quality initiative that allows the success of the quality initiatives to be immediately visible

QITs

Functional and cross-functional QITs are formed at all levels of the organization to address the improvement projects identified in the quality plans. PGBU uses the structured seven-step process shown in Figure 6.7 to address the improvement opportunities, a process that emphasizes the use of facts and logic to maximize the probability of success.

1992 Quality Planning Challenge	1992 Business Unit Targets for Reducing the Cost of Nonconformance	Improvement Projects and Targets of Functional Units that Address the 1992 Quality Planning Challenge and Business Unit Performance Targets to Reduce the Cost of Nonconformance
Reduce costs. **Business Unit Strategy** We must increase our business unit's profitability and price competitiveness by improving every aspect of performance and reducing the cost of nonconformance	• Target 12% reduction in cost of nonconformance as a percent of sales billed. • Sponsor and follow QITs as the functional levels to focus on root causes and implement corrective actions in targeted areas. • Provide management visibility to nonconformance costs through regular publications and briefings.	• Reduce the lost time accident incident rate for Westinghouse and casual employees by 30% in 1992. • Reduce job site tool and equipment loss and damage by 24% in 1992. • Reduce the number of phone calls made to district offices to clarify invoicing data by 50% in 1992. • Reduce manufacturing and vendor nonconformance rates by 30% in 1992 by fully implementing computerized nonconformance and corrective action systems encompassing key vendors and increasing the availability of manufacturing information. • Reduce the cost of manufacturing and vendors' errors by 10% in 1992 by continuing emphasis on statistical process management. • Improve service stock inventory turnover ratio by fully implementing the new inventory management system, and continue inventory QIT initiatives. Improve inventory turnover ratio by 11% in 1992. • Achieve or improve our nonconformance costs goal of $/net allowable hours by improvements through training, SPC expansion, process documentations, and controlled overtime. Reduce nonconformance costs by 31% in 1992. • Control the total spending for nonconformance maintenance accounts by 16% in 1992 by employing preventive maintenance techniques to reduce unplanned downtime. • Reduce the cost of nonconformance by 10% in 1992 through cause and corrective action analysis and process control. • Reduce the total cost of quality by achieving the productivity objective of 60%, capitalizing on product standardization, reducing nonconformance costs by 20%, and reducing product conformance costs by 10% in 1992.

Figure 6.6 The quality improvement priorities and projects focus on satisfying the performance expectations of top management.

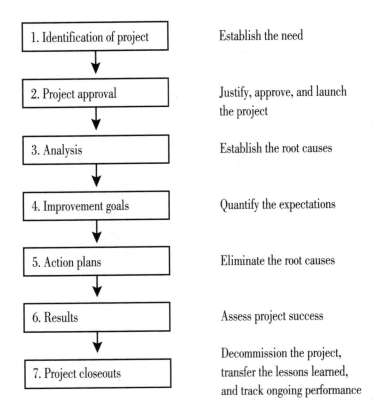

1. Identification of project	Establish the need
2. Project approval	Justify, approve, and launch the project
3. Analysis	Establish the root causes
4. Improvement goals	Quantify the expectations
5. Action plans	Eliminate the root causes
6. Results	Assess project success
7. Project closeouts	Decommission the project, transfer the lessons learned, and track ongoing performance

Figure 6.7 A structured seven-step process guides the improvement teams.

A QIT registration form is used to document the team efforts. The process for registering QITs is shown in Figure 6.8. The benefits of the QIT registration form shown in Figure 6.9 include

- Increased visibility of QITs to PGBU management
- A nomination source for recognition
- A source of periodic statistical reporting

Performance Measurement

PGBU management believes that establishing a total quality culture and achieving the unit's goals requires continual assessment of progress. According to PGBU's quality plan,

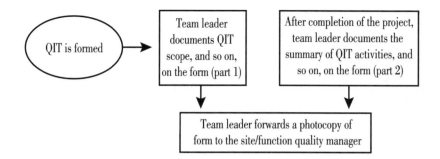

Figure 6.8 The QIT registration process provides progress reporting for teams.

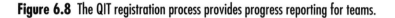

The foundation of total quality is the concept of continuous improvement. It is only through the use of measurement that continuous improvement is gauged. By measuring our various departments' deliverables we can readily see if the necessary progress is being made. Measures are powerful drivers of process improvement. Individuals or departments should ensure that their measurements move them toward results, require efficient work processes, focus on the customer, and meet the departments' needs and objectives.

Quality measurement begins with PGBU's 10 quality success measures, each of which is assigned a "sponsor" who reports directly to the executive vice president. Depending on the measure, the sponsors may include the business unit's controller and total quality director, as well as general managers of the business unit's divisions. Each sponsor's evaluation and compensation is tied in part to the achievement of these goals, providing a powerful signal that quality is a key element in the unit's success.

Each functional organization develops a set of measures to evaluate quality progress in the four imperatives of total quality: customer orientation, human resource excellence, product/process leadership, and management leadership. Lower level measures are tied to specific improvement projects and may be either financial or nonfinancial in nature. For example, PGBU's Fort Payne, Alabama, plant uses the cost of poor quality to measure its progress in

---

Quality Improvement Project

Part 1
Project title _____

Sponsor _____

Team leader _____

Team members _____

Abstract (summary of project scope and expectations) _____

_____

Date initiated _____   Forecasted closure date _____

or

Standing team: _____

Part 2
Date closed _____

Closure summary _____

Team leader signature _____   Date _____

Closure acknowledgment

_____

Team quality manager signature   Date _____

Figure 6.9 The QIT registration form.

achieving specific process improvement goals, while the Charlotte plant tracks cycle-time reductions for the same purpose. Note, however, that both of these metrics tie directly into two of the areas targeted for improvement in 1992—cycle-time and cost reductions. In doing so, the performance measures provide a link between the business objectives of the unit, the quality plan, and the lower level improvement projects.

The Role of the Cost of Poor Quality

PGBU sees three major roles for the cost of poor quality in the overall quality process.

1. To get management's attention and show them the need for quality improvement. Once the scope of the quality problem is revealed in dollars and the potential for improvement is presented, management will understand the opportunity it has to boost profits, increase cash flow, and improve price competitiveness using quality improvement.
2. To provide an objective measurement of quality improvement success. The cost of poor quality provides a yardstick by which management can determine how well the quality improvement process is being implemented. It demonstrates in terms that can be easily understood the effects of quality improvement and the advantages of doing things right the first time.
3. To pinpoint areas where corrective action will be most profitable. Cost-of-poor-quality information can help management set priorities for corrective action. It provides the logic for assigning priorities to problems. Since organizations usually don't have the resources to address all their problems at once, it is necessary to prioritize to eliminate the most serious problem first. The use of the cost of poor quality provides the logic for setting the corrective action priorities by using costs as the decision base. More important, it links quality improvement to the unit's desired end result—increased cash flow.

Given the importance of these uses, cost-of-poor-quality reductions are a key component of the strategic plan for every functional, plant, and divisional organization and are placed on all agendas for evaluating strategic performance. PGBU measures 25 cost-of-poor-quality elements that are grouped into two categories:

conformance costs and nonconformance costs. Standard definitions and measurement techniques have been established for each element to ensure consistency across the functional organizations. The 25 cost-of-poor-quality elements are listed as follows:

Conformance Costs
1. Training
2. Maintenance cost
3. Design verification costs
4. Site quality assurance budget

Nonconformance Costs
5. Manufacturing hourly production labor variance
6. Waiting time
7. Defective purchased material
8. Defective workmanship
9. Other losses
10. Cost of departmental errors in white-collar functions
11. Other inventory losses
12. Material usage—inventory adjustments
13. Surplus inventory
14. Major order cost overruns
15. Overtime bonus
16. Engineering costs to resolve nonconformances
17. Interest lost on uncollectible receivables
18. Field deficiency cost—manufacturing
19. Field deficiency cost—engineering
20. Field deficiency cost—nonengineering
21. Product warranty—manufacturing
22. Product warranty—engineering
23. Product warranty—nonengineering
24. Business policy concessions
25. Contract penalties

PGBU uses a number of methods to calculate the cost of conformance and nonconformace. It is important to remember, however, that the cost of poor quality is primarily a communication and prioritization tool. None of the three purposes requires last penny, or even last dollar, accuracy. Examples of the data sources used by PGBU to collect data for selected quality costs are

Element: training
Data source: training accounts in the financial system

Element: design verification costs
Data source: division specific estimates

Element: site quality assurance budget
Data source: quality assurance budget, including 40 percent
    for benefits minus overtime

Element: manufacturing hourly production labor variance
Data source: plant productivity labor variance

Element: surplus inventory
Data source: calculation from inventory reports

Element: overtime bonus
Data source: budget account variances

Element: interest lost on uncollectible receivables
Data source: aging analysis

Element: product warranty—manufacturing
Data source: accounting statement and the trial balance

Reporting the Costs of Poor Quality

The format of the cost-of-poor-quality report is an important aspect of the system. The report must clearly reflect cost elements so that they can be used in monitoring and managing quality improvement. A typical summary cost-of-poor-quality report for a functional organization of PGBU would include

- Name of the cost-of-poor-quality element
- Definition of each element

- Identification of the calculation method and source of information for each element
- History of prior months and years of cost of poor quality information for comparison and trend information

Examples of detailed cost of quality reports for selected cost elements are shown in Figure 6.10. PGBU views of the cost of poor quality as the price that a company chooses to pay by not preventing errors and by not doing things right the first time. This conveys the belief that none of the costs of poor quality need to be spent and that the cost of poor quality can be eliminated through the systematic quality improvements focused on eliminating the related root causes.

Root-Cause Analysis

Once a cost-of-poor-quality improvement opportunity has been identified and targeted, a QIT is formed to determine and eliminate the root causes of the problem. Figure 6.11 provides the findings of an improvement team that was formed to determine the proportion of overtime costs attributable to problems other than planned overtime to meet accelerated production schedules. Their assessment found that nearly 50 percent of all overtime was unscheduled, providing a significant opportunity for waste reduction. Based on this information, overtime reduction became one of the key success measures within PGBU.

The next phase of the root-cause analysis contained two components: (1) reviewing accounting records to determine the specific reasons that overtime was being incurred and (2) benchmarking the various plants within the business unit to learn how the sites were dealing with overtime issues. The team soon learned that the accounting records only provided information on the symptoms of overtime rather than the causes. Interviews with departmental managers subsequently revealed that overtime was typically worked due to upstream problems in the production process. As a result, the QIT was forced to work its way back through the production process to identify the true root causes.

Element 1: Training

Definition: Total cost associated with both internal and external training (except QA): includes invoicing, travel, salaries, and consulting fees

Data source: 860 and 566 accounts

	Location 1	Location 2	Location 3	Total
19X2	281	115	113	509
19X3	313	119	71	503
19X4	213	145	65	423
19X5	163	46	57	266
19X6	34	149	55	238

Element 21: Product Warranty Manufacturing

Definition: The total cost involved in correcting nonconformances related to manufacturing on products still in warranty

Data source: 50 statement and trial balance

	Location 1	Location 2	Location 3	Total
19X2	202	134	204	540
19X3	142	189	226	557
19X4	118	106	62	286
19X5	320	93	151	564
19X6	102	129	233	464

Note: Numbers and locations disguised

Figure 6.10 Detailed cost-of-poor-quality reporting provides information to monitor progress and identify trends.

Root Cause	**Unplanned Overtime**
Late engineering drawings	33.0%
Late material	24.0%
Defective work	11.6%
Project schedule changes	10.0%
Defective purchased material	5.2%
Waiting time	5.0%
Engineering/manufacturing process problems	2.5%
All other	8.7%
	100.0%

Figure 6.11 Root causes of unplanned overtime.

Using a variety of tools and techniques, including interviews, process flowcharting, and cause-and-effect diagrams, the team concluded that late engineering drawings were the root cause of one-third of the unplanned overtime costs.

The problem of late drawings was turned over to an engineering function QIT. The team began by prioritizing drawings based on how critical they were to ongoing operations. Consistent with the unit's philosophy that continuous improvement requires ongoing measurement, the team also developed an information system to manage and control the engineering drawings process and report drawing status statistics to management. By identifying and minimizing one of the primary causes of unplanned overtime, the QITs were able to significantly reduce the costs arising from unnecessary overtime.

Achievements

Figure 6.12 shows the year-end cost-of-poor-quality status reports from 1989 to 1991, as well as the 1992 plan for this key performance measure. Over the first three years, the cost of poor quality fell by 78 percent, reflecting the significant achievements of QITs such as

1989 Status	1990 Status	1991 Status	1992 Status
Reviewed the COQ report elements to provide meaningful measurement quality costs	Analyzed data and identified major nonconformance elements for improvement	Continued to give visibility to cost-of-quality performance through monthly publication of results and areas for improvement	Target a 12% reduction in cost of nonconformance as a percent of sales billed
Established 25 COQ elements to ensure consistent and accurate data across PGBU	Sponsored spin-off QITs at several locations to address key nonconformance elements	Sponsored and followed QITs at the functional level to focus on root causes and actions that resulted in cost improvements	Sponsor and follow QITs at the functional level to focus on root causes and implement corrective actions in targeted areas
Published monthly reports and identified areas for improvement	Key QIT activities and results were reported on a regular basis	Continued to publicize success stories.	Provide management visibility to nonconformance costs through regular publications and briefings
1989 nonconformance reduction: 15.4%	Published monthly cost of quality reports and identified areas for improvement	Achieved a 1991 reduction in the costs of nonconformance of 30% as a percent of sales billed	
	Achieved a 1990 reduction in costs of nonconformance of 32.5% as a percent of sales billed		

Figure 6.12 The year-end status report to top management shows the growth in the use of the cost of quality to increase profits.

those described above. More important, as the concept continues to evolve, PGBU expects to continue using cost-of-poor-quality measurement to identify and prioritize improvement opportunities in as yet untouched areas of the business.

Conclusion

Market and competitive conditions made investments in new products mandatory if PGBU was to succeed. Westinghouse's corporate office was not in a position to provide the cash for the capital investments necessary to redirect the business. In response, PGBU refocused its total quality process to generate the needed cash. PGBU adopted cost-of-poor-quality reduction as a competitive strategy and established a cause and effect framework to provide the linkage between the quality process and broader business objectives. Strategic quality planning became the means for management to articulate the need to change, set priorities, and allocate resources. This sent the signal to the entire organization that the quality process was a critical part of the unit's long-term competitive strategy for improving financial performance and price competitiveness.

Notes
1. Frank Bakos, speech to Westinghouse Total Quality Symposium, Pittsburgh, Penn., October 1992.

7 Lessons Learned_____

Every company that participated in the study shared lessons that were learned not only through stunning victories and humbling defeats, but also through the hard work required to make the investment in quality pay off. Companies contributed their lessons with the hope that others might avoid some of the sand traps, pitfalls, blunders, rework, learning curves, warts, mistakes, false starts, and potholes that are encountered along the continuous improvement journey. The following points summarize the lessons learned by the participating companies.

- To increase both customer satisfaction and profitability, it is essential to eliminate the distinction between business results and quality results. Strategic business and financial planning must recognize quality as a primary business objective, just as strategic quality planning must recognize business and financial results as a primary quality objective.
- A feeling for "action now" may drive top management to rush into the implementation phase at the expense of cost-driver analysis or project planning. This can lead to the need for midcourse corrections with the attendant lack of focus and additional expenditure of time, money, and effort.
- Delegation of responsibility for the quality process by the CEO, even a step lower in the organization, can seriously

compromise the credibility of the organization's commitment to quality.

- In addition to the commitment of top management, there must be other champions and leaders who provide the additional momentum needed to influence others. Carefully selected pilot sites and projects with a high chance of success help to establish the business value of quality-based cost management and the importance of effective quality improvement for the entire organization.

- Having each improvement team track and report its progress in reducing the poor-quality costs associated with nonvalue-added costs and waste (1) helps the team retain its focus on improving financial performance, (2) eliminates the need for modifying the accounting or financial systems to track the cost of poor quality, and (3) supports the improvement process by establishing a direct connection between the improvement teams and improved financial performance.

- The involvement of the financial or management accounting professional ensures that improvement team reporting, and the subsequent consolidations, represents an unbiased and objective measure of progress that the entire organization can rely on for evaluating the effectiveness of the quality process.

- Beware of setting up the quality process as a "shadow organization" or a separate department.

- To be a useful tool in the day-to-day decision making, the cost-of-poor-quality assessment and cost-driver analysis must be generated by the affected departments, not by an uninvolved staff function.

- One of the most important investments a company can make in the initial stages of quality-based cost management is education and training in preparation for the pilot activities. This provides the people involved with a clear understanding of poor-quality concepts and the objectives to be accomplished. Getting people to buy-in requires, in part, that they understand how quality-based cost management will help them be more successful.

- It is essential that organizations establish a positive and constructive attitude toward cost-of-poor-quality reporting and problem solving to facilitate the identification and prioritization of improvement opportunities. Any hint of coercion, retaliation, or threats based on cost-of-poor-quality data is counterproductive and delays the reporting of reliable information.

- One of the most important applications of cost-of-poor-quality information is educating everyone in the organization about (1) the impact of poor quality on customer satisfaction and profitability, (2) the ways quality improvement contributes to the achievement of business goals, and (3) the importance of quality improvement for the white-collar and indirect functions of the business.

- The vision, strategies, and priorities of top management must be imbedded into the day-to-day management activities of the quality improvement process. For those responsible for implementing quality improvement process to select the vital projects, they must embrace the same business vision, strategies, and priorities as top management. By setting strategies and priorities on the basis of this shared vision, managers move the quality process into the mainstream of decision making for the business. If not, the quality improvement process will never be accepted by top management as a significant element of the business and will remain a fringe activity that exists on a nice-to-have rather than a need-to-have basis.

- A few, well-managed improvement teams deployed against key corporate issues will have a much more positive impact on the bottom line than deploying many teams for many small projects. Unless a company has established a quality strategy based on a reliable understanding of cause-and-effect relationships to improve financial performance, the de facto strategy is simply deploying improvement teams in the hope of doing the right things. Several participating companies referred to this as the field of dreams strategy—if you deploy teams, financial performance will improve. The 70 percent failure rate is evidence that the field of dreams strategy doesn't produce meaningful results.

- White-collar, indirect operations often represent the highest payback opportunities for eliminating the root causes of poor quality. The challenge is educating the people in these areas about the impact of poor quality and their role in improving the productivity, profitability, and competitiveness of the business. Quantifying the financial impact of poor quality in the white-collar, indirect operations provides the information needed to demonstrate the importance of white-collar quality.

- Although world-class companies have learned that the improvement projects most vital to competitive success often rely on solving problems that cross departmental boundaries, creating an environment that encourages such problem solving can be difficult. Top management alone has the prestige, authority, and resources to challenge and successfully change the status quo of an organization. Realistically, top management can only be expected to provide its sustaining support for the difficult challenge of organizational and cultural change when it is clear that its business vision, strategies, and priorities have been adopted by the quality improvement process.

- Management must establish performance measures that tie day-to-day quality improvement activities to the fulfillment of the business vision. The cost of poor quality can be a useful performance measure that allows top management to clearly communicate its strategy and commitment to achieving both increased customer satisfaction and profitability.

The remainder of the book presents the quality-based cost management methodology based on a synthesis of the unique approaches and best practices used by more than 30 successful companies. The methodology is intended to be a practical and effective guide for companies to use in their efforts to lower costs, increase profits, and improve cash flow through quality improvement. Chapter 8 presents a cost-of-poor-quality assessment methodology that blends activity-based costing with quality improvement concepts to identify and quantify the nonvalue-added costs caused by poor quality. Chapter 9 presents the cost-driver analysis methodology for determining the financial impact of potential improvement projects and for setting improvement project priorities on the basis of payback and financial performance. Chapter 10 presents an approach for (1) selecting the improvement projects that can make the greatest contribution to improving profitability, competitiveness, and customer satisfaction; (2) preparing the improvement project plan; (3) monitoring and measuring the progress of the improvement teams; and (4) reporting to top management on the progress and overall effectiveness of the quality improvement effort.

Appendix A provides instructions on how to conduct the cost of poor quality assessment. The appendix emphasizes a team approach that relies on the financial and quality functions to assist in implementing quality-based cost management. Also presented are techniques for gathering data, recommendations for data analysis, considerations for cost-of-poor-quality calculations, suggestions for conducting survey interviews, and a sample format for compiling the postinterview information.

Appendix B provides a listing of common cost-of-poor-quality elements, definitions, and illustrations to facilitate the identification and quantification of nonvalue-added activities and waste caused by poor quality. The listing has been designed so that it can be adapted to the specific needs of an organization when conducting the cost-of-poor-quality assessment.

Part II

Quality-Based Cost Management:
A Methodology

8 The Cost-of-Poor-Quality Assessment _____

Executive Summary

This chapter presents a detailed discussion of the cost-of-poor-quality assessment. Key considerations for conducting a successful assessment are covered, ranging from determining what level of detail meets the needs of the organization to finalizing the presentation of cost-of-poor-quality assessment results.

For many companies, the cost-of-poor-quality assessment may be one of the first quality improvement projects undertaken. The cost-of-poor-quality assessment provides an opportunity for management to (1) set the tone for the improvement process and projects that follow, (2) show its support for the quality process by making resources available, (3) set a constructive attitude for uncovering and dealing with poor quality practices, and (4) demonstrate its commitment to the quality process by encouraging and supporting timely identification and elimination of the root causes of poor quality.

THE COST-OF-POOR-QUALITY ASSESSMENT

Determining the appropriate level of detail for the assessment is one of first issues a company needs to address. The level of detail that a company selects is an important issue and should reflect the following points.

1. *The experience that a company has with the quality process.* A company that is inexperienced with implementing the quality process faces many important organizational, cultural, managerial, and educational issues. A cost-of-poor-quality assessment should complement these early stage efforts and not be so time-consuming and difficult that it detracts from the quality process. A company just beginning a quality initiative should consider limiting its efforts to the assessment of poor-quality costs of internal and external failure. In this way the assessment can be used effectively as both a tool to educate personnel and as a means to assess the nonvalue-added activities and waste due to poor quality. Subsequent assessments can be increasingly more detailed as a company builds a foundation of experience in quality improvement.

2. *The strategic and business requirements of the company.* A cost-of-poor-quality assessment can be conducted at several different levels of detail depending on the requirements of the company, with each assessment level providing an increasingly broader analysis and a correspondingly greater amount of information. The usefulness of the information must be judged against the costs of acquiring the information, as well as strategic and business requirements. For example, an experienced company like Star-Kist has more sophisticated requirements today than it did when it first started to implement quality improvement. Five years ago, Star-Kist's priorities were educating employees and identifying waste and nonvalue-added activities. Now, with a solid quality education and culture in place, the priorities are identifying opportunities to invest in prevention and accelerating value-added quality initiatives.

Cost-of-poor-quality assessments can be broken down into three types or levels. Each successive level is designed to provide an increasing breadth of information to satisfy correspondingly more complex requirements.

Level 1 Assessment. The level 1 assessment is confined to an analysis of internal and external failure costs. Emphasis is placed on identifying and quantifying the waste and nonvalue-added activities driven by the failure to meet internal and external customer requirements, and initially concentrates on identifying the low hanging fruit. This information becomes the basis for prioritizing the poor-quality costs for the next step of quality-based cost management, the cost-driver analysis.

Of the companies participating in the study, it is not uncommon for companies with considerable quality-related experience and success to conduct level 1 assessments. While subsequent assessments grow increasingly detailed as experience is gained, the majority of companies feel an enterprise-wide assessment of poor-quality costs that is limited to internal and external failure costs satisfies their requirements.

Level 2 Assessment. The level 2 assessment combines the analysis of internal and external failure costs with an examination of appraisal costs. The motivation for conducting a level 2 assessment varies according to company requirements.

1. Are costs that had been categorized as appraisal-related costs really due to internal or external failures? Analysis of appraisal costs has proven to be an additional source of identifying internal and external failure costs. One hundred-percent inspection is a good example of a cost that some companies initially classify as appraisal but which, on further inspection, is driven by a failure to meet customer requirements the first time. Recognizing that costs classified as appraisal are often incurred in response to poor quality, some companies routinely include appraisal costs in their assessments.

2. What is the payback from investments in appraisal? The analysis of appraisal costs is conducted to determine if the appraisal costs are being spent in the areas that have the

greatest payback to the company. If not, resources can be shifted to their highest valued use.

Level 3 Assessment. The level 3 assessment combines the analysis of appraisal and internal failure and external failure costs with the quantification of prevention costs. Whether or not a company conducts a level 3 assessment depends on a number of factors. Some companies do not track prevention costs because of the difficulty in distinguishing between prevention activities and normal job requirements. For example, if an engineer does a design review, is that a prevention cost or a normal job requirement? By not measuring prevention costs, arguments over definitions are avoided. Other experienced companies have decided not to assess prevention costs to avoid sending the signal that cutting back on prevention is an effective way to reduce costs. Companies that do conduct assessments of prevention costs generally do so to ensure that investments in prevention are being made in the highest payback areas. Companies have discovered that, unfortunately, not all investments in prevention are made in high payback areas. By routinely assessing whether prevention projects are yielding results, companies are in a more informed position to eliminate organizational barriers that are limiting success or to redeploy the investment to more promising projects.

Selecting the Multifunctional Cost-of-Poor-Quality Assessment Team

Every cost-of-poor-quality assessment team should consist of a member from each of the departments to be assessed, as well as a quality and management accounting team member. Members from each department bring unique departmental perspectives that are needed to develop the customized departmental poor-quality cost element listings and perform critical analyses. In investigating complaint-related information, for example, a marketing department representative would be essential.

The teaming of quality and accounting brings together the specific quality and financial skills that, combined with the experience of departmental personnel, are necessary for the cost-of-poor-quality assessment. Both the accounting and quality professional have roles to play in educating departmental personnel, supporting the departmental assessment team, collecting and analyzing data, helping to prepare the cost-of-poor-quality assessment report, and assisting with the presentation of results to management.

The role of the quality team member is to serve as a guide and resource for all assessment team members by clarifying the cost-of-poor-quality definitions and assisting in the development of examples. The quality professional frequently provides the quality education and training needed to develop the necessary quality skills and capabilities. The role of the management accounting team member is to assist the improvement teams with data collection and calculation of specific quality costs, particularly when allocations or sensitive data are involved. The management accounting team member consolidates the information gathered by the other team members, helps to verify the reasonableness of the calculations and assessment data, assists with the analysis of the information collected, performs cost-benefit analyses, and works closely with the other members of the assessment effort in the preparation of management reports.

The role of the quality and management accounting team members is not to conduct the cost-of-poor-quality assessment for the organization but to facilitate the assessment process. One of the primary benefits from the cost-of-poor-quality assessment is teaching team members from the various departments how to recognize poor quality activities, processes, and practices. This is especially true for team members from service and support areas of the company such as marketing, data processing, shipping, receiving, inventory, advertising, engineering, purchasing, production support, accounting, and administration. While the manufacturing operations are familiar with problems like rework and scrap, these may be new concepts for the indirect, white-collar, and support areas of the company.

Educating the indirect and white-collar areas of the company is crucial to a successful assessment. A variety of studies and experiences show that the majority of the costs of poor quality will be discovered by the team members from the white-collar areas. This discovery process is an important part of creating and instilling a quality ethic that shifts attitudes from good enough to doing the right things right the first time.

Team members should be selected on the basis of a thorough understanding of the actual work performed within their department's operations, activities, and processes. For the initial assessment, it is a good idea to have departmental managers who are interested and supportive of the quality process serve as team members. This helps to educate the managers about the top management objectives for the quality process and the purpose behind the cost-of-poor-quality assessment.

Cost-of-Poor-Quality Training for Team Members

Training is needed to introduce each member of the assessment project to the concepts of poor-quality costs and the purpose of the assessment. The cost-of-poor-quality training begins with the definition of key terms and concepts. The assessment team should prepare examples that are suited to the company's environment. Heinz Pet Products, for example, has translated much of its quality literature and manuals into Spanish for Hispanic employees at its Terminal Island facilities. The effectiveness of the Heinz quality process is a result of the company's willingness to prepare useful quality information for employees, in whatever form or language is most appropriate.

The initial training focuses on key terms and concepts to ensure a solid base of understanding is in place before engaging in the actual assessment activities. In addition to providing an orientation to key terms and concepts, the review and modification of the standard list of cost element definitions and illustrations presented in appendix B are a major part of the training process for assessment team members.

The poor-quality cost element listing should be modified in the following ways.

- The team decides which of the major cost categories (prevention, appraisal, internal and external failure) will be used in the assessment effort. For the initial assessment, the team may want to limit itself to the failure categories, recognizing the learning curve effects. Subsequent assessment teams may decide to add the prevention and appraisal categories as the company and its employees gain more experience in identifying and eliminating poor-quality activities, processes, and practices.
- Once the team determines the major cost categories to survey, the next step is to examine the detailed cost elements within the selected cost categories. Cost elements that are not relevant to the company should be excluded by the team. The assessment team can also add cost elements that it feels should be reflected in the company's customized poor-quality cost element listing.
- The third step is for each assessment team member to provide departmental examples of poor-quality activities and processes that illustrate the cost element. For example, one of the cost elements within the internal failure cost category is rework. The representative from the sales department might identify rework activities or processes such as rewriting sales orders; revisiting customer sites to collect information missed during the initial sales visit; reissuing sales proposals; revising sales materials; redoing mailing lists; and other examples of activities or processes undertaken to repair or correct deficiencies.

Going through the effort to modify the standard poor-quality cost element listing for the department is an educational experience for the assessment team member. This exercise may be the first time anyone has given visibility to poor quality activities or processes. Determining what activities are driven by the failure to meet customer requirements is likely to challenge a number of institutionalized poor-quality habits and practices. Testing the status quo is an important first step in identifying improvement opportunities.

Getting Ready for the Assessment

The assessment guide in appendix A provides additional details to supplement the overview provided in this chapter. The preparation of the customized list of poor-quality cost elements provides examples to help guide assessment team members in conducting the cost of poor quality assessment in their respective departments. The listing contains departmental examples of poor-quality activities, processes, and practices that can be used to educate the members of the department. The department specific examples accelerate the learning process, which is especially useful for those department members selected for interviews. By distributing the customized departmental listing along with the activity log, the interviewees have the opportunity to develop a keener appreciation of quality concepts prior to the interview sessions.

The assessment team should retain copies of each of the customized departmental listings. Subsequent assessments can use the same listing or, based on the previous experiences, can be modified to better meet the needs of a changing business. Maintaining the earlier listings allows the company to consistently track poor-quality costs over time even though additional elements may subsequently have been added. A cost-of-poor-quality baseline can be established and successive assessments plotted against the baseline.

Experience has shown that it is common for the reported cost of poor quality to increase over the first three-year period. The reason is that members of subsequent assessment teams are more experienced, allowing better identification of poor-quality activities and their related costs. Poor-quality practices that may have been overlooked in earlier assessments are often uncovered and reported in subsequent assessments.

Experience also shows that the first cost-of-poor-quality assessment will identify far more improvement opportunities than the organization can handle. The initial emphasis, therefore, should be on education and the identification of *significant* improvement opportunities. It is a fatal mistake to attempt to assess every category and every question, just as it would be a fatal mistake for the company to implement an improvement project for every poor-quality cost element identified during the assessment.

The expectation must be set for management and employees about what the initial assessment can and cannot do. Expectations that the assessment solves poor-quality problems, cures organizational conflicts, or turns up the "miracle" project are unrealistic and must be corrected. The purpose of the cost-of-poor-quality assessment is to identify significant opportunities for improvement, not to develop another accounting system or to conduct a witch hunt. Remember, *it is far more valuable to be approximately right than precisely wrong.*

The first assessment will be a learning experience for the entire organization, so don't make it so difficult that everyone gets frustrated and gives up. The departmental assessments are usually conducted simultaneously and typically require two to three weeks. An additional two to three weeks is required to consolidate the departmental information, analyze the results, and prepare recommendations for the next step. While the first assessment may take slightly longer as personnel become accustomed to the concepts, forms, procedures, and purpose, most cost-of-poor-quality assessments typically can be completed in four to six weeks.

After the assessment team members have modified the standard cost-of-poor-quality element listing to suit their needs, each team member and department manager selects a representative sample of departmental employees to interview. In small departments, it may be possible to interview every employee. In larger departments, the employees selected for the interview should be representative of the various jobs and activities performed within the department.

In a sales department, for example, 100 employees may be involved in selling, order processing, and mailing list maintenance. A representative sample of employees, including supervisors and managers, should be selected for the interview process. For example, if there are 40 sales personnel in the department, and 20 percent of the department personnel are to be interviewed, then 8 salespeople should be selected. If there are both an inside and outside sales force, the selection should reflect the mix of inside and outside sales personnel. The interviewees selected should accurately reflect what goes on in the department, or the results of the assessment may be biased in one direction or the other.

Whenever possible, the department manager should be the departmental representative on the initial cost-of-poor-quality assessment team. If the manager is not an assessment team member, it is important to keep him or her fully informed of the assessment activities. At a minimum, the departmental team member should seek the manager's input in preparing examples for the customized departmental listing.

Before the team begins the assessment, members should anticipate concerns that may be raised. The team needs to decide how it will respond if difficult questions are asked. For example, the interviewees may interpret the cost-of-poor-quality exercise as a prelude to a head-count reduction program; managers may be hesitant to do an accurate assessment for fear that the results of the cost-of-poor-quality assessment may be used to evaluate their performance; or interviewees may feel that this is another "program of the month" and decide that their active participation is a waste of effort. Assessment team members need to be prepared to discuss the overall quality improvement framework within which the cost-of-poor-quality assessment is conducted, how the assessment fits into the broader improvement process, what the results of the assessment will be used for, and what the expected benefits are for both the business and employees.

The Kick-Off Meeting

The assessment team is ready to conduct the kick-off meeting after the training is complete, the departmental listing prepared, interviewees selected, and potential concerns identified. The kick-off meeting is held for each of the departments involved in the assessment. The meeting should be conducted by the assessment team member from that department or jointly by the department manager and the assessment team member. The quality or management accounting assessment team member should also be present at the kick-off meeting to field specific questions or concerns.

The purpose of the meeting is to discuss why the cost-of-poor-quality assessment is being conducted, the type of activity and process-related information the team wants to gather, and what happens once the information is gathered. The length of the kick-off meeting should reflect the needs of the organization and potential concerns to be addressed. Since the meeting is educational, make sure that participants are allowed the time to ask questions and receive complete answers.

In an organization in which an existing quality process has stalled, the kick-off meeting may take longer as the team discusses how top management intends to restart the process and what management is doing differently. The more experienced an organization is with the quality improvement process, the longer the kick-off meeting can take as the interviewees discuss a wide variety of items in greater detail. This meeting sets the tone for things to come, so it is important to do it right the first time.

After the kick-off meeting, the team members begin to work within their respective departments to complete the cost-of-poor-quality assessment. While the quality and management accounting team members can be drawn on for support and guidance, the team members and their respective departments should own the results of the assessment. The ownership of results promotes buy-in to the quality process and forces the department to recognize the need to change activities, processes, and practices to reduce or eliminate the costs of poor quality.

Collecting the Data

There are six primary techniques available for determining the cost of poor quality. These include (1) collection of costs by account,

(2) collection of costs by the "whole person" or equivalent heads, (3) collection of labor costs by project, (4) estimation of costs using the percentage defective, (5) estimation of costs based on the number of occurrences of a poor-quality event, and (6) collection of costs based on interviews and surveys. Each of these costing techniques is discussed here.

The management accounting team member can provide substantial assistance with the *collection of costs by account* technique by identifying financial records in accounting or other systems such as manufacturing, personnel, engineering, sales, or purchasing. Many of the costs of poor quality such as rework, scrap, warranty claims, and quality department expenditures can be easily extracted from the accounting system. It is also common to find substantial internal failure costs in other financial and manufacturing systems. The management accounting team member can often gather the cost data quickly once the team has identified the specific poor-quality activities or processes. Collection of costs by account should therefore be done whenever possible.

The collection of costs by account provides a good starting point for the cost-of-poor-quality assessment. However, studies indicate these easy-to-measure poor-quality costs account for one-fourth of the true cost of poor quality. Although the collection of costs by account is a useful and practical technique, quantification of the hidden costs of poor quality usually requires the use of other cost collection techniques.

The *collection of costs by the "whole person" or equivalent heads* is relatively easy to perform. This technique is based on counting the number of full-time equivalents involved in a poor-quality activity or process. Examples include identifying employees whose job it is to fix defective products, resolve design problems on a failed product, investigate complaints, resolve incorrect invoices, dispose of inferior products, expedite materials or products, set up facilities to handle returned goods, or perform warranty repair operations.

Some of the whole person and equivalent head costs can be easily calculated but not so easily classified. The cost of an internal auditor is an example. Is it a poor-quality activity that should be categorized as an appraisal cost or an internal failure cost? How should the costs of inspection be categorized? Some argue that 100 percent inspection is an internal failure cost because the need to sort good items from bad only arises because internal processes cannot reliably meet customer requirements. On the other hand, in many instances it is not economically viable to ship error-free products to customers without inspection due to inherent imperfections in the manufacturing processes. In other cases, customers such as the U.S. government may require 100-percent inspection. The assessment team has to determine how such costs are to be categorized and then apply the definition consistently.

Often the team member will have to *collect labor costs by project*. Time sheets, time cards, or other documents are useful for providing the breakdown of the time spent on various projects or activities. Time cards, for example, can show what percentage of a person's time is spent on rework or problem correction.

Another technique is *estimation of costs using the percentage defective* relative to the total number of occurrences or instances. The number of defectives is determined and then compared to the total number of occurrences. For example, if a salesperson spends 10 out of 40 available hours per week handling complaints, then 25 percent (10 hours divided by 40 hours) of the salesperson's time would be allocated to external failure. If the purchasing department reissues an average of 20 purchase orders a week because of errors, misunderstandings, and missed communications, and issues an average of 25 purchase orders a day, then 16 percent (20 average purchase order reissues per week divided by 125 average total purchase orders issued per week) of total purchasing costs (people, facilities, and expenses) would be allocated as an internal failure cost due to reworking purchase orders.

Estimation of costs based on the number of occurrences of a poor-quality event is performed by first determining the number of times the event occurs during a specific period and then multiplying the number of occurrences by a standard cost that reflects the estimates that arise due to the problem. For example, a company may already be collecting information on the number of times an engineering change order is issued to correct a quality problem. Using an estimate of the cost of engineering change orders, the assessment team can calculate the associated poor-quality costs.

Hewlett-Packard uses this technique to measure poor-quality costs in its Direct Marketing Division (DMD).[1] Previous measurement efforts using existing quality cost report formats were ineffective because the information was too general and did not indicate specific improvement opportunities. Management decided that a different approach was needed to help the division's management focus improvement efforts in the right areas and measure the performance of the improvement effort.

An enhanced approach called the quality index was developed by Tim Fuller, then DMD's quality manager, to estimate the poor-quality costs caused by process errors and other unsatisfactory conditions. The quality index is based on the number of errors or occurrences of a negative condition in a month, which is then multiplied by the standard cost of the error or occurrence. The result is the identification of high payback activities and process errors, many of which are related to poor quality in indirect and white-collar areas. Some of the most significant process errors and unsatisfactory conditions identified using the quality index approach are

- The cost of orders returned by customers due to incorrect products, damage, and overshipments. DMD's analysis estimates that the total cost of poor quality for processing a customer return is $198 per occurrence, excluding the impact of lost sales, warranty claims, repairs, handling, and replacements. Examples of the white-collar and indirect poor-quality costs related to processing customer returns are shown in Figure 8.1, which includes the costs of unproductive salesperson time, return expenses, paperwork processing, issuing credit memos to customers, and estimates of the costs that incorrect orders create at customer and supplier sites.

Hewlett-Packard: Other than the DMD	$20	Even though a shipment was made from DMD, customers sometimes will call their local sales office for return directions and/or send the item to the sales office. Based on historical data, assume one-third of the customers call their local sales office. Assume one hour of field time at $40. Add $20 for freight and other field costs—$(40 + 20)/3 = 20.
DMD returns department	$35	Department expenses are $25,000 per month. $25,000 for 1,000 returns = $25 per return. Also assume $10 per return for incoming freight.
DMD other departments	$35	The estimated cost of processing the paperwork through the systems and issuing a credit to the customer.
Subtotal for Hewlett-Packard and DMD	$90	
Customer	$90	The best estimate is that the customer incurs about the same cost as Hewlett-Packard and DMD.
Supplier	$18	Assume that 25% of the returns are defective and are returned to the supplier for credit. The best estimate is that the supplier incurs about the same amount of costs as DMD—$(35 + 35)/4 = 18.
Total costs of processing one return, on average	$198	

Adapted from Hawley Atkinson, et al. *Current Trends in Cost of Quality: Linking the Cost of Quality to Continuous Improvement* (Montvale, N.J.: National Association of Accountants, 1991), 44.

Figure 8.1 The total estimated cost of processing a customer return at Hewlett-Packard Direct Marketing Division.

- The cost of both errors and lost sales due to a lack of reliable information in the perpetual inventory system. Unreliable inventory data cause poor-quality costs when the wrong item is shipped to a customer or when sales are lost because the inventory system showed items out of stock when, in fact, the inventory was on hand.
- The cost of inventory over and above what is actually needed to fill customer orders. These costs include the cash tied up in excess asset investments, additional inventory carrying costs, obsolescence, damage, and inventory losses.

Some departments have high costs of poor quality, but it is difficult to determine exactly how high because the amount of time involved in doing things over is not readily apparent. This situation occurs most often in professional, service, support, or white-collar areas such as sales, engineering, accounting, purchasing, administration, and marketing. People tend to go from one project or activity to another project or activity almost continuously. One may be related to nonconformance and the next one to achieving the department's objectives.

In these cases, *collection of costs based on interviews and surveys* is the most effective. An activity log can provide a practical approach for interviewees to track the time spent on various activities. Experience shows that people often do not accurately remember all of the various activities they perform over the course of a day. The activity log is a diary for the participants to record the activities performed and the reason for each activity over a defined period of time, generally one to two weeks. The activity log sensitizes participants to the specifics of their daily work routine, increases their awareness of the activities they performed, speeds up the interviewing process, and improves the accuracy of the interview session. The kick-off meeting is a good time to distribute activity logs to the assessment participants and explain how the logs are used.

The activity logs are designed to assist the interviewees during the interview sessions and should not to be reviewed by supervisory personnel. Objective data recording is essential to remove any potential recording bias. The goal is to have the interviewees gather information as accurately as possible to improve the accuracy of the interview session responses. A sample activity log is shown in Figure 8.2.

The activity recordings should account for the entire day over the time period selected. Examples of recordings are shown Figures 8.3 and 8.4.

After one to two weeks of activity logging is finished, the interviews are conducted. Remember to have the participants bring their activity logs to the interview sessions as a reminder of how their time was actually spent. By recording responses for each of the cost elements, the assessment team can later use the responses and information recorded to determine the cost of poor quality for each department. Unclear or ambiguous responses can be resolved in the interview session.

Managerial Inputs and Assumptions

Once the assessment team members have prepared their departmental listings, the representative salary ranges and labor rates for the employees in the department are needed to determine the cost of poor quality associated with various activities. The management accounting representative on the assessment team can work with the personnel department to gather the salary and labor rate information. Overhead and burden rates can be applied to the salary and labor information to arrive at fully loaded salary and labor rates.

Depending on the culture of the organization, the departmental manager may need to be involved in preparing salary and labor rate inputs. In any case, the salary and labor rate information must be regarded as confidential and handled carefully. The department manager may want to determine salary ranges and labor rates for grades or classifications of employees and then provide that information to the assessment team.

Daily Activity Log

Name _____

Department _____Day_____of_____

Position _____

Time	Activity and Purpose
7:00–7:30 AM	_____
7:30–8:00 AM	_____
8:00–8:30 AM	_____
8:30–9:00 AM	_____
9:00–9:30 AM	_____
9:30–10:00 AM	_____
10:00–10:30 AM	_____
10:30–11:00 AM	_____
11:00–11:30 AM	_____
11:30 AM –12:00 PM	_____
12:00–12:30 PM	_____
12:30–1:00 PM	_____
1:00–1:30 PM	_____
1:30–2:00 PM	_____
2:00–2:30 PM	_____
2:30–3:00 PM	_____
3:00–3:30 PM	_____
3:30–4:00 PM	_____
4:00–4:30 PM	_____
4:30–5:00 PM	_____

Figure 8.2 The daily activity log focuses attention on the daily work routine and activities performed.

Daily Activity Log

Name: Joe Smith

Department: Final Assembly   Day 1 of 5

Position: Welder

Time	Activity and Purpose
9:00–9:30 AM	Welded 7 production frames 15 minutes. Repair of 1 frame from returned goods 15 minutes.

Figure 8.3 Daily activity log example.

Daily Activity Log

Name: Jane Doe

Department: Computer Sales   Day 3 of 5

Position: Senior Salesperson

Time	Activity and Purpose
2:30–3:00 PM	Returned calls to sales prospects 20 minutes. Follow up on late delivery problem 10 minutes.

Figure 8.4 Daily activity log example.

A work calendar should be established to account for plant shutdowns, vacations, holidays, and other nonproduction periods such as maintenance, cleaning, or scheduled downtime. The work calendar helps to prepare cost estimates that reflect vacations, holidays, or time off. Together, the work calendar, salary ranges, labor rates, and burden estimates provide the input for the assessment team to cost out the time spent by employees in poor-quality–related activities, processes, or practices.

Conducting the Interviews

Interviews are conducted with the designated participants and their answers are recorded. Group interviews of five or fewer people are recommended due to the amount of data that needs to be gathered and the importance of obtaining a reasonable degree of accuracy. For departments with more than five or six interviewees, it is best to prepare an interview schedule to make the interview process as efficient as possible. Responses are recorded on listing worksheets and tallied after the interviews are completed. Noting the interviewees on the listing worksheets makes it is possible to go back and confirm details or gather additional information.

The interview process provides a forum for the assessment team members to discuss the examples, definitions, and illustrations of poor-quality costs. The interviewer should use the assessment listing as a tool to relate the activities performed in the department to the concepts of internal and external failure, as appropriate. This improves the accuracy and completeness of the answers received and helps to educate people to identify poor-quality habits, processes, and activities.

Compiling and Analyzing the Information

The departmental worksheets contain the estimates of time, material, and expenses consumed for each activity related to a particular cost element. The management accounting team member can be particularly useful in developing the material cost and expense information needed to measure the waste and nonvalue-added activities driven by poor-quality materials and processes.

Controllable and Uncontrollable Poor-Quality Costs

Once the poor-quality cost data are calculated and tallied for a department, the assessment team member meets with the department manager to review the information. The department manager and assessment team member should ensure that no omissions or double counts have occurred. After the manager and assessment team member agree that the data are reasonable and representative, the various cost elements are classified into controllable or uncontrollable categories.

Controllable poor-quality costs are due to causes within the control of the department, while uncontrollable poor-quality costs are due to causes outside the department's control. The department manager and assessment team member make the classification on a best-efforts basis and note the suspected source of the uncontrollable quality costs. The assessment team member records the information on the departmental worksheet and then supplies the information to the management accounting team member for consolidation.

Recognizing the source of poor-quality costs isn't always easy. For example, assume that a salesperson mixes up the orders of several different customers and mistakenly places an incorrect order for blue widgets when the customer wanted red. The difficulty in determining the source of the poor-quality costs often depends on when and where the company is able to catch the incorrect sales order, shown as follows:

1. *Sales* releases the incorrect order. Poor-quality costs appear as the extra time and expense to fix the incorrect sales order and resubmit the correct order.
2. *Purchasing* processes the incorrect order. Poor-quality costs appear as the time and expense to cancel a purchase order to a supplier, issue a correct purchase order, and pay any restocking or cancellation penalties.

3. *Manufacturing* makes the incorrect order. Poor-quality costs appear as the loss of labor, material, machine time, and overhead required to make the blue widgets, the additional production planning and scheduling required to make red widgets, the production losses due to schedule disruptions and additional setups that arise if the red widgets are done as a rush job, the excess material handling costs to move and store the blue widgets and rehandle the red widgets, and so on.

4. *Shipping* delivers the wrong order. Poor-quality costs appear as the extra time and expense to retrieve the wrong product from the customer, handle the returned widgets, and store the excess inventory.

5. *Accounting* processes the paperwork. Poor-quality costs appear as an uncollectible account receivable, the annual inventory write-down for inventory nobody wants, the cost of processing credit memos and inventory returns, and so on.

6. *Customer* receives the wrong order. Poor-quality costs appear as the extra time and expenses required to respond to customer complaints, penalties for incorrect shipments, lost profit margins from canceled orders, advertising costs to attract new customers because of a lack of repeat business, and loss of sales due to the reputation as a low-quality supplier.

As Figure 8.5 shows, a simple quality failure like an incorrect sales order can affect any department in the organization. The cost of poor quality is a useful tool to help companies establish the culture, set performance measures, and facilitate the cross-functional problem solving to eliminate problems that cut across the entire organization. If the problem of the incorrect sales order is discovered in the manufacturing department, for example, it will be harder to track the problem back to its source in the sales department if purchasing is unwilling to cooperate. The problem solving could still take place on a best efforts basis without the purchasing department, or the problem-solving effort could be dropped altogether.

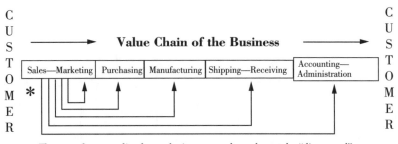

* The cost of poor quality due to the incorrect sales order can be "discovered"
  in any department by an internal customer or an external customer.

Figure 8.5
Poor-quality costs have no respect for organizational charts or boundaries.

Either way, the effect is counterproductive and detrimental to the competitiveness of the entire company. Instead of training the salesperson or upgrading the sales order processes to prevent the error of incorrect sales orders from occurring again, there is no change. Incorrect sales orders continue to be a source of poor-quality costs, measured as rework, scrap, returns, excess inventory, hidden in standards, or buried in some manufacturing or overhead account.

Aggregating the Departmental Cost-of-Poor-Quality Information
The cost collection techniques described previously provide the mechanisms for gathering the necessary labor time, material, and expense information for each of the cost categories being assessed. As shown in Figure 8.6, the departmental cost-of-poor-quality assessment information is then summarized for the entire company. The enterprise-wide cost-of-poor-quality assessment summary displays the total cost of poor quality for the entire business, as well as for each of the cost-of-poor-quality categories and elements. The completed assessment takes the potential value of effective quality management out of the abstract and brings it sharply into focus as cold hard cash.

It is crucial to remember that poor-quality costs have no respect for organization charts. The departmental display of poor-quality

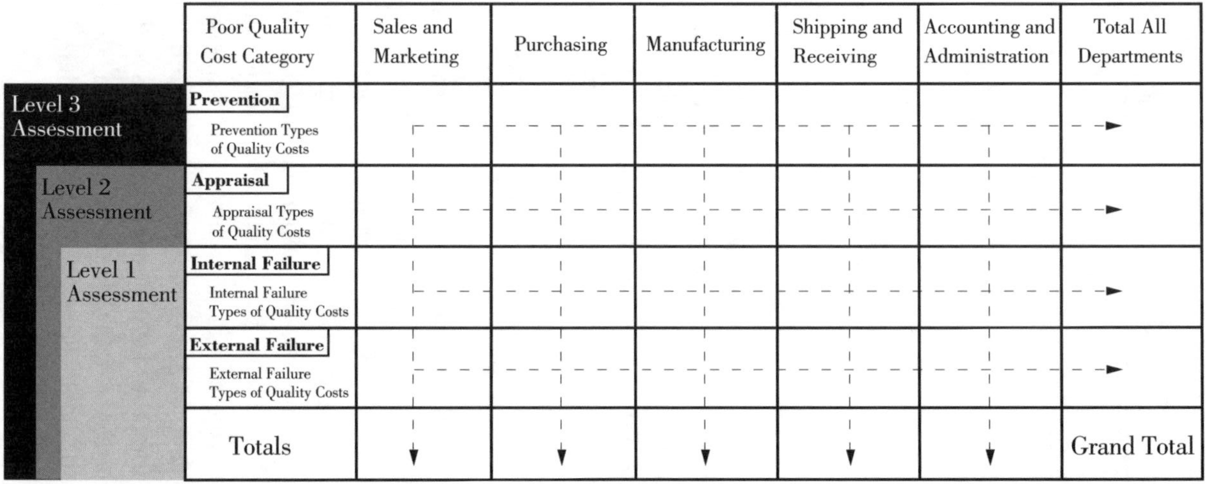

Poor Quality Cost Category	Sales and Marketing	Purchasing	Manufacturing	Shipping and Receiving	Accounting and Administration	Total All Departments
Prevention Prevention Types of Quality Costs						
Appraisal Appraisal Types of Quality Costs						
Internal Failure Internal Failure Types of Quality Costs						
External Failure External Failure Types of Quality Costs						
Totals						Grand Total

Level 3 Assessment

Level 2 Assessment

Level 1 Assessment

Figure 8.6 The cost-of-poor-quality assessment provides a snapshot of poor-quality costs across the entire organization.

costs simply shows where the poor quality costs are reported, not the source of the problem. A cost-driver analysis is required to determine the underlying cause of the poor quality.

Presenting the Cost-of-Poor-Quality Assessment Information

After the cost-of-poor-quality information is collected and analyzed, the next step is presenting the results to top management. The presentation needs to be structured to answer the following critical questions.

1. *What is the purpose of the assessment?* The ultimate goal of the quality process and quality-based cost management is the achievement of business goals and objectives. The purpose of the cost-of-poor-quality assessment is to identify and quantify the non-value-added activities and waste driven by poor quality, thereby supporting the achievement of quality goals and objectives that reflect the broader business goals and objectives.

The cost-of-poor-quality assessment team needs to convey this sense of purpose to top management. To convey that message, however, the assessment team must understand, very specifically, how the results of the assessment support the achievement of business and quality goals and objectives. The team will find it difficult to convey a clear and positive sense of purpose to top management if its members do not understand how and why the assessment fits into the quality and business strategy. Whatever the key strategic and financial imperatives of the business are, the linkage from those imperatives to the cost-of-poor-quality assessment has to be made clear.

2. *What are the assumptions used in the assessment?* Assumptions about wage rates, overhead rates, and allocations need to be documented to answer the questions that will inevitably be asked. For example, if the assessment calculates excess inventory as a cost of poor quality due to unreliable suppliers, what

assumptions are used? The achievable inventory level with reliable suppliers, the cost of carrying excess inventory, the cash tied up in excess inventory, and any other elements that are used to calculate the cost of excess inventory due to quality problems all need to be documented.

Adequate documentation gives the team the opportunity to discuss how the calculations are made. The reasonableness of the assumptions can be verified and, if necessary, changed based on more accurate information. The assumptions used in the cost-of-poor-quality assessment are important to establishing the credibility of the results, so the team should be fully prepared to discuss the calculations for each cost element.

3. *What are the results of the assessment?* When analyzing results, the assessment team should consider what percent of sales is consumed by the cost of poor quality. What other important aspects of the business should be compared to the total cost of poor quality? For example, how much would the cost of poor quality be if it was expressed in terms of lost earnings per share, a percentage of direct labor costs, a percentage of the company's investment in plant and equipment, a percentage of incentive wages or bonuses, or a percentage of the company's cash flow? Are there any other financial or nonfinancial performance measures that are important to top management, middle management, hourly employees, or salaried employees that, when related to the total cost of poor quality, would help people to better understand the financial impact of poor quality?

The assessment team should also consider what the largest poor-quality cost elements for each department are. What are the largest elements for the entire organization? What is the comparison between direct and indirect poor-quality costs? What percent of the poor-quality costs by department are controllable? Uncontrollable? Even though estimates of root causes are educated guesses at this point, is there a pattern to the sources of uncontrollable poor-quality costs? Are any of the assessment results surprising? If so, why?

4. *What actions, if any, should be taken based on the results?*
The assessment team should consider which cost-of-poor-quality
elements relate to priorities that are most important to the business, such as lowering expenses, reducing the level of assets
invested in the business, or increasing customer satisfaction. Are
there any poor-quality cost elements that deserve special attention
given the goals, objectives, and priorities of the business? Which
poor-quality cost elements should be recommended to top management for the cost-driver analysis? Does the cost-of-poor-quality
assessment team have the skills to conduct the cost-driver analysis
or should a different team be assembled?

5. *How does the company benefit from this information?*
Identifying and quantifying the impact of poor quality is the first
step toward improving financial performance through quality
improvement. The benefits of the assessment information arise in
several areas: Personnel are educated about poor quality and its
costs to the business; the financial gain from effective quality management can be quantified; and the cost-of-poor-quality assessment information can be used as a basis for discussing quality in
any department or function of the business using a common language—dollars.

The cost-of-poor-quality assessment allows the quality process
to focus on improving financial performance as well as customer
satisfaction. An emphasis on financial performance provides a signal to everyone involved that the quality process can play an
important part in the competitive success of the company. As members of different departments work together, another benefit is
developing a greater appreciation of how the business operates.
Perhaps most important, the ability to identify the impact of a quality failure shows the importance of doing things right the first time.
The cost-of-poor-quality assessment is often the first time that such
information is available.

6. *How can this information improve the bottom line?* In addition to educating the company about the financial potential of poor

quality, the assessment information may highlight some immediate opportunities for improvement that can produce a positive impact on the bottom line. The cost-of-poor-quality assessment provides the information management needs to begin the cost-driver analysis, which provides the information needed to identify the high-payback improvement projects.

The criteria for selecting poor-quality cost elements for the cost-driver analysis should include consideration of both the strategic and financial imperatives of the business. For example, if cash flow is a priority, then emphasizing the reduction of excess inventory or accounts receivable may have a higher priority. If, on the other hand, additional sales is the priority, then emphasizing lost sales due to quality problems may receive higher consideration. Reflecting the strategic and financial imperatives of the business in the selection of cost elements for the cost-driver analysis helps to ensure that the priorities of the business and the quality process remain aligned.

Another important point to remember is that poor-quality cost elements may share common root causes. Scrap and rework are examples of two poor-quality costs that are often affected by common root causes. By selecting poor-quality costs that may be driven by similar causes, it is more likely that the true financial impact of common root causes will be uncovered. If the cost-driver analysis confirms that common root causes, implementation of a solution may create greater payback and financial leverage than would be available if root causes for individual cost elements were examined independently.

Conclusion

Defining nonvalue-added activities and waste in terms of the failure to meet internal or external customer requirements gives managers the information to focus the quality process on increased customer satisfaction. The ability to quantify the financial impact of nonvalue-added activities and waste provides companies with the direct connection between quality improvement and improved financial performance. Assessing the entire organization gives management a realistic estimate of the impact of poor quality on the business and highlights the key elements. After management confirms the final selection of the key cost-of-poor-quality elements, the assessment team is ready to move into the next phase of quality-based cost management—the cost-driver analysis.

Notes

1. Hawley Atkinson, Gregory Hohner, Barry Mundt, Richard B. Troxel, and William Winchell, *Current Trends In Cost of Quality: Linking the Cost of Quality to Continuous Improvement* (Montvale, N.J.: National Association of Accountants, 1991), 41–47.

9 The Cost-Driver Analysis _____

Executive Summary

Companies have hundreds, possibly thousands, of potential improvement projects from which to select. How, then, does a company select one project over another? Quantifying the cost of poor quality and determining where these dollars are located is an important first step in linking quality to profitability. What the assessment doesn't tell an organization is why the quality problems exist or which projects offer the best potential for improving financial performance. The cost-driver analysis is a powerful technique that integrates the problem-solving and analysis tools of the quality process with the poor-quality-cost assessment. The cost-driver analysis combines these tools and techniques to generate the management information needed to prioritize potential improvements on the basis of improving financial performance.

THE COST-DRIVER ANALYSIS

The cost-driver methodology consists of four steps: (1) determine the root causes of poor-quality costs, (2) identify the activity percentages and calculate the cost of poor quality related to each root cause, (3) combine the financial impacts of common root causes to determine the *total* financial impact of the root cause, and (4) perform a cost-benefit analysis for the high financial impact root causes to determine the financial payback.

1. *Determine the root causes of poor quality.* Before beginning the cost-driver analysis, the objectives need to be understood and agreed on by each member of the analysis team. Confirming the objectives of the cost-driver analysis helps to ensure that the linkage from the business and quality vision to the daily activities of the team is intact and consistent. Understanding the results of the cost-of-poor-quality assessment and the rationale used by management to set priorities for the cost-driver analysis provides the transition from the assessment to the driver analysis. This is especially helpful for members of the cost-driver analysis team who did not participate in the cost-of-poor-quality assessment.

Selection of team members who represent each of the departments that will participate in the analysis is essential. The participating departments can be determined from the assumptions provided by departmental managers about the sources of uncontrollable quality costs. While these assumptions may turn out to be incorrect, the initial selection of team members is based on the best available information at the time. In situations where the team finds that an additional department needs to be involved in the cost-driver analysis, a representative from that department should be identified quickly and integrated into the analysis effort.

Team members need training not only in the basics of quality-based cost management but also in problem-solving techniques. As the cost-driver analysis proceeds, the underlying causes of poor quality may not be obvious. The ability to identify the information needed for analysis, and then apply the appropriate problem-solving technique, is a skill developed through training in problem solving. Team members must either develop these skills or have access to experts who can guide the team in using these techniques. If not, the analysis process gets bogged down and the likelihood of generating useful root-cause information is reduced.

Following training, team members begin the process of identifying and determining the financial impact for each of the cost-of-poor-quality elements selected for the analysis. Chapter 4 presented an overview of cost-driver analysis using an example of the penalties paid for failure to meet customer delivery schedules. This chapter builds on that example to provide a more detailed description of the cost-driver analysis process.

The first steps in the cost-driver analysis are (1) determining the activities that drive the selected poor-quality-cost element and (2) determining the root causes of these activities or cost drivers. Although the specific methods that team members use to identify the cost drivers and root causes vary with the nature of the problem and data availability, the use of quality tools and techniques will generally fall into one of seven categories.

1. Process analysis and documenting
2. Idea generation
3. Data collection
4. Problem solving
5. Analysis
6. Decision support
7. Implementation and analysis

The following list shows a wide array of tools and techniques to provide a sense of the quality tools and techniques available to improvement teams.[1] Some of the tools and techniques require advanced training for effective use while others can be put to use with limited explanation or training. Just as the financial professional brings a variety of skills and experiences, the quality professional is also a valuable resource to draw on when applying the tools and techniques of quality improvement. Many of the tools can be used for multiple purposes, and the following categorization is not intended to limit their use.

Tool or Technique Category	Tool or Technique Description
Process analysis and documenting	Flowchart*
Idea generation	Brainstorming
	Nominal group technique (NGT)
Data collection	Check sheet*
	Survey/interview
Analysis	Affinity diagram
	Benchmarking
	Cause-and-effect diagram (fishbone)*
	Cause-and-effect diagram (fishbone) with addition of cards
	Control chart/run chart*
	Critical path
	Force-field analysis
	Frequency table
	Histogram*
	Interrelationship graph
	Pareto diagram*
	Process capability analysis
	Relational matrix diagram
	Scatter diagram*
	Time line analysis
	Tree diagram
Decision support	Attribute grid
	Multivoting
	Taguchi methods (design of experiments)
Implementation and monitoring	Concurrent engineering
	Objectives matrix
	Quality function deployment
	Statistical process control

*One of the seven basic total quality tools

A brief description of each tool and its use is provided in the tool kit at the end of this chapter.

One tool that is particularly useful in conducting the root-cause analysis is the tree diagram, a technique for displaying cause-and-effect relationships in a logical manner. Because of its inherent ability to clearly display even complex relationships, the technique allows the results of the cost-driver analysis to be explained to team members, affected departments, and management in a straightforward manner. The first branch of the tree diagram is occupied by the cost-of-poor-quality element selected for the cost-driver analysis. As the team identifies the factors that cause or drive these costs, the drivers are recorded in the second level of branches. Returning to the penalties example, the team identified three different drivers of penalties: partial shipments, incorrect shipments, and late shipments. Determining these causes was relatively straightforward. Records in the shipping and accounting departments were analyzed to determine the failures that allowed customers to assess a penalty. The customer records were verified to make sure that all of the penalties were appropriate, and then the reasons were tallied. Figure 9.1 shows the tree diagram following the initial stage of the cost-driver analysis.

The team continued the process of first determining the drivers of the lower branches of the tree diagram and then asking what caused those drivers to occur. The goal was to repeat the process until the underlying root causes of penalties were identified. In this example, partial shipments were a major cause of penalties. But why did partial shipments occur? It turned out that the delivery commitments made to customers were based on unrealistic production standards. The company was unable to meet delivery commitments using these standards, which resulted in a series of partial shipments.

Why were the production standards unrealistic? Investigation showed that the standards did not account for the actual downtime experienced in the factory. Further investigation revealed that the stamping machines were experiencing more frequent damage to the jigs and dies used to stamp parts. After a jig or die was chipped or knocked out of alignment, all of the products produced from that

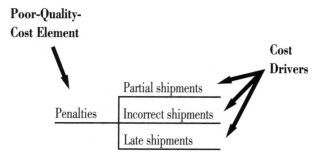

Figure 9.1 The second level of the branches is completed as the team generates the cost-driver information.

point forward were unusable until the press was stopped and the damage corrected.

Even though this process allowed the team to uncover the cause-and-effect relationships that led to excessive downtime, they were still dealing with symptoms of the problem, rather than the underlying root causes. Until the fundamental problem was identified, the process of identifying the cause-and-effect relationships continued.

The next question to answer was what caused the jigs and dies to be chipped or knocked out of alignment. The team compared the timing of tool breaks against the particular source of the raw material used at the time the breaks occurred. This comparison showed that certain raw material suppliers were associated with a much higher incidence of tool breaks than other suppliers. The team then focused on identifying differences in raw material purchases. Further testing showed that small pieces of hardened steel were contained in some of the raw material batches.

The team had now isolated a source of problems that it could target for improvement. By revising its raw material specifications to reflect the required level of raw material purity, the company could eliminate the occurrence of hard spots. Until the team had identified hard spots in the raw material as the real problem, it was still dealing with the symptoms of the underlying root cause of poor quality. Figure 9.2 shows the final results of the team's analysis.

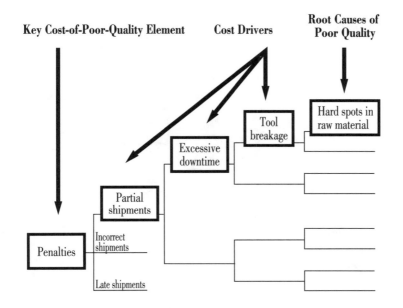

Figure 9.2 Identifying cause-and-effect relationships continues until the underlying root causes of poor quality are identified.

2. Identify the activity percentages and calculate the cost of poor quality related to each root cause of poor quality. After underlying root causes are identified, the next step is determining the cause's financial impact. In the penalties example, records in the shipping and accounting departments showed that 80 percent of the penalties were due to partial shipments. Further analysis of manufacturing, engineering, and purchasing records determined the corresponding percentages for each of the cost drivers and the ultimate root cause. As the tree diagram in Figure 9.3 shows, 90 percent of the partial shipments were caused by excessive downtime. In turn, 75 percent of the excessive downtime in the factory was caused by tool breakage. The next branch shows that 95 percent of tool breakage was caused by hard spots in the raw material.

The total cost of penalties to the company was $198,714. Knowing the percentage of the problem that each cost driver and the root cause accounted for, the team was able to estimate the

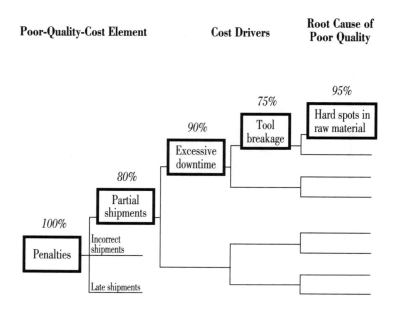

Poor-Quality-Cost Element   Cost Drivers   Root Cause of Poor Quality

Figure 9.3 The activity percentages are added to each successive layer of the tree diagram.

financial impacts by multiplying the total cost of penalties by the following corresponding activity percentages.

• Total penalties	$198,714
• Penalties due to partial shipments	× 80%
Total penalties driven by partial shipments	$158,971
• Partial shipments due to excess downtime	× 90%
Total penalties driven by excess downtime	$143,074
• Excess downtime due to tool breaks	× 75%
Total penalties driven by tool breaks	$107,306
• Tool breaks due to hard spots	× 95%
Total penalties driven by hard spots	$101,940

Figure 9.4 illustrates the completed tree diagram, showing the cost drivers, their related frequencies, and the estimated financial impacts. The completed tree diagram serves two valuable purposes.

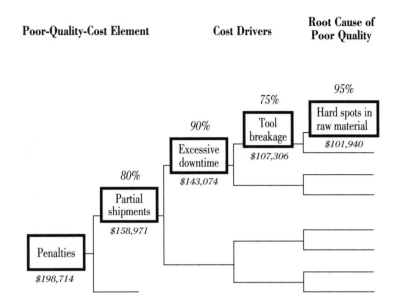

Figure 9.4 The completed cost-driver analysis displays the cost-driver relationships and the financial impact of poor quality.

- It clearly displays the results of the cost-driver analysis. The tree diagram allows team members to easily summarize the results of their work in a simple graphic manner that is easy to understand. The tree diagram also highlights the fact that costly quality problems that appear in one department are frequently caused by root causes in another department. In the early stages of quality-based cost management, many of the case study companies found this to be an important factor in getting the departments to cooperate in solving problems that crossed functional or departmental boundaries.
- It indicates the potential benefits from the elimination of root causes. The tree diagram displays the potential financial benefits from the elimination of various root causes.

This is important not only for determining which projects offer the greatest potential payback but also for setting realistic expectations. Underestimating the potential benefit from a project may cause a company to delay or postpone projects that have a high financial payback. Overestimating the potential of a project is an almost guaranteed disappointment—no matter how well the project turns out, it will fall short of expectations. Realistic expectations are especially crucial in the early stages of implementing quality-based cost management, allowing teams to demonstrate to top management that the quality process can be effectively managed to deliver meaningful results. As improvement teams demonstrate the ability to identify, quantify, and solve meaningful problems, the contribution of the quality process to the achievement of overall business goals is confirmed, thereby reinforcing top management's confidence in the quality process.

3. *Combine common root causes to determine the total financial impact of the root cause of poor quality.* It is important to note that a single root cause may be associated with more than one poor-quality-cost element. Table 9.1 shows the large number of cost elements and departments that were negatively affected by hard spots in the raw material. Viewed from the perspective of the organization as a whole, it was obvious that the benefits from eliminating hard spots would extend far beyond merely reducing penalties. Because selected cost elements often have common root causes, the results from individual cost-driver analyses must be combined to evaluate a root cause's overall financial impact.

4. *Perform a cost-benefit analysis for the high financial impact root causes to determine the financial payback.* Knowing the savings or cash flow that an improvement project might generate is only half of the information required to prioritize improvement opportunities. To determine if a project has a positive or negative payback, the cost to implement the improvement needs to

Effect of Hard Spots on Poor-Quality Costs	Department Affected
Penalties	Accounting
Sales returns	Sales
Complaint investigation	Sales
Scrap Manufacturing	
Rework	Manufacturing
Corrective actions	Manufacturing
Uncontrolled material losses	Purchasing
Field performance evaluations	Engineering
Planned inspections, tests, and audits	Quality
Excess and uncollectible accounts receivable	Accounting
Excess and obsolete inventory	Accounting

Table 9.1   A root cause of poor quality can impact multiple cost elements.

be estimated. The estimated investment to eliminate hard spots included all necessary expenditures such as the cost of time, material, expenses, and capital equipment, which totaled $145,000. Compared to the payback of $1,363,480, which was discussed in chapter 4, the expected net benefit to the company of implementing updated material specifications was

Estimated financial benefit – Estimated investment =
Estimated net financial benefit

$1,363,480 – $145,000 = $1,218,480

Estimating the net financial benefit allows a company to prioritize potential quality improvement opportunities using financial criteria. Selecting improvement projects on the basis of financial criteria such as net present value, internal rate of return, or payback, is the same process that companies typically use to select other investment alternatives such as making capital investments, expanding product lines, or opening new markets. By attaching financial expectations to the quality process, it is possible for the quality process to compete against other alternative investments for available resources.

Conclusion

The cost-driver analysis uses the combined skills of the quality and financial professionals along with the other team members to identify the cost drivers and underlying root causes of poor quality. Grouping the common root causes provides organizations with the information needed to quantify the cost of not doing things right. The ability to demonstrate the negative financial impact of poor quality is a major step forward in gaining the organizational support necessary to solve problems that cross functional boundaries. An accurate understanding of the sources of poor quality, and their related costs to the organization, is often the base from which industry and market leaders coordinate and communicate the need for cross-functional cooperation to solve problems.

The next step in the quality-based cost management approach is selecting the improvement projects that can make a genuine contribution to improving the competitiveness of the company. The issues of project selection, planning, project monitoring, and reporting to top management are discussed in the next chapter.

THE PROBLEM-SOLVING TOOL KIT

The problem-solving tool kit[2] presents a one-page description of various continuous improvement tools and techniques. A graphic illustration of each tool is provided along with a brief description of what the tool is, why the tool is useful, and how the tool is used.

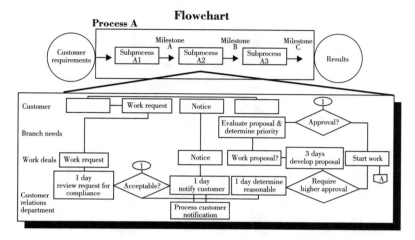

What
A visual representation of how work gets done.

Why
To answer analytical questions about the efficiency and effectiveness of a work process in order to improve the process.

How
1. Identify key processes based on importance to the business, products, or customers.
2. Establish the scope of the process to be analyzed.
3. Establish the teams and document the process.
4. Identify any problem areas.
5. Gather data required to determine the root cause of the problem.
6. Select the appropriate improvement to the process that eliminates the problem.
7. Implement the improvement and compare to expected results.
8. Institutionalize the continuous improvement process.

Figure 9.5 Process analysis and documenting.

What
A free-form method of generating ideas/solutions used to equalize involvement and generation of original thoughts.

Why
Brainstorming produces many ideas/solutions in a short time.

How
1. Review the topic and "why, how, or what" question.
2. Give everyone a minute or two of silence to think about the question.
3. Invite everyone to call out their ideas. (Important: There should be no discussion of ideas until session is complete.)
4. Write down every idea.
5. Consolidate like ideas and discuss the complete list.

Figure 9.6 Brainstorming.

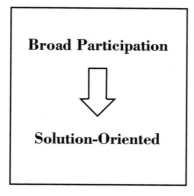

What

A technique similar to brainstorming. A structured approach to generate ideas and survey the opinions of a small (10 to 15 people) group.

Why

NGT produces many ideas/solutions in a short time. Structured to focus on problems, not people; to open lines of communication; to ensure participation; and to tolerate conflicting ideas. Builds consensus and commitment to the final result.

How

1. Present issues, instructions.
2. Generate ideas during 5 to 10 minutes of quiet time, no discussion.
3. Gather ideas round-robin style, one idea at a time, written on a flip chart and posted.
4. Process/clarify ideas—duplicates are eliminated, like ideas are combined. Limit discussion to brief explanations of logic or analysis of an item and brief agreement statements. Focus on clarifying meaning, not arguing points.

Figure 9.7 Nominal group technique (NGT).

Problem	Month			
	1	2	3	Total
A	||	||	|	5
B	|	|	|	3
C	ЖЖ	||	ЖЖ	12
Total	8	5	7	20

What
Simple, easy-to-understand form used to answer the question, How often are certain events happening? It starts the process of translating opinions into facts.

Why
When you need to gather data based on sample observations to begin to detect patterns.

How
1. Agree to exactly what is to be observed. Everyone has to be looking for the same thing.
2. Determine the time period during which the data will be collected.
3. Design the form so that it is easy to use and so that everyone has the same interpretation of each data item.
4. Collect data.
5. Analyze and evaluate the data.

Figure 9.8 Check sheet.

```
┌─────────────────────────────────┐
│                                 │
│   Name _____          │
│   Address _____        │
│                                 │
│                                 │
│   1. _____     │
│   2. _____     │
│   3. _____     │
│                                 │
│                                 │
└─────────────────────────────────┘
```

What
Questionnaire designed to gather information on customer/supplier/process worker needs, expectations, and opinions.

Why
To provide information that can help guide the formulation of solutions to problems with products, services, and work processes.

How
1. Use existing data to determine where holes in the data might exist that can be filled through feedback.
2. Design questionnaire to gather information that will fill in holes in the existing data.
3. Solicit questionnaire responses through mass distribution or personal contact.
4. Collect responses and analyze for useful feedback.

Figure 9.9 Survey/interview.

Administrative Processes

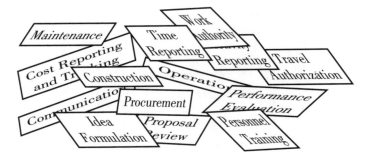

Administrative Processes Groupings

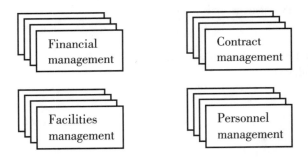

What
A tool to sell ideas generated through brainstorming or NGT.

Why
To group ideas into logical sets.

How
1. Use an idea-generation technique to address a problem.
2. Place each generated idea on a card or self-adhesive note and spread the cards on a table or pin them up on the wall.
3. Allow group participants to move the cards around into groups until there is consensus on the groupings.
4. Generate a title card for each group of ideas.
5. Use grouped ideas to address large parts of the problem.

Figure 9.10 Affinity diagram.

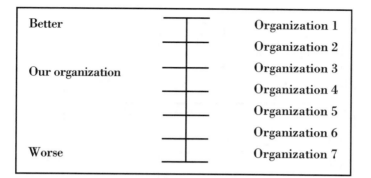

What

Method of measuring your processes against those of recognized leaders. It helps you to establish priorities and targets, leading to improved quality.

Why

When you know where you stand with respect to your competitors, you can target various processes for improvement.

How

1. Identify items to benchmark and their key characteristics.
2. Determine whom to benchmark—companies, organizations, or groups.
3. Determine benchmarks by collecting and analyzing data from direct contact, surveys, interviews, and technical journals.
4. From each benchmark item identified, determine the best-in-class target.
5. Evaluate your process in terms of the benchmarks and set improvement goals.

Figure 9.11   Benchmarking.

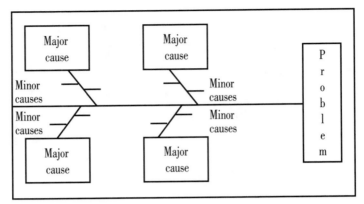

What
Represents the relationship between an effect (problem) and its potential causes.

Why
The diagram is drawn to sort and relate the interactions among the factors affecting a process. Assist in determining root causes.

How
1. Name the problem.
2. Decide the major categories for causes. Major causes may include data and information systems, dollars, environment, hardware, materials, measurements, methods, people, and training.
3. Brainstorm for more detailed causes.
4. Eliminate causes that do not apply.
5. Discuss the remaining causes and decide which are most important.
6. Work on most important causes (for example, use of design experiments).
7. Desensitize, eliminate, or control causes.

Figure 9.12 Cause-and-effect diagram (fishbone).

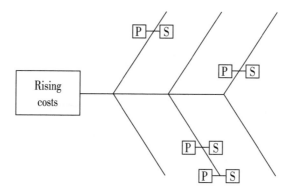

What
CEDAC is a large cause-and-effect diagram with problem and solution cards placed next to each other along the cause lines.

Why
To identify problems and integrate solutions that all contribute to some undesirable effect.

How
1. Determine the major problem (effect).
2. Prepare a large cause-and-effect diagram for wall hanging or flip chart.
3. Use idea-generating techniques to identify causes and potential solutions to each cause.
4. Group causes and potential solutions along the cause lines in logical groupings.
5. Rank potential solutions using multivoting or other decision tools.
6. Selectively implement top-ranked solutions.
7. Maintain cards for historical purposes.
8. Evaluate solution effectiveness after some period of time.

Figure 9.13 Cause-and-effect diagram (fishbone) with addition of cards (CEDAC)

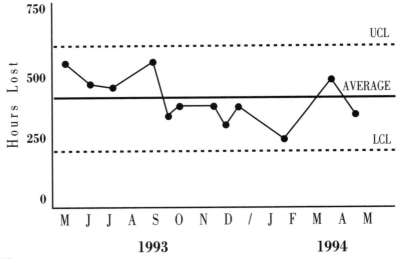

What

A line chart in which the data points represent some measurement and the average, upper control limit (UCL), and lower control limit (LCL) are depicted. It indicates the range of variation built into the system (an output of SPC).

Why

To distinguish between variation inherent in a process from a common cause and the variation arising from sources that come and go unpredictably—special causes.

How

1. Determine the measurement indicating a problem.
2. Gather the trend data over time and plot on the chart.
3. Compute the average and the UCL and LCL using statistical formulas, and plot on the chart.
4. Determine if there are any common causes and continue to investigate the root problem using other tools and techniques.
5. Identify special causes of variation. It should be relatively easy to track down these sources and prevent their reoccurrence.

Figure 9.14   Control chart.

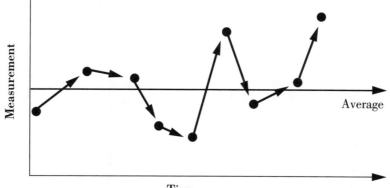

Measurement

Average

Time or sequence

What
A visual monitoring of a process to see whether or not the long-range average is changing (an output of an SPC).

Why
When you need to do the simplest possible display of trends within observation points over a specified period of time.

How
1. Agree on what is to be measured.
2. Determine time frequency of measurement.
3. Gather and plot data.
4. Analyze and evaluate data.

Figure 9.15   Run chart.

Activity	Expected Time	Shortest Time	Longest Time	Preceding Activities
A	2	1	3	
B	4	2	6	A
C	3	2	5	A
D	4	2	5	B
E	4	1	6	C, D
F	2	1	3	E
G	5	3	6	F
H	7	3	9	G
I	2	1	3	H
J	6	5	7	F
K	4	3	5	I, J

What

The critical path is the longest set of contiguous tasks within a work process.

Why

The critical path determines the cycle time for the process. Hence, if the tasks comprising the critical path can be shortened, then the entire process time can be reduced.

How

1. Identify and list all of the tasks involved in a work process and assign an identifier to each task (for example, A, B, C, and so on).
2. Create a table that identifies
    - Each task
    - Expected completion time for each task
    - Shortest completion time for each task
    - Longest completion time for each task
    - Preceding tasks
3. Determine the critical path. This usually can be done by inspection. However, computer programs are available for large complex processes.
4. Draw a critical path diagram if necessary

Figure 9.16 Critical path.

Improving Process Quality

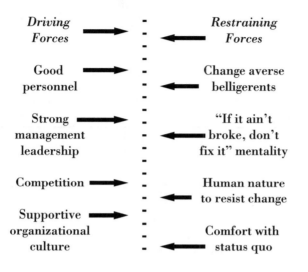

What
A tool to assist in examining the driving and restraining forces of change.

Why
1. To force creative thinking focused on the issues of change.
2. To build organizational consensus concerning the fuel for and the barriers to change.
3. To provide an entry point into process improvement initiatives.

How
Simply list all of the driving forces and all of the restraining forces to change. Brainstorming and/or NGT can be used to assist in list development.

Figure 9.17   Force-field analysis.

Number of Changes per Document	Frequency	Relative Frequency
0–10	12	12/136 = 0.088
11–20	21	21/136 = 0.154
21–30	27	27/136 = 0.199
31–40	38	38/136 = 0.279
41–50	23	23/136 = 0.169
51–60	10	10/136 = 0.074
61–70	5	5/136 = 0.037
Total	**136**	**1.0**

What
To organize data before placing on a histogram or to illustrate other useful data such as relative frequency.

Why
To assist in turning gathered data into useful information.

How
1. Arrange the discrete or range of values to be analyzed in ascending or descending order along the left side of the table.
2. Indicate the frequency for each value in the table and look for frequency concentrations or patterns.
3. Option: Compute relative frequency for each value by dividing each value's frequency by the total number of data points.

Figure 9.18   Frequency table.

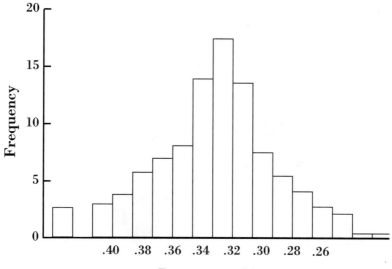

What

A diagram used to visually represent how the products of a process meet the goals or specifications.

Why

To analyze and evaluate the quality of the process and the products.

How

1. Determine goal or specification to be measured.
2. Measure product in terms of the goal or the specification.
3. Plot data and goal on the chart.
4. Analyze and evaluate how well actual products meet goals or specification.
5. When necessary, determine reasons for nonconformance using other tools.

Figure 9.19   Histogram.

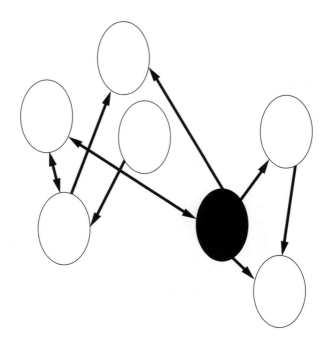

What
Planning tool to organize related ideas.

Why
To illustrate dependencies between ideas to pinpoint areas where improvements can make the greatest impact.

How
1. Draw circles on page and enter one idea gathered earlier in each circle.
2. Discuss relationships between ideas and draw lines to indicate dependencies.
3. Focus discussion on the idea with the largest number of interdependencies.

Figure 9.20   Interrelationship graph.

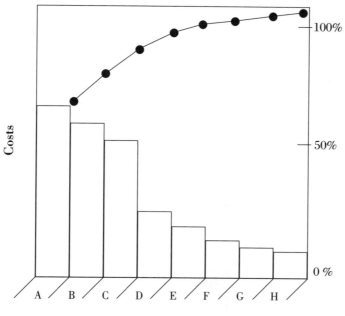

Problems

What

A bar chart in which the bars are arranged in descending order, with the largest to the left. Each bar represents a problem (cause). The chart displays the relative contribution of each cause to the total problem.

Why

The Pareto chart makes clear which vital few problems (causes) should be addressed first. This technique is based on the Pareto principle, which states that a few of the causes often account for most of the effect.

How

1. Measure the elements of interest.
2. Measure the elements, using the same unit of measurement for each element.
3. Order the elements according to their measure, not their classification.
4. Create a cumulative distribution for the number of items and elements measured and make a bar and line graph.
5. Work on the most important elements first.

Figure 9.21 Pareto diagram.

Process capability   = C_p
Upper specification limit   =   USL
Lower specification limit   =   LSL
Process standard deviation   = σ

$$C_p = \frac{USL - LSL}{6\sigma}$$

σ can be determined from
control charts

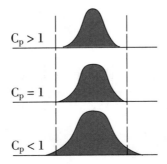

What
To determine whether a process is capable of meeting customer requirements.

Why
Good processes are not good enough if they cannot meet customer requirements.

How
Take samples of process output and determine if the sample, and therefore the process, is within specification limits. Statistical methods are applied to sample data.

Figure 9.22   Process capability analysis.

			Operating System	Languages	Diagnostics	Microcode	Cooling Tower
Total Cost of Ownership	Price Facility	Price of product	○	○			△
		Warranty					△
		Cheap repairs	◎		◎		◎
		Weight					◎
		Footprint					◎
		Cooling					◎
		Power consumption					◎
	People	Operations staff	◎				◎
		Programming staff	◎	◎			
		Training costs	◎	◎			

Key: ◎ = strong relationship   △ = possible relationship
      ○ = moderate relationship   = no relationship

What
Use of the familiar device of a matrix to map ideas in one dimension against ideas of another dimension.

Why
To provide a structure for systematically evaluating the relationship between ideas in the two dimensions.

How
1. List one set of ideas along the vertical axis and one set of ideas along the horizontal axis.
2. Ask the question at each row and column intersection, What is the relationship between these two ideas (that is, strong, moderate, possible, or no relationship)?
3. Document the answers using some type of key notation.
4. Review and evaluate those areas where the two different older sets have significant relationships.

Figure 9.23 Relational matrix diagram.

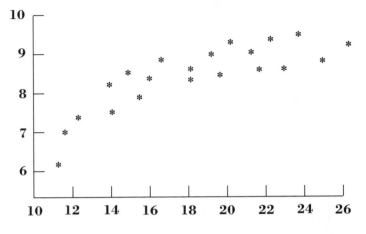

What
A plotting technique that lets you look at the relationship between two process characteristics. Can support cause-and-effect diagramming.

Why
To determine if two characteristics are related or unrelated. Used to test for possible cause-and-effect relationships.

How
1. Determine the two characteristics to be related.
2. Gather data.
3. Plot the data on the *X* and *Y* axes.
4. If unrelated, the points will be randomly scattered around the graph. If related, the points will form a band or line running either upper left to bottom right or bottom left to upper right. In this case, the characteristics are related.

Figure 9.24 Scatter diagram.

Process Time Line

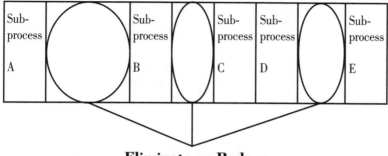

Eliminate or Reduce

What
A systematic method for reducing process cycle time.

Why
Time line analysis focuses on eliminating the "dead" time between subprocesses thereby reducing cycle time.

How
1. Identify all subprocesses.
2. Assign approximate completion time for each subprocess.
3. Determine approximate total time process.
4. Place subprocesses on a process time line.
5. Identify dead time and reasons for dead time.
6. Identify methods for dead time elimination or reduction.

Figure 9.25   Time line analysis.

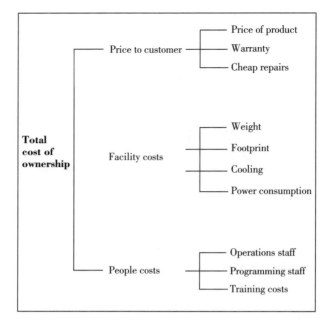

What
Hierarchical method of structuring ideas.

Why
Visually represent thoughts and ideas and their relationships to look for gaps and omissions at every level of the hierarchy used to help structure ideas and map their relationships.

How
1. Generate thoughts and ideas utilizing brainstorming or the NGT.
2. Organize the data in a hierarchical structure by categorizing and grouping like things.
3. Draw the hierarchical structure.
4. Scan and review for gaps and omissions.
5. Fill in gaps and omissions.

Figure 9.26 Tree diagram.

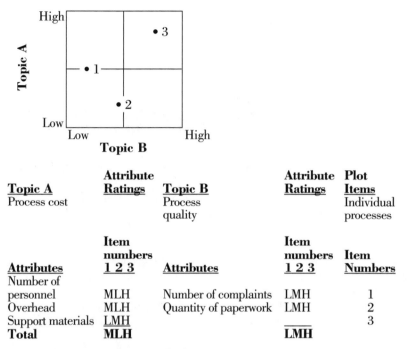

Topic A	Attribute Ratings	Topic B	Attribute Ratings	Plot Items
Process cost		Process quality		Individual processes

	Item numbers		Item numbers	
Attributes	**1 2 3**	**Attributes**	**1 2 3**	**Item Numbers**
Number of personnel	MLH	Number of complaints	LMH	1
Overhead	MLH	Quantity of paperwork	LMH	2
Support materials	LMH			3
Total	**MLH**		**LMH**	

Key: L = low, M = medium, H = high

What
The attribute grid is used to graphically analyze the relationships between different topics of interest.

Why
The attribute grid provides a means to synthesize many attributes and their complex relationships in a manner that facilitates decision making.

How
1. Determine the topics of interest for a given set of items.
2. Determine the attributes of topics that will provide differentiation among the items to be plotted.
3. Develop a rating system for each attribute that will provide differentiation among the items to be plotted.
4. Rate attributes, calculate item totals, and plot grid.
5. Use information contained in grid to make decisions.

Figure 9.27   Attribute grid.

Alternative A	ͰͰͰ
Alternative B	III
Alternative C	IIII
Alternative D	II

What

A method for selecting or narrowing a set of alternatives. Can be used to prioritize a list.

Why

Improve the team's ability to reach consensus. Allow each team member to express strength of opinion through voting

How

1. List all alternatives and count them, that is, N number of alternatives.
2. Give each number $N/3$ votes (or whatever number seems reasonable given the number of alternatives).
3. Have each member cast a vote given the following guidelines.
   - The member can cast all, some, or none of his or her votes for any alternative.
   - When all votes (the sum) are cast, the member is done.
4. Rank order the alternatives based on the number of votes received.
5. Repeat the process until the desired result is accomplished.

Figure 9.28   Multivoting.

Robust design techniques to
minimize production and
operational variability

What

A body of knowledge used to improve the process of learning from experimentation. This learning enables improved process design.

Why

Improve design-to-production transition. Quickly optimizes product designs (robust design) and production processes. Reduces costs, stabilizes production processes, and desensitizes production variables.

How

1. Identify controllable and uncontrollable noise factors that influence the product's functional characteristics.
2. Set up an experiment to discover interactions and effects between controllable and uncontrollable factors.
3. Study the factor variation in step 2 and determine the factor levels that optimize the product's financial characteristics, while minimizing the influence of uncontrollable factors.

Figure 9.29   Taguchi methods.

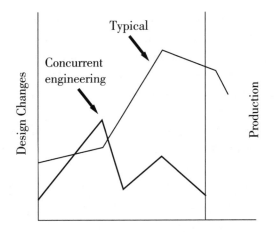

What
A method for integrating functional disciplines such as manufacturing and design. It is a systematic approach to product design that considers all elements of the product life cycle. Concurrent engineering defines the product, its manufacturing process, and other required life-cycle processes such as maintenance.

Why
This approach can be used to shorten the design-to-development life cycle and reduce costs by examining the interaction of functional disciplines from the perspective of a cross-functional process.

How
1. Use cross-functional teams.
2. Identify and reduce variation in production and use through adroit selection of design parameters.
3. See also tools, design of experiments, and transition from development to production templates.
4. Team building.

Figure 9.30 Concurrent engineering.

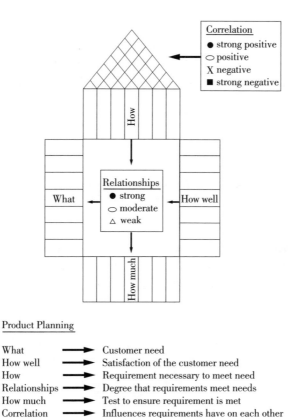

Product Planning

What	→	Customer need
How well	→	Satisfaction of the customer need
How	→	Requirement necessary to meet need
Relationships	→	Degree that requirements meet needs
How much	→	Test to ensure requirement is met
Correlation	→	Influences requirements have on each other

What
A conceptual map that provides the means for cross-functional planning and communications. A method for transforming customer wants and needs into quantitative, engineering terms.

Why
Products should be designed to meet customer wants and needs so that customers will buy products and services and continue to buy them. Marketing people, design engineers, manufacturing engineers, and procurement specialists work closely together from the time a product/service is first conceived to be able to meet customer requirements. QFD provides the framework for the cross-functional teams to work.

How
QFD is a rigorous process and beyond the scope of this text. Training for QFD is available and should be obtained prior to implementation.

Figure 9.31   Quality function deployment.

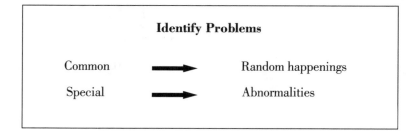

What
Method for determing the cause of variation based on a statistical analysis of the
problem. SPC uses probability theory to control and improve processes.

Why
SPC is an effective tool for improving performance of any process. It helps identify
problems quickly and accurately. It also provides quantifiable data for analysis,
provides a reference baseline, and promotes participation and decision making by
people doing the job.

How
1. Identify problems or performance improvement areas. Identify common and
   special causes. Common causes are random in nature, often minor. Special
   causes result from an abnormality in the system that prevents the process from
   becoming stable.
2. Diagram the process.
3. Collect data.
4. Apply statistical techniques (may need a statistical specialist).
5. Analyze variations.
6. Take corrective action. Fix special causes.

Figure 9.32   Statistical process control (SPC).

Notes

1. KPMG Peat Marwick, Federal Services Group, *Work Process Improvement Reference Guide* (Houston Tex.: KMPG Peat Marwick, 1991.) Portions of the reference guide and the process reengineering methodology were developed with the assistance of the Management Assistance Office of the NASA Johnson Space Center under contract NAS9-18239.

2. The following sources are included for additional information on the tools described in the chapter 9 problem-solving tool kit.

   Blackburn, Joseph. "The Time Factor." *National Productivity Review* (Autumn 1990).

   Brassard, Michael, ed. *The Memory Jogger.* Methuen, Mass.: Goal/QPC, 1988.

   Burr, John T. "The Tools Of Quality—Part I: Going with the Flow (chart)." Quality Progress (June 1990).

   Conti, Tito. "Process Management and Quality Function Deployment." *Quality Progress* (December 1989).

   Department of Defense. *Total Quality Management—A Guide for Implementation.* Covina, Calif.: Procurement Associates, 1989.

   Hauser, John R. and Don Clausing. "The House of Quality." *Harvard Business Review* (May–June 1988).

   Johnson Space Center Team Excellence Action Process—Six-Step Continuous Quality Improvement Strategy. Houston, Tex.: NASA–Lyndon B. Johnson Space Center, September 1989.

   Moen, Ronald D. and Thomas W. Nolan. "Process Improvement—A Step-by-Step Approach to Analyzing and Improving a Process." *Quality Progress* (September 1987).

   Scholtes, Peter and Heero Hacquebord. *A Practical Approach to Quality.* Madison, Wis.: Joiner Associates, Inc., 1987.

   Scholtes, Peter. *The Team Handbook.* Madison, Wis.: Joiner Associates, Inc., 1988.

Strickland, Jack C. "Total Quality Management—Linking Together People and Processes for Mission Excellence." *Army Research, Development & Acquisition Bulletin* (May–June 1989).

Thor, Carl G. *Using Nominal Group Technique to Establish a White-Collar Productivity Measurement System.* Houston, Tex.: American Productivity Center, 1987.

10 Project Selection, Measurement, and Reporting _____

Executive Summary

This chapter completes the description of quality-based cost management by presenting an approach for selecting improvement projects that offer the greatest contribution to improved profitability and competitiveness. We first review the elements of an effective project plan that describes how, when, and why a particular improvement contributes to the achievement of quality and business goals. A process is then described for monitoring and measuring the progress of the improvement teams to facilitate the improvement process and ensure greater success. The final element is reporting to top management on the overall effectiveness of the quality improvement effort and its contribution to the achievement of overall business goals, which concludes our description of the principles of quality-based cost management.

PROJECT SELECTION, MEASUREMENT, AND REPORTING

The cost-of-poor-quality assessment and cost-driver analysis teams begin the quality-based cost management process by quantifying the financial impact and root causes of poor quality. This information serves as the basis for selecting improvement projects to improve financial performance. After management has ranked projects according to their relative financial and competitive importance, the remaining task is evaluating the capability of the organization to successfully implement the potential projects. Management's final choice of projects must balance the competitive importance of the project with the organization's implementation capabilities.

Determining the Competitive Impact of Potential Projects. The most important factors in the selection of improvement projects are the strategic requirements of the business. In order to align business and quality priorities, management must consider the financial and nonfinancial goals in the strategic plan when choosing improvement priorities. In determining the competitive impact of potential projects, two lessons were learned by the case study companies: (1) to achieve competitive success, the selection of significant projects is much more important than the total number of projects selected, and (2) it is essential that everyone involved in the selection process understand the achievement of specific strategic and financial results will only occur if the project selection is based on logical cause-and-effect relationships.

The strategic requirements of the business determine whether a project is important or not. If, for example, the strategic and financial imperatives of a business call for increased cash flow, then projects that provide cash flow are more important and should be given a higher priority. The purpose of strategic quality planning is to clearly focus the quality process on the strategic and financial imperatives of the business and address these imperatives through the project selection process. To do so, the relationships that link strategy, productivity, profitability, and competitiveness must be clearly understood if the strategic or financial imperatives and the quality process are to be linked through project selection.

The market and industry leaders participating in the study all recognize that the critical success factors for their particular businesses are the key to effective project selection. Westinghouse captures this concept in its formal definition of total quality: "Total

quality is performance leadership in meeting customer requirements by doing the right things right the first time."

Doing the right things means setting proper performance
requirements for the total quality process. The performance
requirements must embrace every aspect of the organization,
including internal and external customer satisfaction, profitability,
employee relations, image, community relations, and government
affairs.[1]

As discussed in chapter 6, the PGBU of Westinghouse has
identified three strategies to accomplish its corporate goal of
becoming the supplier of preference through total quality. Doing the
right things at PGBU means initiating and implementing quality
improvements to ensure that the unit achieves its goal of becoming
the supplier of preference. As a part of its total quality process, the
unit's top management challenged each of the functional organizations to develop quality plans and select quality initiatives that
focused on PGBU's key objectives. These include

- Cycle time and cost reductions
- PGBU strategic plan support
- Improving customer satisfaction

The quality initiatives selected by each functional organization
focus on areas that are specifically designed to be linked to the key
improvement initiatives. Each quality initiative is supported by an
improvement strategy and a measurable goal that allow the success
of the quality initiative to be visible to everyone in the organization. PGBU's Winston-Salem plant, for example, developed the key
quality initiatives, strategies, measures, and goals illustrated in
Figures 10.1 to 10.4 to meet the unit's key quality objectives.

As companies gain experience using the quality-based cost
management, project selection can be used to accomplish more
sophisticated financial strategies. Among these strategies is using
the cash flow generated by shorter-term improvement projects to
fund longer-term, more capital-intensive projects. The timing of
project implementation is determined by its cash flow characteris-

Strategy: Complete the integration of all small tuned parts into the computer integrated manufacturing (CIM) cell; optimize facilities layout and utilization to support the strategic objectives of cost and lead time reductions in response to customer requirements and market demands.

Measures: For all parts "loaded" on the CIM cell, compare CIM versus standard.

Goals: (1) Achieve cost reduction of 30% and (2) achieve lead time reduction of 70%.

Figure 10.1   Key quality initiative at Winston-Salem: improving customer satisfaction.

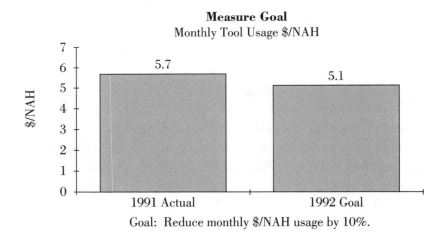

Measure Goal
Monthly Tool Usage $/NAH

Goal: Reduce monthly $/NAH usage by 10%.

Strategy: Involve the entire plant community in reducing the cost and usage of tooling.

Measures and goals: Measure the $/net allowable hours (NAH) with a goal of achieving a 10% reduction compared to 1991.

Figure 10.2   Key quality initiative at Winston-Salem: human resource excellence.

Measure Goal

Minutes of Hand Grinding Reduced

Goal: Reduce 1.0M minutes of hand grinding.

Strategy: Reduce the amount of hand grinding required by improving machining processes to more closely produce a net shape product.

Measures and goals: Measure the minutes of hand grinding with a goal of reducing hand grinding by 1 million minutes in 1992.

Figure 10.3   Key quality initiative at Winston-Salem: product and process leadership.

tics and its relationship to other projects. For example, Boeing Canada de Havilland Division (de Havilland), a manufacturer of aircraft for the regional market, began a massive turnaround improvement effort to reduce manufacturing costs, improve cycle time, and increase throughput. The turnaround plan prioritized the operations improvement projects using the following criteria: (1) time required for completion, (2) investment required, and (3) financial payback measured in terms of increased cash flow and profits.

The initial priority was immediate operations improvement projects that required little or no capital investment but were capable of reducing costs and improving production flows. Particular emphasis was placed on implementing planning, scheduling, and production improvements that provided quick payback. As the first

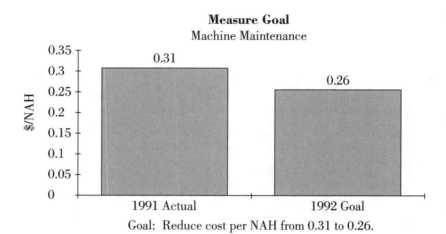

Goal: Reduce cost per NAH from 0.31 to 0.26.

Strategy: Control the total spending for maintenance accounts 587 and 593 on a monthly basis during 1992 by employing preventive maintenance techniques to reduce unplanned downtime.

Measures and goals: Measure the $/NAH with a goal of reducing the $/NAH by 15% in 1992.

Figure 10.4 Key quality initiative at Winston-Salem: management leadership.

phase of the turnaround, the immediate operations improvement projects provided a short-term, cost-effective fix that generated the cash flow required to fund longer-term projects, such as those in materials management.

Important changes were made in a variety of areas based on the required investment and payback profile of a project. Long-term improvement projects related to effectivity and configuration management were implemented based on short-term financial impact. For example, the project team revised the process for releasing engineering change orders (ECOs) to the shop floor. By limiting the release of engineering change orders to those that were either federally mandated, safety related, or customer requested, de Havilland was able to reduce the number of ECOs by 85 percent. As a result of the significant decrease in the flow of engineering change orders to the shop floor, de Havilland experienced a significant drop in final assembly rework and overtime. The net result was improved throughput, substantially lower labor costs, and higher material utilization.

Quick payback projects, such as immediate operations improvements and the revisions to the ECO process, were implemented with the realization that longer-term improvement might alter the short-term fixes. While a sophisticated manufacturing planning, scheduling, and control system were the solution to many of the operations problems, it was unrealistic to begin the implementation of this system any earlier than the second year of the turnaround. The short-term fixes were used to create the cash flow necessary to finance longer-term solutions such as the manufacturing systems implementation.

The project sequencing reflected the overall financial strategy and allowed de Havilland top management to balance a series of complex challenges, ranging from managing organizational change and upgrading computer systems to hiring the necessary expertise and maintaining the production flow. The financial payback from lower manufacturing costs, reduced inventory, and faster cycle time generated a payback of more than \$10 for each dollar de Havilland invested in the turnaround improvement projects.

Improvement projects must be ranked not only on their capability to contribute to improving financial performance, but also on their ability to satisfy the strategic and nonfinancial requirements of the business. How important is the project to internal or external customers? The financial impact of failing to meet the requirements of the customer is partially measured using the cost of poor quality, but a company may also want to consider other criteria as well. The more important a product or service is to a customer's success, the greater the financial impact of failing to meet the customer's requirements. Frequency of use is also a consideration, particularly where repeat business is important. Determining the impact and importance of specific failures to meet customer demands allows a company to prioritize problem-solving efforts by first eliminating failures that matter the most to customers.

For example, the most important quality improvements at Star-Kist and Heinz Pet Products are those projects that focus on employee safety. A safety-related improvement project is the only type of project that can be approved without financial justification. Dick Wamhoff, then the executive vice president of Heinz Pet Products as well as president and chief operating officer at Star-Kist, emphasizes that safety improvements are the company's most important projects because a safe environment is the first prerequisite for any productive and profitable operation. Employees can concentrate on the tasks at hand, be imaginative, and find new ways to do jobs better in a safe environment. Getting hurt on the job is unacceptable, and management treats an injury even more seriously than a production stoppage or the use of the wrong ingredients.

Heinz Pet Products stresses a preventative approach to safety and conducts monthly safety training. Job descriptions have been modified to make safety a responsibility of each person in the plant. The emphasis on safety as an integral part of the quality process produced a 63-percent reduction in Occupational Safety and Health Administration (OSHA) recordable accidents from 1989 to 1991. A by-product of the safety emphasis has been a 72-percent reduction in workers' compensation claims and the related costs of medical expenses, lost wages, rehabilitation, and other incurred costs. Figure 10.5 shows total workers' compensation reductions between 1989 and 1992, with 1993 workers' compensation costs projected to be 50 percent lower than those in 1992.[2]

In summary, an understanding of the broader business goals must be reflected through the quality planning process. Establishing a logical cause-and-effect framework between broader business objectives and project selection ensures that projects are related to the overall goals that the organization wants to achieve. Linking business goals to project selection ensures that the projects selected for implementation can make a genuine competitive impact.

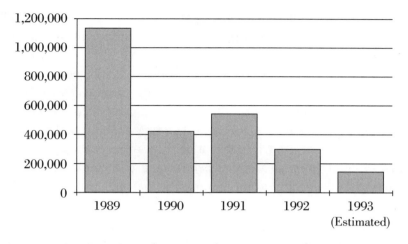

Figure 10.5 A 72-percent reduction in workers compensation from 1989 to 1992 is achieved through improved safety.

Determining the Chances of a Successful Implementation. The second major facet of project selection is determining the likelihood that the organization can successfully implement the high-impact, vital projects identified by management. Management needs to carefully consider a variety of factors in making its final choices, including organizational readiness, time requirements, resource availability, track record, degree of difficulty, and size of the project.

• Organizational readiness. How prepared is the organization to change? Is top management prepared to support the organizational alterations required to eliminate the root causes of poor quality? In the initial stages of the quality-based cost management process, the trend in the research sites was to select pilot projects with a high probability of success. This provides a positive learning experience for the team members and establishes a positive track record for quality-based cost management. A series of pilot proj-ects was also frequently used to refine processes and procedures and train additional personnel. Once the pilot projects were complete, the trained personnel applied the proven processes and procedures to roll out quality-based cost management throughout the organization.

Training is typically conducted just before team members need the knowledge, rather than mass training programs with little immediate application after the training is completed. Several of the research sites refer to this as just-in-time training, where training is given just prior to application. The primary difficulty with mass training programs is that people tend to forget material that isn't applied, leading to the impression that quality training programs are neither cost-effective nor useful.

The phased quality-based cost management implementation coincides with the growth in organizational readiness. This, in turn, produces a higher success rate for the projects. As skills and experiences are gained, the projects can become increasingly complex while retaining a high probability of success.

•   Time requirements. One of the major sources of failure identified in studies of quality processes is the frustration associated with projects that have time horizons stretching into years. Many companies have found that in the initial stages of a quality process, it is better to select projects that have a shorter time line and thus a quicker payback. A series of shorter-term projects creates a track record of success that reinforces the value of quality as a competitive tool. The risks associated with longer-term projects, such as technological changes or shifts in competitive strategies, are minimized by selecting projects that require less time to implement. Projects with shorter time requirements also allow companies to rotate more people through the quality process and build a base of trained and experienced personnel.

•   Resource availability. An organization may not currently have the personnel, financial resources, or facilities to implement a desired project. Projects that require resources beyond the capability of an organization can be postponed until the resources are available. A strategy observed at several research sites is the allocation of a portion of financial gains toward either longer-term projects or capital-intensive projects. In this way, shorter-term projects provide a funding mechanism to pay for projects that are only feasible in the longer run.

- Track record. If the track record of a company's quality process is littered with failures and ineffective implementations, then the sources of failure need to be determined. Whatever the reason— overenthusiastic management, unrealistic expectations, shortage of resources, lack of organizational readiness, unmanageable project difficulty, overly long project horizons, lack of strategic importance, or other reasons—it makes sense to address the sources of failure to ensure that the barriers to success are eliminated. After the barriers have been addressed, the likelihood of project success increases dramatically.

- Degree of difficulty. Is the project within the skills and experience available to the company, or does it require a technological breakthrough? While breakthrough projects may offer a significant payback, the probability of success may be so low that the project should be rejected in favor of projects with a higher probability of success. In addition to technical or operational difficulties, the degree of organizational adaptability should also be considered. If an organization is not ready to change, then projects requiring a high degree of organizational adaptability should be postponed to a later time when the organization may be more capable of making the necessary changes.

- Size of the project. Larger projects require more sophisticated project management and coordination than smaller projects. Adding in one more level of complexity to an improvement project that already requires new skills, attitudes, and organizational changes increases the risk of failure. It is better to postpone large, complex projects until the organization has proven skills and capabilities, demonstrated through successes with smaller projects. An alternative is to break a large project down into a series of smaller, more manageable proj-ects. Doing so increases the likelihood of success as it lessens the reliance on sophisticated project management skills and expertise the organization may not yet have acquired.

An alternative for a project that cannot be broken down into smaller components is a series of transition projects, the sum of which is a breakthrough for the organization. A project plan can be developed to address the phases that the project must go through to accomplish a final result. Transition projects should be structured so that completion of each transition phase represents a genuine contribution to the organization, but kept at a manageable level to ensure success. Improvements to computer systems and major capital expenditures are examples of improvement projects that can be phased to make both the required investment and the subsequent learning curves manageable for the organization, while still making value-added contributions to improved competitiveness.

Harvesting the Low-Hanging Fruit

A misconception that has hampered quality processes is the idea that an organization can't expect to see results for a long period of time, often years. Part of the explanation for the failure of 70 percent of quality processes to produce meaningful results is the level of expectations many companies have set for the quality process. The companies participating in the best practices study all agree that quality is a long-term journey—a process of continuous improvement that never ends. However, the actions and attitudes of the participating companies directly contradict the notion that "results take a while, sometimes as long as two to five years." On average, the research sites reduced total reported poor-quality costs by 11 percent in the first year of quality-based cost management.[3] One of the important lessons learned by these companies is that the quality process, like any other process, has to be actively managed and updated to continuously deliver meaningful results.

In the early stages of the quality process, many significant quality problems are relatively easy to solve. In subsequent years, however, there are fewer and fewer low-hanging fruit to harvest. As the case study companies moved into the "higher branches of the tree," the cost-of-poor-quality assessments were refined to identify opportunities in the higher branches. These refinements typically took one of two forms.

First, many companies gradually added new elements to the assessment as experience in problem identification and data gathering was gained. This often entailed adding appraisal elements to the existing assessment of failure cost categories, allowing the teams to identify opportunities to eliminate inspection activities that were carried out to compensate for quality shortcomings. Second, as the companies' quality initiatives have matured, more and more companies are expanding the assessments even further by broadening the definition of poor quality to encompass *any* activity that does not add value to the customer. For example, the Industrial Systems Division of Texas Instruments (now a part of Siemens) revised its definition of poor quality to include the costs of product development overruns, a significant improvement opportunity that reflected the division's inability to do it right the first time.[4] Once the magnitude of this problem was highlighted, an improvement team was established to attack the root causes, with stunning results. The project management system that was developed as part of the solution proved to be so successful that it was adopted by a number of other Texas Instruments divisions. By updating cost-of-poor-quality elements in this way, companies can continue identifying and quantifying new layers of improvement opportunities, fostering a climate of continuous improvement.

Preparing the Project Plan—Building a Mechanism to Tackle Vital, Cross-Functional Problems

Combining the elements of strategic importance, financial payback, and organizational readiness provides the basis for selecting projects that have a high likelihood of increasing the competitiveness of the business. Management needs to concentrate on selecting projects that address and resolve problems that are vital to the organization rather than diffusing the organization's resources with projects that are useful but not vital to the organization's success.

The next step is preparing a project plan for each of the projects selected for implementation. If a project is important enough to merit the commitment of scarce resources, then it is surely important enough to merit a thorough project plan that increases the likelihood of success. The trend toward fewer, more crucial projects places a greater priority on project planning as a means to improve the success ratio of the vital few improvement projects.

As discussed in chapter 4, the project plan establishes the game plan for improvement project implementation, setting realistic expectations, time frames, and responsibilities for the improvement team. The project plan also provides an explanation of the importance of the project to everyone involved, and serves as the organizational mechanism that establishes the merit of the improvement project, identifies the departmental participants, and specifies resource requirements. Moreover, issues that have historically stalled the resolution of vital, cross-functional problems are addressed in the project planning process by placing these issues on an authoritative agenda for resolution.

At the research sites, it is common for the final selection of the improvement projects to be the responsibility of senior management due to the strategic importance of the projects. Improvement projects approved or sponsored by senior managers are elevated to a level where the authority exists to cross functional boundaries and gain cooperation.

The quality improvement project plan outline shown in Table 10.1 incorporates ideas from several of the research sites. The

Table 10.1 Quality improvement project plan outline.

Project title _____
Sponsor _____
Team leader _____
Team members _____
Summary of project scope _____
Expectations—financial _____
Expectations—nonfinancial _____
Resource requirements _____
Date initiated _____   Forecasted closure date _____
                                  or
                                  Standing team _____

project plan summarizes much of the information developed during the cost-of-poor-quality assessment and cost-driver analysis, and identifies potential barriers, issues, and considerations directly affecting the success of the project. Considerations in preparing a project plan are listed in the following paragraphs.

Project title. What the team is going to do and why. The Evansville Division of Whirlpool shows how project titles can convey a clear message of the project's activities and purpose.

- Improve resistance of door gasket for rolling.
- Define the proper heat/process to eliminate stile/mullion sweating.

Sponsor. The sponsor of a project is a senior manager who can provide both personal and organizational support to the team. Personal support may include helping the team develop better decision-making skills or acting as a sounding board for ideas or recommendations. Organizational support includes gaining the cooperation of senior managers to eliminate barriers or ensure that required resources are available. High-level sponsors are the primary means for building senior management awareness and buy-in of the improvement process. In turn, high-level sponsorship is one important means for top management to show ongoing interest and support in the quality process.

Team leader. The team leader is selected to guide the day-to-day efforts of the improvement process. Companies participating in the study often select the team leader from the department that is most affected by the improvement project. Selecting the team leader from the most affected department ensures that the concerns of that department will be represented in the final solution.

Team members. Team members are selected from all of the departments that will be affected by the improvement project. This ensures that each department will be represented in the development of a solution. The best source of information about the departments that will be affected by the proposed improvement project is the cost-driver analysis, as shown in Figure 10.6.

Summary of project scope. The project plan must clearly define the scope of the project to avoid confusion at a later date about

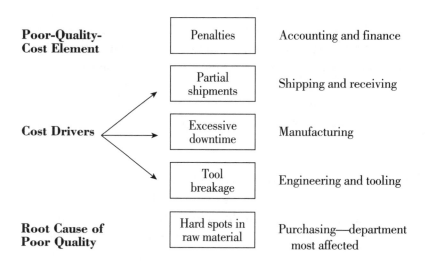

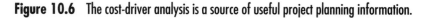

Figure 10.6   The cost-driver analysis is a source of useful project planning information.

what the project was or was not intended to accomplish. Setting boundaries around the project helps ensure that teams are not sent out to attack amorphous problems that cannot be completed in a reasonable amount of time. Breaking a large or complex project into several smaller, more manageable projects with specific goals and objectives is a common practice at this stage.

Expectations—financial. The financial expectations section details the estimated costs and benefits for the selected improvement project. Efforts should be made to include all costs, including any required capital expenditures, travel, and consulting fees. Companies commonly break the estimated financial impacts into income statement and balance sheet effects to more clearly indicate where the costs and benefits will subsequently appear in the financial statements. The financial justification for the material specifications upgrades discussed in chapter 4 provides a typical example of the methods used to determine financial expectations for a project.

Expectations—nonfinancial. Nonfinancial project expectations typically include criteria such as reduced defects, reduced customer complaints, faster cycle time, improved customer satisfaction, or increased on-time delivery.

Resources required. This section provides a specific listing of the labor, capital, and material resources that will be required to complete the project.

Date initiated. Indicates the date the project is scheduled to begin. Setting realistic starting dates helps ensure that the necessary resources are available to accomplish the project within the specified time frame.

Forecasted closure date or standing team. Whether the project has a standing team assigned or is given a specified closure date depends on the nature of the problem, the importance of the problem's resolution to the company and its customers, the time required to complete the project, and the project's complexity.

In the case of the team working on the reduction of penalties due to delivery problems, the assigned closure date was 90 days beyond the date the project was initiated. The project time frame was arrived at by estimating the interval between each step in the improvement process. As shown in Figure 10.7, the overall time required to decrease penalties was estimated at 50 days using the following methodology. Assuming that it takes 10 days to establish material specifications for the raw material suppliers, the first material orders using the new specifications will occur on the eleventh day of the project. Since the average order takes 10 days to manufacture, and surface delivery of the finished goods requires an additional seven days, the ultimate customer won't receive the conforming parts for nearly three weeks. Typically, it takes an additional two weeks for a customer to notify the company of a penalty assessment. Using these assumptions, it would realistically take 50

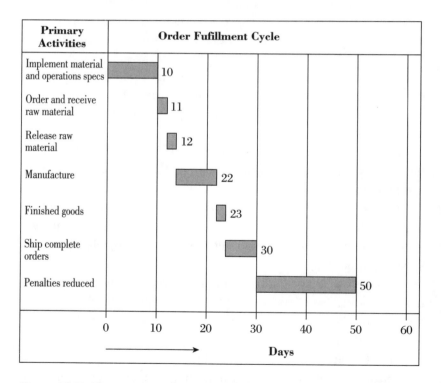

Figure 10.7   The time required to generate benefits and institutionalize the improvement establishes the project time frame.

days before penalties would begin to drop. An additional 40 days was authorized to allow the team to finalize implementation of the revised specification and evaluate the results of its efforts.

Understanding a project's time line gives a company the information needed to determine when the team should be disbanded. If, for example, there is 100-percent conformance to the new material specifications within the first 50 days of the project, the team can be suspended while the benefits work their way through the organization. By monitoring the financial and nonfinancial performance measures associated with the project, management can determine if the improvement has taken hold. If not, the team can be reactivated to implement further changes to ensure that the improvement becomes permanent.

The last element of the project plan is consideration of intangibles that may have a very real impact on the success of the quality improvement. For example, excessive downtime was not a new problem for the high alloy shaft manufacturer. Previous attempts to solve the problem had centered around the purchase of more powerful machines with greater capacity. The failure to meet schedules would disappear for a short period as the extra capacity covered the excessive downtime. When the additional capacity was no longer adequate to mask the problem, the company's performance in meeting schedules would again start to deteriorate. This cycle of masking delivery problems with additional capital investment had continued over a three-decade period. It was only after the loss of a major contract and the ensuing financial problems that management challenged this approach to solving delivery problems.

As this example shows, some of the intangibles that need to be considered include (1) top management's commitment to the quality process and (2) the competitive necessity to improve quality. If top management recognizes that quality-based cost management is a powerful means of linking quality and profitability, then it is likely that the changes that are needed to transform the company into an effective competitor can occur. If, on the other hand, top management is committed to fire fighting, with the intention of returning to the old ways of doing business once the quality problem is solved, then the likelihood that the quality process will stall or fail is high. Without top management's sincere commitment to implementing quality-based cost management, it is unlikely that the necessary cross-functional cooperation and coordination will occur. For example, if the vice president of manufacturing is adamant about not changing manufacturing standards as a result of a specific improvement project, or feels that the resources requested by the quality team will be wasted, or refuses to provide qualified personnel to participate on the improvement project, then those responsible for implementing quality-based cost management may be better advised to delay the project. Time and resources will be much better spent in areas of the company where the improvement projects have a reasonable likelihood for success.

The project plan provides the organizational mechanism to address the financial, nonfinancial, and intangible issues that will ultimately determine the success of the quality process and quality-based cost management. Careful project planning provides the opportunity to assess the organization's needs and capabilities objectively to make informed decisions about where to begin implementing the quality process and quality-based cost management.

Monitoring and Measuring Project Performance

Monitoring and measuring project performance occurs at both the team and management levels. Significant differences exist in team- and management-level reporting with respect to frequency, amount of detail, required degree of precision, relative importance of financial and nonfinancial measures, and, most important, purpose.

Team-level reporting is concerned with ensuring that the right steps are being taken to eliminate the targeted root cause and tracking the resulting improvements in quality and costs. Much of the reporting at the team level is concerned with the nonfinancial *process* measures, that is, measures of progress for processes that must be improved before better results occur. These processes may be either production processes or business processes such as purchasing or accounts payable.

The goals of team-level reporting are (1) to identify the processes that must be improved and (2) to measure the extent to which these improvements are made. In general, team-level reporting relies on numerous measures and is quite detailed. For example, a team might use a number of measurement techniques ranging from simple check sheets to control charts to determine why the root cause identified in the cost-driver analysis arises. Based on this information, the team may determine that several actions must be taken to eliminate the root cause, such as additional training, improved procedures, and reduced variability in a critical parameter of a production process. As a result, a series of new measurements such as monthly totals of the percentage of employees trained in a new technique, weekly status on the number of revised procedures issued, and real-time process control charts for the critical process parameter may be tracked. In this way, team-level reporting is evolutionary, with the required level of detail, accuracy, and frequency determined by the specific process and improvement being addressed.

Management-level reporting, in contrast, is primarily concerned with *results* measures. Did the improvement project achieve its ultimate financial and nonfinancial objectives? At this level, the concern is less with how the improvement was made and more with whether the improvement is contributing to broader business goals. At Heinz Pet Products, for example, management-level reporting is limited to the corporate goals of reducing the cost of poor quality and increasing customer satisfaction, with one page provided for each.

Two elements that must be carefully considered in management reporting are the frequency of reporting and the level of data accuracy. One of the most frequent criticisms of traditional cost-of-poor-quality applications is that monthly reporting drives managers to emphasize short-term quick fixes or fire fighting while ignoring longer-term improvement projects that may have a greater impact on company performance. In fact, many of the companies we studied are abandoning monthly or quarterly reporting in favor of the less frequent semiannual or annual reviews. The United States Customer Operations at Xerox is an example of a company that only reviews the performance of improvement teams on a yearly basis. Group management believes that many improvement projects can take months to identify the underlying reasons for the problem and implement the changes necessary. By limiting management-level reporting to once a year, management gives the improvement teams the time needed to implement modifications that result in lasting gains.

Heinz uses a different approach to management reporting but places a similar emphasis on allowing teams the time needed to implement the necessary changes. CATs report monthly to the sponsoring QIT, allowing any impediments to the improvement process to surface at a higher level in the organization. The QITs consolidate the monthly data and report quarterly to the quality improvement councils. These councils, however, only report to the TQM steering committee every six months, thereby avoiding the short-term mentality that has plagued many traditional cost-of-poor-quality applications.

A second consideration is the level of accuracy required for management reporting. As we noted in chapter 1, any improvement data that are used for performance evaluation and compensation must be accurate and objective to avoid jeopardizing the credibility of the entire quality process. While estimates and judgments may be beneficial when used to identify improvement opportunities and underlying root causes during the assessment, cost-driver, and team reporting stages, these same estimates and judgment cannot be used for performance evaluations. Instead, "hard" financial and nonfinancial measures such as verifiable reductions in the cost of poor quality and defect rates should be used for management-level reporting.

Figure 10.8. illustrates how the high alloy shaft manufacturer developed an effective management-level system to evaluate performance. The financial and nonfinancial performance measures for each department were identified from the cost-driver analysis. By sequencing the high-level departmental performance measures according to the cause-and-effect relationships, management could determine if benefits were cascading down to the income statement and balance sheet. If not, corrective actions could be taken to remove any barriers or impediments.

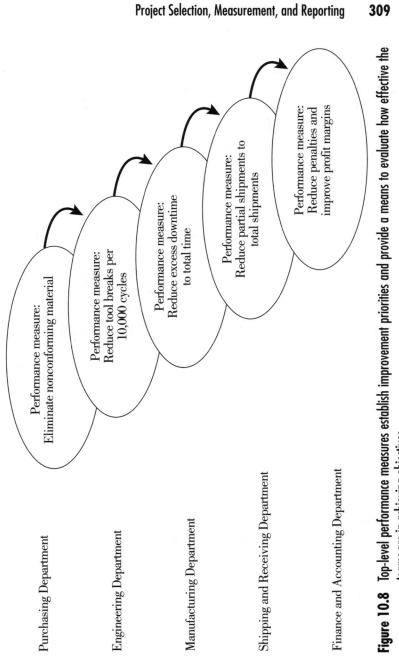

Purchasing Department

Engineering Department

Manufacturing Department

Shipping and Receiving Department

Finance and Accounting Department

Performance measure:
Eliminate nonconforming material

Performance measure:
Reduce tool breaks per
10,000 cycles

Performance measure:
Reduce excess downtime
to total time

Performance measure:
Reduce partial shipments to
total shipments

Performance measure:
Reduce penalties and
improve profit margins

Figure 10.8 Top-level performance measures establish improvement priorities and provide a means to evaluate how effective the teams are in achieving objectives.

The key to this system's success was understanding that improvements in financial performance measures could only be accomplished by improving the upstream, nonfinancial performance measures first. The starting point for improving operating profitability was changing raw material specifications for the suppliers to eliminate the hard spots causing the various problems encountered by the company. If operating profitability improved, then it was clear that the benefits from eliminating hard spots had worked their way through the entire organization. If not, then the reason for the breakdown could be identified and eliminated. For example, if the number of tool breaks dropped significantly but the number of excessive downtime hours continued at historical levels, then the team knew to investigate the link between engineering and manufacturing. Either the incorrect cause-and-effect relationship had been identified between tool breakage and excessive downtime, or an organizational blockage existed to prevent the improvement from taking effect.

Figure 10.9 shows the specific cause-and-effect relationships and performance measures for each step in the improvement process. By using a cause-and-effect framework to develop performance measures, the failure to achieve financial improvement can be traced to the point where nonfinancial performance fails to improve. Identifying the breakdown in the causal chain of events pinpoints where action should be taken to correct whatever problem is preventing the improvement from occurring.

It is important to note that companies are not building elaborate financial or manufacturing information systems to monitor team performance. Instead, existing or temporary systems are being used. Many of the measurements for the team's use are gathered by the team members themselves. This allows teams to gather performance information for their own analysis and problem-solving purposes, without being constrained by the level of detail or frequency of financial or manufacturing reporting cycles. For management-level reporting, most companies use existing financial or operational data where possible. If additional measures are needed, temporary reporting mechanisms are established, often with the assistance of the accounting or quality organizations. After the improvement team

Improvement Project Plan: Eliminate Hard Spots in Raw Material				
Flow of Benefits	Cause-and-Effect Relationships	Performance Measures	Participating Departments	Additional Considerations
Profitability and cash flow +$1,218,480 Net	Profitability and cash flow improve as penalties decrease	Operating profit margin increases as penalties decline	Accounting monitors margins for improvement	Cash flow increases, inventory purchases decline, and gross profit margins improve with fewer labor costs, fewer setups, and improved machine productivity
Penalties <$198,714>	Penalties decline due to fewer partial shipments	Penalties to operating costs decline	Accounting monitors penalties	Shift personnel as returns and partial shipments decrease
Partial Shipments	Fewer partial shipments as downtime decreases	Partial shipments to total shipments decline	Shipping monitors delivery performance	Work with production scheduling to update output rates for improved productivity
Excessive Downtime	Improve as tool breaks decline	Downtime to total hours decline	Operations monitors downtime	Shift personnel as need for setups and repair drops
Tool Breakage	Reduce as hard spots are eliminated	Tool breaks per 10,000 cycles decline	Engineering monitors tool breaks	Reduce amount purchased as scrap and waste decreases
Hard Spots in Raw Material	Eliminate as the material specifications are implemented	Nonconforming material to total receipts decline	Purchasing monitors supplier performance	

Figure 10.9 The project plan is an important tool to monitor and manage the improvement process to increase the overall probability of success.

has completed its mission, the temporary reporting system is disbanded along with the team.

Commercial Nuclear Fuel Division (CNFD), the Westinghouse unit that won the Malcolm Baldrige National Quality Award in 1988, provides an example of how one company measures and monitors both short- and long-term performance. In 1987, after three years of steady growth and margin improvement, CNFD management observed that market forces were beginning to adversely impact its operating profit margins.[5] By 1990 estimates of operating profit margins showed a marked deterioration compared to historical standards. CNFD management conducted a two-day workshop that identified 60 opportunities to improve operating margins. The 60 opportunities were distilled down to 12 potential projects. The 12 improvement projects and their primary improvement targets are listed as follows:

Project Description	*Primary Improvement Target*
1. Improve product efficiency	Cost reduction
2. Reduce assessments, general and administrative, and other fixed costs	Cost reduction
3. Reduce direct materials and plant and fixed expenses costs	Cost reduction
4. Reduce finished parts costs	Cost reduction
5. Reduce engineering costs	Cost reduction
6. Achieve price increase	Price
7. Reduce raw material holding time	Price
8. Increase manufacturing volume	Volume
9. Increase engineering service technology transfer sales	Volume
10. Reduce engineering development cycle time	Cycle time
11. Reduce premanufacturing engineering cycle time	Cycle time
12. Reduce manufacturing cycle time	Cycle time

The potential projects were then analyzed and their impact quantified. The cumulative impact of the 12 projects was then added to the 1990 plan. The result was a forecasted improvement in excess of highly profitable historical standards. The new plan called for complete implementation of all 12 projects by 1990, providing a clear, quantitative road map to achieve the three-year strategic goals—and the direct linkage between the individual improvement projects and the overall financial goals.

Since 1990 CNFD has continued to link quality improvement to financial goals. Each of CNFD's individual projects has specific financial and nonfinancial objectives and related performance measures to monitor and measure progress. Collecting and analyzing data, monitoring trends, and taking action are essential parts of CNFD's quality improvement process. At the production level, daily and weekly trends are used to verify that projected quality improvements are actually being achieved and to identify areas where further actions are required. This monitoring occurs over the life of the project. When the project is completed, its measurement system is eliminated.

CNFD relies on a unique system of measures to monitor the long-term progress of its quality improvement process on a division-wide basis.[6] This system identifies eight key factors that measure the health and vitality of its overall business. These factors, illustrated in Figure 10.10, are called pulse points and serve as top-level measures in the division's quantitative evaluation system.

CNFD has developed a system to monitor and measure performance that balances established measures, such as the eight top-level pulse points, with temporary measures, such as those required by a particular improvement project. Improvement projects are selected on the basis of contributing to the accomplishment of strategic and financial objectives, and monitored to determine the effectiveness of the project to meet those expectations. Short-term measurement processes for an improvement team are set up to monitor performance and feed performance information into a more formal, structured system used to monitor and report performance on a long-term basis.

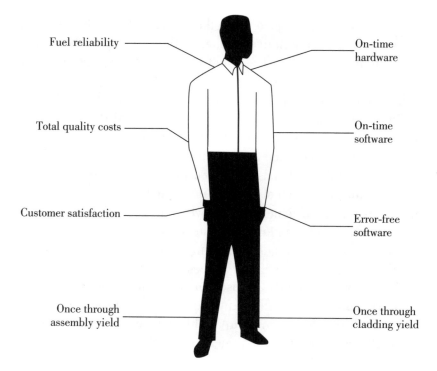

Adapted from *Performance Leadership Through Total Quality,* Westinghouse Electric Corporation, Commercial Nuclear Fuel Division, A Case Study in Quality Management.

Figure 10.10 CNFD established eight top-level pulse points to monitor the vitality and health of the overall business.

Reporting to Top Management

Top management reporting must focus on the contribution the quality process makes to the strategic and financial goals of the business. The quality plan states the priorities and objectives for investments in the quality process. Top management reporting provides an update on the achievement of those objectives to date.

Heinz Pet Products illustrates how reports to top management concentrate on accomplishments. As discussed earlier, the two original goals for the Heinz quality process were a 50-percent reduction in poor-quality costs and a 50-percent reduction in customer complaints in a four-year period. A single-page report, shown in Figure 10.11, presents the progress in achieving the corporate quality goals.

Figure 10.12 illustrates how Heinz Pet Products reports to top management on the progress of specific projects for reducing the cost of poor quality and customer complaints. The vital few projects are described, noting key measures for each project and the cost-of-nonconformance element that the project is targeting.

Similarly, the vital few projects for reducing customer complaints are described in Figure 10.13, noting current projects and the projects for the next six months.

Reporting focuses on the progress that investments in quality and quality-based cost management have made in achieving corporate goals and objectives. Only at the lower levels of the organizational and quality structure are detailed operating statistics reported. While these statistics are quite useful for assessing whether the required process improvements are taking place, only

---

Heinz Pet Products

Cost-of-Poor-Quality Information
Cost of nonconformance: $63MM
Cost of nonconformance reduction achieved to date: $27MM; *43% reduction*

Customer Complaint Information
Complaints per 100M units have *decreased by 33%* for the latest period reviewed.
The vital few targeted complaint categories have *decreased by 86%*.

Figure 10.11 Reporting to top management concentrates on progress in achieving goals and objectives.

Heinz Pet Products

**Key Projects: The Vital Few
Cost-of-Nonconformance Reduction**

Projects in Progress	Key Measures	Cost of Nonconformance
Distribution efficiencies	• Mode utilization • Use of full truckload rates • Overflow warehousing • Customer returns	$6.1MM
Ingredient yield loss	• Overfills/spillage • Ingredient quality • Ingredient substitution • Material quality	$5.1MM
Direct labor efficiency	• Direct labor variances • Line efficiency rates	$2.2MM
Purchasing efficiencies	• Inventory levels • Fresh meat utilization • Expediting costs • Spot market grain purchases	$3.0MM
Workers' compensation	• Total incident rates	$800M
General and administrative costs	• Staffing/sales ratios	$2.4MM

Figure 10.12   Reporting to top management identifies the actions for continued reduction in poor-quality costs.

Heinz Pet Products

Key Projects: The Vital Few
Customer Satisfaction Improvement/Complaint Reduction

Projects in Progress
Toll-free number implemented for Reward and Meaty Bone

Customer satisfaction drivers identified

Trade customer satisfaction survey completed. Corrective actions to date include
- Key account visits by top-level management
- Negotiation of structure and timing of promotions deals with trade and Heinz Pet Products
- Cross-functional teams to support each sales territory

Next-Six-Month Focus
- Trade deals effectiveness
- Finished goods inventory reduction and sales forecasting accuracy
- Functional benchmarking
- Safety management

Figure 10.13   Reporting to top management identifies the actions for continued increase in customer satisfaction.

actual results in terms of profitability and competitiveness are reported to top management. The top-level pulse points of CNFD are examples of the concise top management reporting that helps the organization concentrate on the achievement of meaningful results rather than merely undertaking activities that may or may not be related to the organization's key financial and nonfinancial goals and objectives.

A SUMMARY OF QUALITY-BASED COST MANAGEMENT—XEROX USCO

The experiences of Xerox, Heinz Pet Products, Texas Instruments, Star-Kist Seafood Company, Heinz World Headquarters, McDonnell Douglas, Hewlett-Packard, Commercial Nuclear Fuel Division, Power Generation Business Unit, Westinghouse Productivity and Quality Center, Pacific Bell, and others illustrate the capability of quality-based cost management to improve financial performance. This final chapter closes with an overview of how Xerox USCO has implemented quality-based cost management to improve financial performance as a part of its quality process.

A service organization is selected for the quality-based cost management overview to demonstrate that (1) the concepts and application of quality-based cost are important for service companies as well as manufacturing companies, and (2) the service component of most manufacturing companies offers an opportunity for rapid and significant improvement. The hidden costs of poor quality, which often account for more than 75 percent of the true costs, illustrate the difficulty manufacturing companies have in quantifying the impact of poor quality in the service and support segments. One of the major quality challenges facing manufacturing companies is to integrate the service segments of their businesses into the quality process with the same intensity associated with the shop floor.

The summary of quality-based cost management in USCO will follow the structure used in the detailed case studies.

- Background and quality planning
- Cost-of-poor-quality assessment
- Project selection
- Team deployment
- Monitoring and measuring progress
- Results from quality-based cost management

Background and Quality Planning

USCO had seen the successes of the manufacturing divisions of Xerox but had delayed involvement with the quality improvement process until 1987.[7] Senior management questioned whether or not a quality process could be successfully applied in a marketing organization and viewed quality-based cost management as a manufacturing tool. While USCO had seen the benefits that quality improvements had provided to the manufacturing divisions, the quality process didn't move ahead until the chief financial officer (CFO) of USCO recognized the competitive potential of quality-based cost management. The president of USCO had recently challenged his senior managers to improve profitability in response to pressures from corporate headquarters for improved financial performance. Based on this challenge, the CFO accepted the responsibility for implementing quality-based cost management and funded the investment needed to get the process started. Funding for the quality-based cost management process was established outside the normal operating budget process, and, from its beginning, the emphasis was placed on providing a tool to assist line managers and improve business practices.

Cost-of-Poor-Quality Assessment

Since USCO is strictly a sales and marketing organization, the group had to redefine accepted manufacturing poor quality definitions for use by a service operation. In late 1988, the USCO cost-of-quality team published *Cost of Quality: A Guide to Application* to define quality costs in service-related terms. Scrap, rework, and quality-related downtime all had to be defined in terms that made sense for a service organization that had no manufacturing operations. Reliability was recast in terms of predictability and accuracy, completeness of service was defined as integrity, and, most important, timeliness was operationalized as the time required to deliver the service or complete a service.[8]

The loss of a dominant market share to competitors like Cannon, Minolta, and Kodak in the 1970s and the entrance of new competitors in the late 1970s and 1980s had created an intensely competitive market environment, making USCO very sensitive to the impact of lost sales due to poor quality. Consequently, USCO added a new dimension by quantifying the impact of lost revenues and profits in addition to the traditional conformance and nonconformance cost categories.

USCO relied on the test of meeting, or failing to meet, customer requirements as the means of identifying value-added or nonvalue-added activities and waste. The USCO approach to developing quality cost definitions consisted of verifying customer requirements to ensure that (1) the supplier understood the use of the output produced for the customer, and (2) the customer had a complete understanding of the output to ensure the output of the supplier was both necessary and usable by the customer.

The costs of training, operations reviews, and preinstallations to avoid failure costs or check work were considered costs of conformance. The costs of nonconformance included rework and waste in the service delivery process, such as aborted installs and broken installs due to incomplete parts, introduction failures, accounts receivable write-offs, lost equipment, inventory write-offs, retrofits, parts failure within warranty, commission overpayments, overtime, and premium freight. Examples of lost-opportunity costs included lost work time, sales returns, order cancellations, invoice errors, equipment constraints, and lease cancellations.

Measurement of the cost of poor quality was done on a "roughly right" basis rather than requiring a high degree of accounting precision. The "roughly right" measurement emphasized process over goals and positive change over measurement, and minimized the incremental workload by avoiding changes to the financial systems. By keeping quality-related reporting distinct from the regular financial reporting systems, USCO was able to maintain the focus of cost-of-poor-quality measurement on identifying opportunities and supporting the improvement process.

In early 1989, USCO conducted its first cost-of-poor-quality assessment using representatives from the various functions, and determined the total cost of poor quality to be $1.05 billion, nearly 25 percent of sales. Not surprisingly, the financial impact of poor quality got the attention of top management. Senior management soon became active in the quality process and provided its support for a quality-based cost management approach, thereby raising the priority and importance of the entire quality process. The results of the first cost-of-poor-quality assessment are shown in Figure 10.14. The figure displays the financial impact of the 11 improvement opportunities that were selected for the cost-driver analysis based on their dollar magnitude. In total, the 11 elements represented nearly $250 million, or nearly 25 percent of the total cost of poor quality for the entire division.

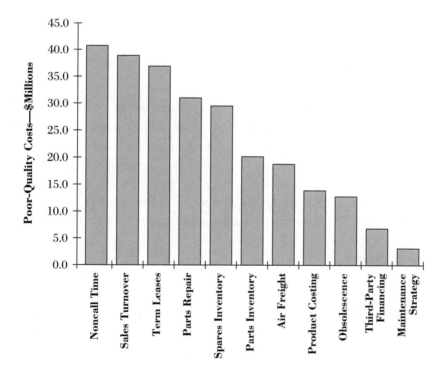

Figure 10.14   The 1989 USCO asessment established the financial impact of the key cost-of-poor-quality elements.

Project Selection
The top quality problem areas that were selected for quality-based cost management in 1989 based on the magnitude of financial impact included

1. Time spent by sales and service personnel on work other than customer calls
2. Salesperson turnover
3. Management of equipment term leases
4. Parts repair
5. Spare parts usage
6. Spare parts inventory
7. Air freight charges
8. Product costing
9. Obsolescence
10. Third-party financing arrangements
11. Maintenance strategy

The CFO chaired the initial meetings in which senior staff members and representatives from each department gathered to prioritize the improvement opportunities based on the estimated cost of poor quality for each opportunity, the estimated payback from reducing or eliminating the root causes of poor quality, the degree of external customer impact, and the level of difficulty, using a project selection worksheet similar to Figure 10.15.

Team Deployment
Two aspects of the deployment of the quality-based cost management process are credited with contributing to the success of the teams. First, the process was not implemented as another cost-reduction program, but rather as a series of improvement projects that focused on eliminating the nonvalue-added activities and waste caused by poor quality. The cost-of-poor-quality assessment was not used to judge individual performance, nor was quality-

Directions: In boxes across the top, write the outputs/problems your group is considering. Then rate them against the listed criteria by working across each row. The higher the total score, the greater the likelihood that the output/problem is appropriate for your group to work on.

Problem Statement Output →

External Customer Impact
1   2   3   4   5
Little   Great

Ability to Control
1   2   3   4   5
Little   Great

Cost of Poor Quality
1   2   3   4   5
Little   Great

Degree of Difficulty
1   2   3   4   5
Little   Great

External customer impact: The seriousness or urgency of the problem as perceived by the external customer.

Ability to control: The extent to which the group controls the problem or processes and can control the solution

Cost of poor quality: The approximate, expected cost of poor quality from solving the problem, improving processes, or reducing the number of errors.

Degree of difficulty: A judgment about the relative difficulty of working through the problem to a solution considering both the time to resolve the problem and the amount of resources required.

Courtesy of Xerox Corporation. *Cost of Quality: A Guide to Application;* Prepared by the USCO Cost of Quality Team; Xerox Corporation; 1987; Page 21.

Figure 10.15   The USCO quality improvement project selection worksheet.

based cost management used to eliminate jobs. Once the work force realized that the emphasis was on the elimination of poor quality and not jobs, the process gained rapid acceptance.

The second aspect of quality-based cost management's success was the ability of the teams to take appropriate actions and make necessary changes. The president of USCO empowered the teams to plan and execute changes that would lower the cost of poor quality. More significantly, the teams were empowered to make revisions to policies and procedures and, when appropriate, incur expenses to help make the necessary changes.

The problems tackled by the teams were clearly cross functional in nature. By giving the teams the authority to take appropriate actions and make necessary changes, top management sent a clear signal to the entire division that functional barriers needed to be removed to ensure the success of the quality initiative. As such, the quality-based cost management process acted as a change agent for the division. By quantifying the impact of long-standing operating problems that had been hindering the division, then deploying teams to address the key problems, an organizational mechanism was put in place that provided cross-functional cooperation and coordination.

The improvement team structure at USCO is critical to promoting cross-functional cooperation. For example, the team that developed the cost of quality application guide was composed of team members from marketing, quality, distribution, finance and administration. Similarly, the team responsible for the external lease improvement opportunity consisted of representatives from finance, pricing, product marketing, and major account marketing. Each team had a controller assigned to the team to estimate costs, obtain needed information from the financial systems, and provide support to the line managers involved in the projects. One of the roles performed by the controllers was to support the line managers in charge of the teams by actively facilitating the quality process. Controllers were involved in scheduling meetings, coordinating attendance, and providing interim status reports to the team leaders. Finally, a senior staff member was assigned to provide the overall team leadership.

The authority to make policy and procedural changes, incur expenses, and staff the teams with cross-functional membership, as well as the visible support of senior management were the keys to the improvement team success. The cost-of-poor-quality and cost-driver analysis focused the teams on the high payback opportunities and, combined with management's support, provided USCO with an effective problem-solving resource.

Monitoring and Measuring Progress

The quality-based cost management process called for top management progress reporting on an annual basis. The year-end results were evaluated by comparing the initial cost-of-poor-quality assessment for a particular problem with the associated cost of poor quality at the end of the year. The controllers assigned to the teams were responsible for gathering the financial data and helping the teams track interim results.

Results from Quality-Based Cost Management at USCO

In its first year, quality-based cost management reduced the cost of poor quality by $53 million (Figure 10.16). Although dramatic, these results were achieved without layoffs or drastic cost-cutting measures. The payback was accomplished by quantifying poor-quality improvement opportunities, and then taking action through the deployment of empowered improvement teams that focused on reducing or eliminating the root causes of poor quality.

Prior to the implementation of quality-based cost management, no functional manager had the authority to solve the cross-functional problems identified in the cost-of-poor-quality assessment. The assessment quantified the impact of problems that had existed for years but had never been put on an authoritative organizational agenda for improvement. Quality-based cost management provided the organizational mechanism to establish the cross-functional teams with the authority and responsibility to make the necessary changes.

For example, excessive air freight charges were a well-known problem that had existed within USCO for a number of years. In

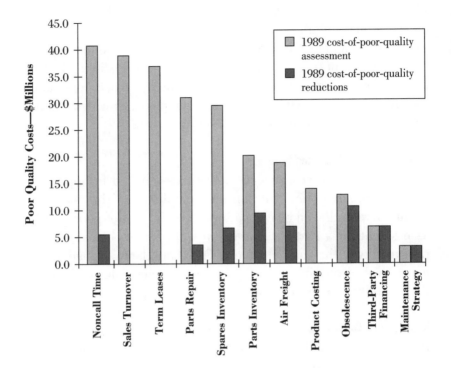

Adapted from Lawrence P. Carr, "Applying the Cost of Quality to a Service Business," *Sloan Management Review*, Spring 1992, page 76 by permission of publisher. © 1992 Sloan Management Review Association. All rights reserved.

Figure 10.16   USCO eliminated $53 million in poor quality costs by concentrating on short-term, high-payback improvement projects.

1988 the year prior to the implementation of quality-based cost management, air freight charges for purchased parts and equipment were $11.2 million. A multifunctional team was selected to examine the problem and develop solutions. After conducting its analysis, the team implemented a solution that called for a single focal point within each USCO organization to manage air freight. The result was a reduction in air freight charges of $6.5 million in 1989. Air freight expenses were reduced even further in 1990, producing an additional savings of nearly $5 million.

The improved financial performance from quality-based cost management is attributed to a number of factors.

1. The strong and visible support of USCO senior management, coupled with an effective training program, has given credibility to the quality-based cost management process. The training sessions and active involvement of senior managers send a clear signal to all employees that cross-functional, quality-based cost management is a priority for the entire organization.

2. Project planning, as an element of the quality-based cost management process, aids in setting priorities for resource commitment. More important, it furnishes the organizational vehicle to facilitate improvements that cross the traditional functional boundaries of the business.

3. The authorization of the multifunctional improvement teams to coordinate changes in policy and procedures that cut across functional lines sends further reinforcing signals. Quality-based cost management has become a part of the quality culture and management process at USCO. As a part of the TQM approach, quality-based cost management serves as a change agent and helps to overcome the inhibitors to quality progress.

Conclusion

The success of Xerox USCO in achieving significant financial improvement using quality-based cost management is impressive but in no way unique. Other companies participating in the study have achieved equally impressive results. Heinz, which set a corporate goal to eliminate $250 million in poor quality costs over four years, reached that goal nearly one year ahead of schedule. In 1990, Motorola credited quality-based cost management with saving the company $942 million over the previous three years.[9]

McDonnell Douglas eliminated of $72 million in poor-quality costs over the first eight production aircraft of the C-17 program. These experiences show that improved financial performance is a natural output of the improvement process once management has taken the necessary steps to link the quality process to broader organizational goals. By identifying the opportunities and focusing its efforts, companies don't have to wait years to significantly improve financial performance through quality improvement.

Notes

1. Westinghouse Electric Corporation Productivity and Quality Center, "Total Quality: A Westinghouse Imperative," Executive Overview, February 1992, 4.
2. Workers Compensation Expense and Recordable Accidents Report, John Sterrit, Director of Plant Safety, Heinz Pet Products, 1992.
3. Christopher D. Ittner, *The Economics and Measurement of Quality Costs: An Empirical Investigation* (doctoral thesis, Harvard University Graduate School of Business, June 1992).
4. Robin Cooper and Robert S. Kaplan. *The Design of Cost Management Systems: Text, Cases, and Readings* (Englewood Cliffs, N.J.: Prentice-Hall, 1991), 252.
5. Westinghouse Electric Corporation Productivity and Quality Center, "Performance Leadership Through Total Quality," 2.
6. Westinghouse Electric Corporation Productivity and Quality Center, "Commercial Nuclear Fuel Division—A Case Study: Putting It All Together: A Baldrige-Winning Performance," 11.
7. Lawrence P. Carr, "Applying the Cost of Quality to a Service Business," *Sloan Management Review* (Spring 1992): 72–77. Also notes prepared by Professor Carr providing further details regarding quality-based cost management at Xerox United States Customer Operations.
8. J. M. Juran, "Service Industries," chapter 33 in *Juran's Quality Control Handbook, 4th ed.* (New York: McGraw-Hill, 1988).
9. Garrett DeYoung, "Does Quality Pay?" *CFO Magazine* (September 1990): 24–31.

Conclusion

The goal of this study was to identify best practices in managing the cost of poor quality. We studied more than 30 different companies to understand how they manage the quality process to improve financial performance. For many of these companies, the answer is focusing quality tools and techniques on eliminating the excess costs of nonvalue-added activities and waste caused by poor quality. By adding a financial dimension to the quality process, these companies are able to simultaneously improve both customer satisfaction and financial performance.

Our experiences with these companies indicate that the first major phase companies go through to reach world-class levels of performance is significantly reducing the nonvalue-added activities and waste in their current business processes. Quality-based cost management can provide the information necessary to identify, quantify, and eliminate nonvalue-added activities and waste to reach the next higher level of productivity, profitability, and competitiveness. For many of the participating companies, educating everyone in the company about the negative impact of poor quality provided the initial momentum for changing the established cultural, strategic, and operational priorities. The ability to demonstrate the business value of quality through improvement in financial performance and customer satisfaction provided the sustaining momentum to become an industry leader.

For the first four to seven years of effective quality-based cost management, the participating companies experienced significant increases in productivity and profitability as they eliminated the high payback root causes of poor quality. As the low hanging fruit was harvested, companies began expanding the definition of non-value-added activities and waste beyond the traditional definitions of quality failure. The result was a gradual shift in emphasis toward increasing the value-added aspects of the business to reach higher levels of both customer satisfaction and profitability. Reaching world-class levels of performance using second- and third-generation business process reengineering was built on the foundation of first-generation gains that were achieved using quality-based cost management. The purpose of this book is to help guide managers in making the organizational changes and decisions needed to achieve these first-generation gains through the elimination of the high payback root causes of poor quality.

Appendix A

Cost-of-Poor-Quality Assessment Guide ___

The goal of quality-based cost management is to focus quality and process improvements on eliminating the root causes of poor quality and their related costs. By understanding where the costs of poor quality occur—whether in manufacturing departments or in indirect and white-collar departments such as purchasing and marketing—a company can take control of and manage one of the largest cost items in the entire business.

The cost-of-poor-quality assessment provides the starting point for implementing a quality-based cost management process that can make a significant positive impact on a company's productivity, profitability, and overall competitiveness. Though the assessment is simple in concept, the task takes time and effort. The following guidelines are provided to ensure that this time and effort is well directed.

Assessment Planning

The three keys to an effective assessment are planning, planning, and planning. Adequate planning can reduce the amount of time required for the assessment, improve the accuracy of the data, and increase the organizational buy-in. While the plan's specific details will vary with each company's needs and circumstances, five common steps are critical to success.

1. *Determine the required level of detail.* As discussed in chapter 8, determining the appropriate level of detail for the assessment is one of the first issues that a company needs to address. Three levels of detail are typically used in cost-of-poor-quality assessments. A level 1 assessment focuses on internal and external failure costs. Many companies have found that a level 1 assessment can identify a wealth of improvement opportunities, especially in the early stages of a quality process, while minimizing implementation costs. A level 2 assessment offers greater detail, analyzing appraisal costs as well as failure expenditures. Assessing appraisal costs allows a company to (1) determine the extent to which inspection activities are driven by poor quality and (2) evaluate the payback from specific investments in appraisal. A level 3 assessment provides the most comprehensive estimate of poor-quality costs, encompassing prevention, appraisal, internal failure, and external failure costs. Like the level 2 assessment, the evaluation of prevention and appraisal costs allows a company to determine whether investments in quality improvement are being effectively allocated. In general, companies that are just beginning their quality journey usually limit their assessment efforts to level 1. As the low hanging fruit identified in the level 1 assessment is harvested, additional cost elements are evaluated to uncover additional improvement opportunities.

2. *Determine how the project will be organized.* The project organization provides the link between the assessment team and top management. The assessment team is headed by a team leader who is responsible for successful completion of the assessment. The team leader should possess leadership skills, a solid understanding of quality-based cost management, and knowledge of the company's activities and products. To enhance commitment to the quality process, the team leader should not come from the quality or accounting functions. Instead, the team leader should come from one of the functions or organizations that will actually be implementing the resulting improvement projects.

The team leader reports to a steering committee that oversees planning and implementation of quality-based cost management.

The steering committee is typically composed of upper management, which provides an important link to the company's president. The committee reviews the project plan prior to its acceptance and meets periodically to review progress.

3. *Select team members.* Team members should be selected from each of the departments to be assessed. The departmental representatives bring valuable knowledge of processes within their functions and increase departmental ownership for the results. More important, cross-functional assessment teams increase the probability that problems crossing organizational boundaries will be identified and eliminated.

Representatives from the quality and accounting functions should also be included on the assessment teams. Quality and accounting team members possess extensive experience in cost estimation and quality improvement techniques, experience that can be put to use in educating other team members, collecting and analyzing data, and preparing final reports.

4. *Determine training requirements.* Training is crucial to the successful implementation, acceptance, and use of quality-based cost management. Training requirements differ depending on the audience. Managers at all levels of the organization must be exposed to the fundamentals of quality-based cost management and the potential benefits from quality improvement. Assessment team members require more extensive training in key terms and concepts, data-gathering techniques, and interviewing skills. Finally, users of the data should understand what information is provided by the assessment and how that information should be used in decision making.

5. *Complete the assessment plan.* The finalized assessment plan summarizes the tasks that must be accomplished to complete the project, the estimated time required for each task, and the anticipated costs to complete the assessment. These costs may include the wages of the team members, support resources and materials (for example, secretary time, supplies, graphics, and so

on), training programs and seminars, computer hardware and software, travel, and consulting expenses. By identifying the required resources and setting realistic schedules, the completed assessment plan helps to ensure that the project stays on schedule and within budget.

Collecting the Information

Once the assessment plan is finalized, data collection can begin. This section reviews the following elements of effective data collection.

- How to collect the information
- Who to interview
- How to prepare for the interview
- How to conduct an interview

1. *How to collect the information.* Chapter 8 discusses the six primary techniques available for identifying the costs of poor quality: (1) collection of costs by account, (2) collection of costs by the "whole person" or equivalent heads, (3) collection of labor costs by project, (4) estimation of costs using the percent defective, (5) estimation of costs based on the number of occurrences, and (6) estimation of costs based on interviews and surveys. Figure A.1 provides a data-gathering checklist for the assessment team members to begin gathering the information needed to implement these techniques.

The first step in collecting cost-of-poor-quality data is determining the elements that will be examined. Appendix B contains a standard list of cost-of-poor-quality elements that can be used to develop a customized list of elements that reflect a company's specific circumstances. By modifying the standard list and adding organization-specific examples, the assessment team can create a list of poor-quality cost elements to which the employees can relate.

Of the many data-gathering techniques, collection of costs by account and estimation of costs using interviews and surveys are the

- Organization charts
- Listing of accounts in the accounting system
- Department job descriptions, budgets, and head counts
- Existing performance measures
- Existing quality measures
- Process flowcharts
- Salaries or wages by employee or labor grade
- Work calendar
- Customized list of cost-of-poor-quality elements and examples

Figure A.1 The data-gathering checklist.

most frequent. Assessment team members should be made aware of the fact that interviewing is more than just a data-gathering technique. Interviews allow information to flow both ways. The assessment team member can use the interview to educate users on the value of cost-of-poor-quality information and to answer questions, address concerns, and build ownership for the assessment output. In return, information is gathered from reliable sources that actually perform the work.

2. *Whom to interview.* Interviews should be held with a representative sample of employees in each department. In small departments, this may include all employees. In larger departments, interviews should be conducted with each manager and a representative selection of subordinates. Subordinates are particularly valuable in less proceduralized support and white-collar areas, where managers may not know exactly how each employee spends his or her time.

3. *How to prepare for the interview.* The kick-off meeting educates all departments about the basic concepts of quality-based

cost management, the objectives of the assessment, the purpose of the interviews, and the information that is needed. The kick-off meeting also serves as a good venue for distributing "to do" lists to interviewees covering relevant material such as organization charts, existing quality measures, job descriptions, activity logs described in chapter 8, and notices stating the time and place of the interviews. In addition, interviewers can prepare themselves by determining what information they are looking for, what questions they need to ask, and what supporting documentation is necessary.

4. *How to conduct an interview.* Interviews typically last between one and two hours each. This allows the participants enough time to carefully consider their responses while keeping the interview focused. Beyond two hours, participants tend to lose concentration. If the interview is not completed in a reasonable time frame, consider rescheduling the completion for another time.

In order to make the interview a positive experience for interviewees, as well as a useful data-gathering technique, the following steps should be taken.[1]

1. Explain the purpose. Interviewees should understand why the interviewer is there. Concerns about the assessment can be addressed at this time.
2. Review the benefits. Explain the importance of quality-based cost management to the company. Give examples of how the assessment results will benefit the interviewee's own work area and assist in the achievement of strategic goals and objectives.
3. Discuss the process. Review the requirements of the assessment, emphasizing its dependence on the knowledge and input of the interviewees. Note that the objective is reasonable estimates of poor quality rather than precise figures.
4. Ask key questions. Focus questions on the desired objectives of the assessment. What are the products and services

that their department supplies? Who are their internal and external suppliers and customers? Which of the customized cost-of-poor-quality elements apply to their department? What existing data are available on these elements? How much time is spent on these activities? Remember to have interviewees bring along their activity logs as a reminder of how their time is spent.

5. Facilitate the answers. "Help the interviewees answer the questions. Ask follow-up questions if you sense that an answer is incomplete or reflects misunderstanding of the original question. Provide technical assistance if the interviewees cannot respond because of a lack of [quality-based cost management] knowledge. Keep the interview on track."[2]

Compilation and Reporting on the Findings

Once the data-gathering process is completed in each department, team members should discuss the results with departmental representatives to verify that the information is reasonably accurate. The initial departmental assessment should take approximately four to six weeks. Subsequent assessments usually require less time as the organization becomes more experienced in the process.

The individual departmental worksheets are first consolidated, then combined for the presentation to top management. A sample departmental worksheet for a level 1 assessment is illustrated in Figure A.2. The suggested contents for the presentation to senior management include

- Total cost-of-poor-quality for the unit or company
- Comparison of the ratio of total cost-of-poor-quality to relevant benchmarks, such as sales, employee wages, manufacturing costs, earnings before interest and taxes, earnings per share, profit sharing, and so on
- Breakdown of poor quality costs into categories corresponding to the assessment level

Accounting and Administration						
Category	Labor	Materials	Equipment	Expenses		Comments/Source
1. **Internal Failure Costs**						
1.1 Product and service design failure (internal)	8,000	0	0	0	8,000	10% of VP/GM
1.1.1 Investigation and redesign: corrective action	34,569	0	0	0	34,569	803 hrs/yr
1.1.2 Rework due to product and service design changes	0	0	0	0	0	
1.1.3 Scrap due to product and service design changes	258	0	0	0	258	6 hrs/yr
1.1.4 Production liaison costs (design related)	0	0	0	0	0	
Total	**42,827**	**0**	**0**	**0**	**42,827**	
1.2 Purchased product and service failure costs	1,200	0	0	0	1,200	
1.2.1 Purchased product reject disposition costs	0	0	0	0	0	
1.2.2 Purchased product and service replacement costs	0	0	0	0	0	
1.2.3 Purchased product and service failure analysis: corrective actions	2,725	0	0	0	2,725	150 clerical hours, 25 controller hours
1.2.4 Rework of internal and external supplier rejects	0	0	0	0	0	
1.2.5 Uncontrolled material, equipment, or parts losses	1,200	73,000	0	0	74,200	50% of inventory adjustment
Total	**5,125**	**73,000**	**0**	**0**	**78,125**	
1.3 Operations failure costs due to defective products and services	20,000	0	0	0	20,000	25% of VP/GM
1.3.1 Product and service review and corrective action costs	16,487	0	0	0	16,487	273 hrs/yr cntrlr, mngmnt. accountant, 226 hrs/yr staff
1.3.1.1 Disposition costs	0	0	0	0	0	
1.3.1.2 Investigation costs	0	0	0	0	0	
1.3.1.3 Operations corrective action	0	0	0	0	0	
1.3.2 Rework and repair costs	0	0	0	0	0	
1.3.3 Reinspection and retest costs	1,894	0	0	0	1,894	44 hrs/yr
1.3.4 Extra activities to complete inadequate business, production, work, or operations processes	0	0	0	0	0	
1.3.5 Scrap costs	4,875	0	0	0	4,875	4 hrs/wk clerical for scrap and NCMR's, 1.5hrs/wk controller
1.3.6 Downgraded end product or service	0	0	0	0	0	Included in 3.3.2
1.3.7 Internal failure labor losses (downtime)	0	0	0	0	0	

Figure A.2 Sample cost-of-poor-quality departmental worksheet.

	Category	Labor	Materials	Equipment	Expenses	Total	Comments/information source
1.3.8	Standards, variances, and allowances establishing acceptable levels	0	0	0	0	0	
1.3.9	Material, overhead, or labor waste	353	0	0	0	353	2 hrs/yr cntrlr, cost acct, 10 hrs/yr staff
	Total	**43,608**	**0**	**0**	**0**	**43,608**	
1.4	Manpower failure costs	0	0	0	0	0	
1.4.1	Manpower replacement costs	0	0	0	0	0	
1.4.2	Loss of production due to manpower failure	147,000	0	0	0	147,000	Write-off of accounts receivable due to quality problems
	Total	**147,000**	**0**	**0**	**0**	**147,000**	
1.5	Excess facilities, equipment, assets, personnel, or other resources required as a result of operating inefficiencies	0	0	0	0	0	
1.6	Other internal failure costs	0	0	0	0	0	
	Total internal failure costs	**238,561**	**73,000**	**0**	**0**	**311,561**	

	Category	Labor	Materials	Equipment	Expenses		Comments/Source
2	**External Failure Costs**						10 hrs/yr cntrlr, cost acct, 20 hrs/yr mgr, 60 hrs/yr staff
2.1	Complaint investigations	2,921	0	0	0	2,921	30 hrs/yr staff + 22 hrs/yr
2.2	Returned goods	20,190	200	0	653,289	673,679	600 hrs/yr clerical, 100 hrs controller, and 2.3% sales
2.3	Retrofit costs	0	0	0	0	0	
2.4	Recall costs	0	0	0	0	0	
2.5	Warranty claims	0	0	0	0	0	
2.6	Liability costs	0	0	0	9,000	9,000	Insurance premiums
2.7	Penalty costs	0	0	0	0	0	
2.8	Maintaining customer goodwill	30,000	0	0	0	30,000	30% of president time
2.9	Lost sales due to lack of productivity or availability	0	0	0	0	0	
2.10	Lost sales due to lack of capability	0	0	0	0	0	
2.11	Lost sales due to a damaged reputation or tarnished image	0	0	0	105,000	105,000	
2.12	Other external failure costs	0	0	0	0	0	
	Total External Failure Costs	**53,111**	**200**	**0**	**767,289**	**820,600**	

Figure A.2 *(continued).*

- Changes in the category since the last assessment, if applicable, and a discussion of why the changes have occurred
- Breakdown of poor quality costs into direct versus indirect and white-collar costs
- Identification of key cost-of-poor-quality elements
- Assumptions used in calculating the cost of poor quality
- Recommendations for the cost-driver analysis

Conclusions and Lessons Learned

A good implementation plan provides the foundation for a successful cost-of-poor-quality assessment. Using these data, a company can begin to identify the root causes of poor quality and, ultimately, begin to link quality to profits. But to ensure success, the following dos and don'ts should be kept in mind.

- Do keep the assessment simple. Use existing information whenever possible.
- Do use the assessment in a positive and constructive fashion to facilitate the improvement process.
- Do measure all poor-quality costs within the department or function. Controllable and uncontrollable cost designations can be applied by the departmental or functional manager later.
- Do communicate the results and their meaning to the entire organization.
- Do consider setting reduction targets for the cost-of-poor-quality, but remember to be realistic in setting expectations and time frames.
- Do encourage departmental and functional managers to be team members. Their participation is essential.
- Don't make the cost estimates too detailed or down to the last penny. Be approximately right rather than precisely wrong.
- Don't exclude any department or function—including quality and finance.

- Don't dollarize trivia. If a disagreement can't be resolved over a cost element or a definition, then it probably should be dropped.
- Don't make the assessment a witch hunt. It is counterproductive to use the results of the assessment to assign blame or measure the performance of an individual or department. Used as a weapon, the assessment becomes a part of the problem and not a part of the solution.
- Don't use the cost of poor quality to compare departments. The uncontrollable costs make the comparisons meaningless. Moreover, departmental comparisons breed competition, reducing the likelihood that successful cross-functional teams can be formed to eliminate quality problems that cross departmental boundaries.
- Don't create a new accounting system. Doing so reduces the value of quality-based cost management by diverting precious resources away from reducing or eliminating the root causes of poor quality.

Notes

1. The list is loosely adapted from Peter B. B. Turney, *Common Cents: The ABC Performance Breakthrough* (Portland, Ore.: Cost Technologies, Inc., 1991), 251–253.
2. Peter B. B. Turney, *Common Cents: The ABC Performance Breakthrough*, 252–253.

Appendix B
Standard Cost-of-Poor-Quality Element Listing_____

The springboard for the financial success achieved by companies participating in the study is provided through the elimination of nonvalue-added activities and waste, which then frees scarce resources for deployment into value-added activities that increase productivity, profitability, and competitiveness. Establishing the direct link between higher quality processes and improved financial performance, however, requires that an organization possess the capability to define, identify, and quantify the nonvalue-added activities and waste that are driven by poor quality.[1]

The foundation for defining nonvalue-added activities and waste is the test of whether or not an activity or cost is associated with the failure to meet customer requirements. If so, the activity or cost is classified as nonvalue-added or waste. This definition provides the breakthrough thinking that case study companies employed to

- Build a consensus on the definition of nonvalue-added activities and waste. If not, the lack of a company-wide consensus seriously diminishes or invalidates the usefulness of the assessment because of the confusion and controversy created by the results.

- Establish both improved customer satisfaction and financial performance as a natural consequence of an effective quality improvement process. Otherwise, companies sometimes find themselves forced into a situation where they increase customer satisfaction at the expense of improved financial performance or vice versa, rather than implementing strategies that will improve both at the same time.

Consensus on the definition of nonvalue-added and the emphasis on increasing both customer satisfaction and financial performance helped the case study companies to neutralize or eliminate the barriers that have caused many quality processes to stall or fail in their effort to produce meaningful results.

Build a Consensus on the Definition of Nonvalue-Added Activities and Waste. By classifying activities and costs as nonvalue-added based on the criteria of failing to meet internal and external customer requirements, the confusion and controversy of unclear or arbitrary classification schemes is avoided. Companies have found that an approach that asks managers and supervisors to define the value of activities performed by their groups often leads to widely varying replies. Rather than relying on classification schemes where essentially similar activities are defined differently by different people, controversy is avoided by defining nonvalue-added activities in terms of their failure to meet internal and external customer requirements. Confusion is eliminated by using a standard classification scheme that is applied consistently across all activities and levels of the company.

For example, the lack of a consensus regarding nonvalue-added activities and waste leads to inconsistent reporting which, in turn, leads to results that are questionable or controversial. A recent study cites just such a problem where the final tabulation showed that managers and supervisors believed that only 4 percent of their activities were nonvalue-added.[2] The percentage was much lower than expected and caused the company to question the results. The results were attributed to the fact that the ranking of activities was done relative to each group's own mission, where each group was responsible for writing its own mission statement. The company finally agreed that future assessments should classify an activity as value-added or nonvalue-added on the basis of whether an activity directly supports corporate objectives. Everyone involved in the study agreed that had such a criterion been used, the percentage of nonvalue-added activities would have been much higher. Since the objective of the assessment is to find ways to measure, analyze, and manage costs, the information generated would have been much more useful had a more relevant criterion been used.

In another example, the team was frustrated in its attempt to rank activities and learned how difficult it is to classify activities as providing little or no value.[3] The team subsequently decided that value classification was not an important objective. For this company, the value ranking of activities was not attempted because of the difficulty in building a consensus about the definition of value-added versus nonvalue-added within the organization.

In another study to identify process improvement and cost reduction opportunities, the team wrestled with the problem of defining a scheme to classify activities as value-added versus non-value-added.[4] The value ranking assigned by the assessment team to each activity "was a painful process. Everyone had a different definition of what's valuable to them." In the end, a value classification scheme was developed for activities based on their importance to accomplishing the business mission and objectives, and providing value to the internal and external customers. This new classification scheme is now tied to the quality improvement process and is able to gain the attention and support of management and the workforce.

Establish Both Improved Customer Satisfaction and Financial Performance as a Natural Consequence of an Effective Quality Improvement Process. Conducting a cost-of-poor-quality assessment where a nonvalue-added activity is defined in terms of the failure to meet customer requirements establishes very clearly that the impact of poor quality is twofold: Customers are dissatisfied and costs are higher. Customers are dissatisfied because the company has failed to meet their expectations for products and services. Costs are higher because the failure has consumed valuable resources and provided little or no value. The only things the company has to show for its failure to meet customer requirements are fewer resources and dissatisfied customers.

The realization that poor quality drives customer dissatisfaction and higher costs is key to shifting the priorities of the quality improvement process. The new priority must be to simultaneously achieve increased customer satisfaction and improved financial performance by implementing improvement projects that have been selected on the basis of logical cause-and-effect relationships. As new priorities are established, the challenge is to develop the means to gather meaningful information to take effective actions.

Standard Cost-of-Poor-Quality Element Listing

Companies participating in the study have relied on an assessment approach that uses a standard listing of definitions as the means to gather useful information. The standard listing defines the categories and cost elements that will be included in the assessment and provides representative examples of each cost element. Companies have found that precise definitions of nonvalue-added activities and their costs dramatically simplifies the assessment process. Figure B.1 shows the structure of the standard element listing.

The listing begins with the major category (internal failure, external failure, appraisal, or prevention) followed by the subcategory, in this case "operations failure costs due to defective products and services." After defining the cost element scrap costs, department-specific examples from a typical manufacturing company are presented as a training aid to help the assessment team translate the standard element listing and definitions into familiar terms that are useful and meaningful for people who participate in the departmental assessments.

The assessment team should not hesitate to eliminate, supplement, modify, or enhance the illustrations to make the element listing

Category
1.0 INTERNAL FAILURE COSTS—General Definition

The sum of all costs incurred for activities caused by or resulting from the failure of a product or service to meet customer requirements prior to shipment or delivery. Internal failure costs include the costs required to evaluate, dispose of, and either correct or replace defective or deficient products or services prior to delivery to the internal or external customer. Also included are the costs required to correct or replace inaccurate or incomplete product or service descriptions or documentation.

Internal failure costs also include all the material, labor, and expenses wasted due to defective or otherwise unacceptable work received from internal or external suppliers.

Subcategory
1.3 Operations Failure Costs Due to Defective Products and Services

Operations failure costs can generally be viewed as the costs associated with defective products or services discovered during normal operating processes of a department or function.

Cost Element
1.3.5 Scrap Costs

The total cost (including material, labor, and overhead) for defective products or services that is wasted or disposed of because the product or service cannot be reworked to conform to requirements. The unavoidable losses of material (such as the turnings from machining work or the residue in a food mixing pot) are generally known as waste (check company cost accounting definitions) and are not to be included in the cost of poor quality.

Figure B.1 The standard element listing presents the cost categories, cost elements, definitions, and illustrations to assist in creating the customized departmental element listings.

Cost Element Illustrations

Accounting: Time and materials consumed to produce daily, weekly, monthly, or annual financial reports, statements, and such that are thrown away due to missing or incorrect information.

Data Processing/MIS: Producing reports and computer runs for people who have left the company or that no longer support any customer-specified or business need.

Engineering: Resources spent on project designs that are discontinued due to the lack of understanding the customer requirements or inability to accurately identify market requirements.

Operations: Production of undersized parts that can not be reworked.

Purchasing: Purchase orders that are subsequently canceled due to errors, omissions, or misunderstandings about internal or external customer requirements.

Quality: Ineffective quality training resulting from a misunderstanding of the trainee's requirements.

Sales/Marketing: Proposals, sales literature, or mass mailings thrown out due to misunderstandings, lack of timeliness, product changes, price changes, and the like.

Figure B.1 *(continued).*

a more effective tool to support the quality process. It may be appropriate to have two or three illustrations for a cost element. Once the departmental illustrations for the cost-of-poor-quality elements and definitions are developed, each department has a customized listing and set of definitions taken from everyday operations, which provides the basis for future assessments.

The relationship between the assessment levels and the major quality cost categories are as follows:

Assessment Levels	*Major Quality Cost Categories*
Assessment Level 1	1.0 Internal Failure Costs
	2.0 External Failure Costs
Assessment Level 2	3.0 Appraisal Costs
	1.0 Internal Failure Costs
	2.0 External Failure Costs
Assessment Level 3	4.0 Prevention Costs
	1.0 Internal Failure Costs
	2.0 External Failure Costs
	3.0 Appraisal Costs

The standard cost-of-poor-quality element listing starts with assessment level 1 and concludes with assessment level 3. The following standard cost-of-poor-quality elements and descriptions are provided to assist in the development of customized lists tailored to the unique circumstances of the business.

Assessment Level 1

1.0 Internal Failure Costs—General Definition

The sum of all costs incurred for activities caused by or resulting from the failure of a product or service to meet customer requirements prior to shipment or delivery. Internal failure costs include the costs required to evaluate, dispose of, and either correct or replace defective or deficient products or services prior to delivery to the external customer. Also included are the costs required to correct or replace inaccurate or incomplete product or service descriptions or documentation.

Internal failure costs also include all the material, labor, and expenses wasted due to defective or otherwise unacceptable work received from internal or external suppliers.

1.1 Product and Service Design Failure (Internal)

Design failure costs can generally be considered to be the unplanned costs incurred because of inherent design inadequacies in released products or services. They do not include billable costs associated with customer-directed changes (product or service enhancements) or major redesign activities (product or service upgrading) that are part of a company-sponsored marketing plan.

1.1.1 Investigation and Redesign

After initial release of a product or service design, the total cost incurred for all activities associated with problem investigation and redesign activities, including requalification as necessary, required to completely resolve product or service problems inherent in the design.

Accounting: Investigation of management reporting labor inefficiencies, scrap, or unplanned overtime due to an inadequate or faulty customer requirements definition or product design.

Data Processing/Management Information Services (MIS): Investigation of errors to determine if the source of the design failure is at the user interface level or the programming level.

Engineering: Investigation of failures and redesign of deficient product or service features discovered prior to shipment to customers.

Operations: Investigation of product flaws due to production deficiencies.

Purchasing: Investigation of slow inventory turnover, obsolete inventory, missed delivery dates, or other failures due to the improper design of a reorder system.

Quality: Root-cause analyses and the application of problem-solving methodologies due to product or service failures. Ineffective quality tool and technique training resulting from not understanding the trainee's requirements.

Sales/Marketing: Sales literature thrown out due to errors, outdated information, or failure to meet management's expectations.

1.1.2 Rework Due to Product and Service Design Changes
The cost of all rework activities, such as materials, labor, and applicable overhead specifically required as part of resolving design problems and revisions to the implementation plan for required design changes.

Accounting: Correction of reporting errors and reissue of reports and information due to faulty product design, such as a payroll system.

Data Processing/MIS: Reinput of data lost due to system design failure. Reverification of the system requirements.

Engineering: All subsequent design modifications to the initial design due to design deficiencies.

Operations: Rework resulting from failure of the operations plan, routings, or production schedules.

Purchasing: Expediting or slowing down shipments due to reorder system design failure.

Quality: Rework resulting from a design failure.

Sales/Marketing: Reprinting of sales and marketing materials, reassignment of personnel, and costs incurred due to a change in the design of a promotional or advertising program.

1.1.3 Scrap Due to Product and Service Design Changes
The cost of all materials, labor, and applicable overhead scrapped or disposed of as a result of resolving product or service design problems or implementation plan changes.

Accounting: Unusable forms, manuals, excess personnel, and other costs incurred as a result of changes required to resolve service design problems and implement changes required.

Data Processing/MIS: Unusable forms, manuals, excess personnel, and other costs incurred as a result of changes required to resolve system design problems and implement changes required.

Engineering: Design deficiencies that are not repairable.

Operations: Disruption of work effort and obsolescence of inventory, tools, facilities, and products due to engineering changes required to correct design deficiencies.

Purchasing: Restocking charges incurred due to incorrect product design specifications.

Quality: Scrap resulting from design changes.

Sales/Marketing: Loss of marketing program development time, competitive advantage, and investments due to changes in product designs.

1.1.4 Production Liaison Costs (Design Related)

The cost of unplanned support activities required because of inadequate, incomplete or deficient designs, descriptions, or documentation by the engineering or product development department or organization.

Accounting: Liaison costs with MIS to correct design deficiencies of accounting or financial management systems.

Data Processing/MIS: Liaison costs with departments affected by MIS design failures.

Engineering: Administrative or support time spent related to redesign efforts.

Operations: Liaison resources required to reschedule staff, equipment, or other resources.

Purchasing: Cancellation of purchasing actions due to changes or respecification of materials due to design errors.

Quality: Additional training of operators resulting from inadequate design, description, or documentation by the engineering or product development organization.

Sales/Marketing: Coordination with engineering on customer-required changes due to inadequately designed product offerings.

1.2 Purchased Product and Service Failure Costs

Costs incurred due to the rejection or failure of purchased products or services to meet internal or external requirements.

1.2.1 Purchased Product Reject Disposition Costs

The cost to sort and dispose of incoming inspection rejects. Includes the cost of reject documentation, review and evaluation, disposition orders, handling, and transportation (except as recovered from the supplier).

Accounting: Cost of activities associated with changes in accounts payable due to returned goods and resulting credit memo processing.

Data Processing/MIS: Cost of electronic data interchange capability dedicated to the disposition of reject material.

Engineering: Review and evaluation of reject materials.

Operations: Handling, storing, and returning rejects to suppliers.

Purchasing: Nonchargeable costs for coordination with suppliers regarding disposition of materials.

Quality: Sorting incoming rejects.

Sales/Marketing: Identification of alternative sales outlets to dispose of purchased product rejects.

1.2.2 Purchased Product and Service Replacement Costs

The added cost of replacement for all items or services rejected. The cost of items replaced and not returned to the supplier, and items rejected and returned to supplier are counted. Includes replacement costs if not paid for by the supplier, plus additional transportation, expediting, and other associated expenses.

Accounting: Clerical activities related to the payment of replacement goods.

Data Processing/MIS: Test run of replacement software.

Engineering: Determination of replacement options.

Operations: Premium freight charge for quick delivery of replacement items.

Purchasing: Acquisition of replacement items and cost of negotiated settlements.

Quality: Added inspection costs associated with the receipt of replacement materials.

Sales/Marketing: Added proofing and inspection costs associated with receipt of replacement sales brochures.

1.2.3 Purchased Product and Service Failure Analysis
The cost of activities for failure analyses and investigations into the causes of internal or external supplier rejects to determine necessary corrective actions. Includes the cost of visits to supplier plants for this purpose and the cost to install necessary added inspection protection while the problem is being resolved.

Accounting: Investigation of root causes of supplier billing error.

Data Processing/MIS: Determination of root causes of faulty information.

Engineering: Failure analysis of supplier rejects.

Operations: Failure analysis of supplier rejects.

Purchasing: Costs associated with negotiating settlements for nonconforming products or services.

Quality: Failure analysis of supplier rejects.

Sales/Marketing: Failure analysis of ineffective mailing list information purchased from outside sources.

1.2.4 Rework of Internal and External Supplier Rejects
The total cost of necessary supplier item repairs incurred by the company and not billable to the supplier—usually due to production or service delivery expediencies.

Accounting: Correction of untimely, incorrect, or inadequate supplier billing information.

Data Processing/MIS: Correction of supplier information errors.

Engineering: Determination of how or whether to rework nonconforming products.

Operations: Rework of nonconforming supplier products not billable to suppliers.

Purchasing: Documentation of supplier-related rework costs.

Quality: Rework of supplier rejects not billable to suppliers.

Sales/Marketing: Repair of exhibition materials not billable to suppliers.

1.2.5 Uncontrolled Material, Equipment, or Parts Losses

The cost of material, equipment, or parts shortages due to damage, theft, or other known or unknown reasons. A measure of these costs may be obtained from reviews of inventory adjustments, annual inventory write downs, consignment inventory adjustments, lost-in-shop situations not accounted for by inventory adjustments, fixed-asset record adjustments, and physical inventory records or adjustments.

Accounting: Record keeping of material losses.

Data Processing/MIS: Cost of disaster recovery.

Engineering: Theft, loss, or accidental disposal of engineering blueprints.

Operations: Damage to finished goods inventory.

Purchasing: Additional purchases to replace equipment missing from uncontrollable losses.

Quality: Theft of measurement equipment.

Sales/Marketing: Damage and loss of material, equipment, or parts used for sales demonstrations or display.

1.3 Operations Failure Costs Due to Defective Products and Services

Operations failure costs can generally be viewed as the costs associated with defective products or services discovered during the normal operations processes of a department or function.

1.3.1 Product and Service Review and Corrective Action Costs

Costs incurred for activities in the review and disposition of nonconforming products or services and the corrective actions necessary to prevent recurrence. (Include investigating the failure, the cost of disposing of the rejected parts, and steps taken to eliminate the root cause.)

1.3.1.1 Disposition Costs

All costs incurred in the review and disposition of nonconforming products or services.

Accounting: Credit memo processing and related record keeping associated with the review and disposition of nonconforming products or services.

Data Processing/MIS: Programming developed to monitor and measure nonconformance occurrences within a department or the company.

Engineering: Analysis required to establish adequate disposition or disposal procedures, practices, or policies.

Operations: Expense associated with waste disposal of rejected goods.

Purchasing: Sale of scrapped materials back to suppliers

Quality: Review and disposal of nonconforming work-in-process and finished goods.

Sales/Marketing: Disposition of inappropriate or ineffective advertising material.

1.3.1.2 Investigation Costs

Costs incurred in the investigation of failures. Including the cost of failure analyses (physical, chemical, and so on) conducted by or obtained from outside laboratories, sources, or experts in support of defect cause identification.

Accounting: Audits by public accounting firms for the specific purpose of identifying causes of accounting errors, financial systems failures, or financial reporting deficiencies.

Data Processing/MIS: Systems audits to investigate data processing and system applications errors.

Engineering: Experiments conducted to determine the root cause of product failures.

Operations: Production runs for the purpose of determining process failures.

Purchasing: Purchase of laboratory support for internal customers.

Quality: Failure analysis of defective goods.

Sales/Marketing: Investigation to identify causes of decline in market share.

1.3.1.3 Operations Corrective Action

The actual cost of corrective actions taken to remove or eliminate the root causes of nonconformances. This item can include such activities as rewriting operator instructions, redeveloping specific processes or flow procedures, redesigning or modifying equipment or tooling, and developing and implementing specific training. Does not include design (item 1.1.1) or supplier (item 1.2.3) corrective action costs. (Some consider these prevention costs.)

Accounting: Redeveloping staff guidelines to eliminate procedural errors.

Data Processing/MIS: Debugging of software after the release of the production code.

Engineering: Redeveloping a manufacturing process or product.

Operations: Rewriting operator guidelines.

Purchasing: Redevelopment of purchasing guidelines to eliminate clerical and procurement errors.

Quality: Implementation of new training procedures to correct defects.

Sales/Marketing: Redevelopment of sales territory guidelines to eliminate intra- and interdepartmental conflicts.

1.3.2 Rework and Repair Costs

The total cost (labor, material, and overhead) of reworking or repairing defective products or services discovered during the business, service, work, or delivery process. Does not include rework due to product or service design change (item 1.1.2).

Accounting: Recalculation of payroll expenses due to errors in the time sheets and expense records.

Data Processing/MIS: Rerunning programs due to errors such as out-of-sequence processing.

Engineering: Development of repair methods.

Operations: Rework of previously completed products due to delay in receipt of engineering change orders.

Purchasing: Reissue of purchase orders.

Quality: Rework resulting from operations failures.

Sales/Marketing: Resubmitting customer sales orders due to errors in gathering the necessary customer, service, or product-related information.

1.3.3 Reinspection and Retest Costs

Inspection, test, and audit labor that is incurred because of product or service rejects or failures, including documentation of rejects, fault analysis, inspection or test after rework/repair, and sorting of defective lots.

Accounting: Inspection of reworked financial reports or analyses.

Data Processing/MIS: Inspection and testing of regenerated output.

Engineering: Inspection of redrawn blueprints.

Operations: Inspection of reworked parts.

Purchasing: Inspection of reprocessed purchase orders.

Quality: Reinspection of reworked parts.

Sales/Marketing: Inspection of reprinted sales brochures.

1.3.4 Extra Activities to Complete Inadequate Business, Production, Work, or Operations Processes

The total cost of extra activities, such as trimming excess or document completion, added because the basic business, production, work, or operations processes are deficient, error-prone, or inadequate and, as a result, are not able to produce products or services that conform to customer requirements. These costs are often hidden in the accepted or standard cost of the operations or appear as additional steps in a process.

Accounting: Revising financial forecasts due to incomplete or inadequate preparation of related data by other departments.

Data Processing/MIS: Manual inspection of output due to lack of automated test procedures.

Engineering: Manual input of the engineering bill of materials because of a CAD system deficiency to complete the task.

Operations: Trimming of excess material from a formed part due to the poor condition of molds, machinery, plant equipment, or tooling.

Purchasing: Expediting of orders resulting from errors in the inventory system.

Quality: Analyzing receiving records to verify material on hand due to a lack of timely receiving information.

Sales/Marketing: Calling the warehouse to verify inventory quantities because the information in the computer is unreliable.

1.3.5 Scrap Costs

The total cost (including material, labor, and overhead) for defective products or services that is wasted or disposed of because the product or service cannot be reworked to conform to requirements. The unavoidable losses of material (such as the turnings from machining work or the residue in a food mixing pot) are generally known as waste (check company cost accounting definitions) and are not to be included in the cost-of-poor-quality.

Accounting: Time and materials consumed to produce daily, weekly, monthly, or annual financial reports, statements, and such that are thrown away due to missing or incorrect information.

Data Processing/MIS: Producing reports and computer runs for people that have left the company or that no longer support any customer-specified or business need.

Engineering: Resources spent on project designs that are discontinued due to the lack of understanding the customer requirements or inability to accurately identify market requirements.

Operations: Production of undersized parts that can not be reworked.

Purchasing: Purchase orders that are subsequently canceled due to errors, omissions, or misunderstandings about internal or external customer requirements.

Quality: Ineffective quality training resulting from a misunderstanding of the trainee's requirements.

Sales/Marketing: Proposals, sales literature, or mass mailings thrown out due to misunderstandings, lack of timeliness, product changes, price changes, and the like.

1.3.6 Downgraded End Products or Service

The price differential between a normal selling price and a reduced selling price due to nonconforming or off-grade end products or services because of quality reasons. This also includes any costs incurred to bring nonconforming or off-grade end products or services up to salable condition.

Accounting: Accounts payable discounts not taken.

Data Processing/MIS: Changes in data input to reflect new price guidelines.

Engineering: Design efforts to upgrade defective products to a salable condition.

Operations: Resources spent on upgrading defective products to salable (discounted) condition.

Purchasing: Cost of improvements to components required due to improper purchasing specifications.

Quality: Resources spent on upgrading defective products to salable condition.

Sales/Marketing: Price reductions made to customers to compensate for poor quality.

1.3.7 Internal Failure Labor Losses (Downtime)

When labor is lost because of nonconforming products or services, there may be no concurrent material losses or such losses may not be reflected on scrap or rework reports. Typically, such labor losses or downtime occur because of equipment shutdowns, the failure to provide accurate or timely schedule information, requirement to perform repeat setups, or line stoppages for quality reasons. Costs are the efficiency losses and may be hidden by an allocation for labor allowances.

Accounting: Downtime due to failure to receive closing information as required.

Data Processing/MIS: Downtime due to a programming or system error.

Engineering: Downtime related to uncertainty of corrective action.

Operations: Downtime due to machine breakdown.

Purchasing: Downtime due to computer failure.

Quality: Downtime resulting from faulty measurement data or equipment.

Sales/Marketing: Forced sales slowdown due to insufficient production capacity resulting from an order fulfillment process failure.

1.3.8 Standards, Variances, and Allowances Establishing Acceptable Levels of Material, Overhead, or Labor Waste

Any production, accounting, or engineering standards, variances, and allowances establishing "acceptable" levels of material and labor waste based on historical, institutionalized, or other similar practices or experiences.

Accounting: Additional staffing required to complete the monthly closing due to the unanticipated errors and corrections that occur during the closing.

Data Processing/MIS: Additional hardware or software maintained for backup due to inadequate maintenance resources, procedures, or processes.

Engineering: Resources dedicated to generating and supporting engineering change orders not specified by the customer, federally mandated, or related to safety.

Operations: Established rework facilities and related personnel requirements.

Purchasing: Variances built into material standards to account for supplier rejects.

Quality: Training courses repeated because the training was forgotten due to a lack of application.

Sales/Marketing: Resources consumed in following up on unqualified prospects.

1.4 Staff Failure Costs

Costs incurred from not having adequate staff capacity. This includes the cost of having to replace employees, equipment shutdowns, and process defects or failures due to labor shortages or having employees with the wrong skills.

1.4.1 Staff Replacement Costs

Cost of losing employees due to a failure in the hiring process such as hiring the wrong employee, or the inability to keep valued employees. Include the cost of search firms to replace dismissed or resigned employees and severance costs.

Accounting: Clerical activities related to adding and deleting employees from the company's payroll.

Data Processing/MIS: Severance pay to dismissed employees.

Engineering: Executive search firm fees.

Operations: Added cost of temporary agency to fill unplanned labor shortage.

Purchasing: Contracting with search firms.

Quality: Training of replacement employees.

Sales/Marketing: Executive search firm fees.

1.4.2 Loss of Production Due to Staff Failure

Loss of production and process capacity due to shortage of employees and/or shortage of employees with required skill sets. Include the cost of lost sales, overtime, and other related costs.

Accounting: Slow invoicing or excessive accounts receivable due to shortage of accounts receivable staff.

Data Processing/MIS: Overtime to compensate for staff shortage.

Engineering: Delays in product development due to the shortage of qualified engineers.

Operations: Overtime due to the shortage of qualified production employees.

Purchasing: Higher material costs from expediting or premium costs due to inexperienced purchasing personnel.

Quality: Slowdowns in production schedules due to the shortage of quality professionals.

Sales/Marketing: Lost sales due to a shortage of properly trained or available sales representatives.

1.5 Excess Facilities, Equipment, Assets, Personnel, or Other Resources Required as a Result of Operating Inefficiencies

Costs of excess facilities, equipment, assets, personnel, or other resources required to meet customer requirements as a result of operating inefficiencies.

Accounting: Handling and distributing payroll checks due to deficient automatic deposit capability.

Data Processing/MIS: Manipulation or conversion of data due to processing errors or inefficiencies.

Engineering: Reassigning sales liaison personnel to correct misunderstanding between the customer, sales person, and engineering staff.

Operations: Expediters and supporting resources.

Purchasing: Excess inventory held in the event that excess scrap or reject levels occur.

Quality: Engineering liaison due to design-related problems.

Sales/Marketing: Manually reentering sales order information into backlog, sales reporting, or other support systems because the systems are unable to share common data or information.

1.6 Other Internal Failure Costs

Other internal failures costs incurred for activities resulting from the failure of a product or service to meet customer requirements prior to shipment or delivery. These may be identified by the assessment team as relevant to specific departments and the company. Examples could include redundant products or services. For example, if a company subscribes to three different pricing services or information sources for essentially the same activity, the confusion that arises from different data describing the same activity has a cost to the organization. It may be appropriate to classify the costs created by lower productivity or rework as a poor-quality cost due to redundant or duplicate services. Also include the cost of the service that would be eliminated.

2.0 External Failure Costs—General Definition

The sum of all costs incurred for activities resulting from a product or service failure shipped or delivered to the external customer. These costs consist primarily of costs associated with the product or service not meeting customer or user requirements.

2.1 Complaint Investigations

The total cost of investigating, resolving, and responding to individual customer or user complaints or inquiries, including necessary field repair or corrective services related to a complaint investigation.

Accounting: Investigation of payroll errors.

Data Processing/MIS: Generation of customer complaint data file information.

Engineering: Investigation of a design failure with external customers.

Operations: Investigation of customer complaints.

Purchasing: Material review analysis.

Quality: Investigation of and response to customer complaints.

Sales/Marketing: Liaison efforts in resolving customer complaints.

2.2 Returned Goods

The total cost of activities for evaluating, repairing, or replacing products or services not acceptable to the internal or external customer or user. It does not include repairs accomplished as part of a maintenance or modification contract.

Accounting: Resources dedicated to accounting for returned goods transactions.

Data Processing/MIS: Capability required to process returned goods information, track returned goods status, and generate related reports.

Engineering: Evaluation of returned goods.

Operations: Repair of returned goods, including material handling and storage.

Purchasing: Rework of purchasing commitments or purchasing budget due to effect of returned goods.

Quality: Time required for the evaluation of returned goods.

Sales/Marketing: Evaluation of customer reported deficiencies causing returned goods.

2.3 Retrofit Cost

Costs of activities to modify, replace, or update products, field maintenance facilities, or service offerings to a new design level because of deficiencies that require a major redesign. Including that portion of retrofits due to quality problems.

Accounting: Modification of financial statements to incorporate changes in inventory valuation methods.

Data Processing/MIS: Recall of software to repair design flaws.

Engineering: Major redesign of products in the field due to design deficiencies.

Operations: Modifications of product design because of design deficiencies.

Purchasing: Acquisition of parts used for modifications.

Quality: Product modifications due to major redesign to correct deficiencies.

Sales/Marketing: Update of sales literature to incorporate missing information.

2.4 Recall Costs

Include costs of recall activity due to quality problems.

Accounting: Resources consumed in estimating and accounting for the financial effects of a recall.

Data Processing/MIS: Recall of reports issued to users that contain material errors.

Engineering: Preparation of plans and coordination with sources to handle any hazardous or toxic material associated with the recall.

Operations: Production of suitable replacement products or material to customers effected by the recall.

Purchasing: Activities associated with the timely acquisition of conforming products or services.

Quality: Activities to specify actions plans to prevent the recall from recurring.

Sales/Marketing: Notification of customers about the recall of an inferior product or service.

2.5 Warranty Claims

The total cost of customer or user claims after acceptance of a product or service, including repair costs such as removing defective hardware from a system, and cleaning costs due to a food or chemical service accident. In cases where a price reduction is negotiated in lieu of a warranty claim, the value of this reduction should be counted.

The write-off of accounts receivable due to a quality problem, providing a customer with additional products or services at a reduced or no-cost basis, and extending a warranty or guarantee period are examples of costs incurred as a result of warranty claims.

Accounting: Activities involving the accounting and paying of claims.

Data Processing/MIS: Collecting and processing of data related to the recall including report generation and additional hardware or software capacity needed.

Engineering: Responding to questions about short-term adjustments or fixes customers can make to minimize damage and losses associated with the warranty claims.

Operations: Production planning and schedule changes required in response to warranty claims.

Purchasing: Coordination of claims against suppliers.

Quality: Investigation of warranty claims to verify claims are reasonable and not due to other causes such as customer misuse.

Sales/Marketing: Coordination with customers on the payment of claims. Including negotiation costs.

2.6 Liability Costs

Costs due to liability claims or expected liability claims, including the cost of product or service liability insurance.

Accounting: Clerical activities involved with paying liability costs. Payment of liability claims.

Data Processing/MIS: Additional resources consumed responding to requests for information regarding a liability claim.

Engineering: Litigation support efforts required to defend against liability claims.

Operations: Assessment of current manufacturing procedures or practices in question as a result of the liability claims.

Purchasing: Acquisition of liability responsibility from suppliers.

Quality: Resources required to develop revisions to company or customer operating guidelines or procedures to minimize the damage or losses from a liability claim.

Sales/Marketing: Coordination of claims with customers and any costs of negotiation.

2.7 Penalty Costs

Cost of any penalties incurred due to something less than full product or service performance. Penalties can be required by contracts with customers, government rules and regulations, or payments made to customers as compensation for a product or service failure.

Accounting: Managerial and clerical activities involving payment of penalties.

Data Processing/MIS: Collecting and processing information regarding penalties.

Engineering: Reassessing customer requirements due to penalties.

Operations: Production changes required as a result of penalties.

Purchasing: Cost of assessing and collecting penalties from suppliers who have not fulfilled their agreements such as a breach of contract or termination for default.

Quality: Analysis or damages or losses that affect the amount of penalties claimed or paid.

Sales/Marketing: Coordination with customers on the payment of penalties.

2.8 Maintaining Customer Goodwill

Costs incurred, over and above normal selling costs, to customers or users who are dissatisfied or not completely satisfied with the quality of delivered products or services. Such costs are incurred because customers' expectations are greater than what they receive from the product or service.

Accounting: Relationship rebuilding with customers who receive inaccurate or untimely billing information.

Data Processing/MIS: Changes to programming undertaken in response to a service failure with customers.

Engineering: Meeting with customers to showcase the features of the product or service after a complaint.

Operations: Product giveaways to customers.

Purchasing: Meeting with customers who are not satisfied with the service provided by the purchasing department.

Quality: Activities related to regaining lost customer goodwill.

Sales/Marketing: Efforts designed to appease customer complaints and concerns.

2.9 Lost Sales Due to Lack of Productivity or Availability

Costs including the value of profit margin lost due to a sales reduction or lost sales because of a lack of productivity or unavailability of revenue-generating resources such as sales and service personnel, demonstration equipment, service engineers, inventory, financial, or other resources.

Accounting: Lost sales due to failure to correctly anticipate the current working capital requirements of business.

Data Processing/MIS: Untimely software release.

Engineering: Failure to deliver a product design on time due to a diversion of engineering resources to respond to customer complaints.

Operations: Inability to meet current sales demand due to higher than expected reject rates caused by inexperienced production personnel.

Purchasing: Failure to deliver the proper materials to the operations department.

Quality: Failure to achieve a customer's specified level of conformance, resulting in a delay or loss of a supplier certification by the customer.

Sales/Marketing: Estimate of lost profit margin or lost sales due to excessive development time where the time-to-market is a key determinant of profitability.

2.10 Lost Sales Due to Lack of Process Capability

Costs including the value of profit margin lost due to a sales reduction, or lost sales resulting from inadequate process capability due to process design deficiencies, inadequate staffing, delays, errors in information, or failures to meet current or changing customer requirements.

Accounting: Errors in sales invoices that cause sales to be underbilled due to lack of timely sales pricing information.

Data Processing/MIS: Customer switching to competitors because of an improperly functioning electronic data interchange capability.

Engineering: Inadequate product development capability.

Operations: Shipping errors due to inaccurate or untimely master file updates.

Purchasing: Late product delivery resulting from late receipt of materials.

Quality: Poor appraisal effectiveness.

Sales/Marketing: Lost sales due to insufficient customer contact.

2.11 Lost Sales Due to a Damaged Reputation or Tarnished Image

Costs including the value of a profit margin lost due to a sales reduction. Lost sales related to a damaged reputation or tarnished image with customers due to the failure of a product or service. Including the costs related to restoring or correcting the damaged reputation or tarnished image.

Accounting: Customers switching to competitors over concerns about the continued financial health of business.

Data Processing/MIS: A reputation for inadequate data processing causes customers to place orders with competitors.

Engineering: Company sales losses due to reported design flaws.

Operations: Canceled customers orders due to reported failures of the product in the field.

Purchasing: Lost sales from the inability to obtain material on credit terms because of slow pay reputation.

Quality: Lost sales due to inferior quality rating from an independent product testing or consumer research organization.

Sales/Marketing: Lost sales due to current customers telling potential customers about problems with a product or service.

2.12 Other External Failure Costs

Other external failures costs incurred for activities resulting from a product or service failure shipped or delivered to the external customer that is identified by the assessment team as relevant to specific departments and the company. An example of this might be the external failure costs from setting unrealistic expectations on the part of the customer. The unrealistic expectations could come from a variety of sources such as inadequate training of sales personnel or attempts to justify mispriced products or services with unsupportable claims.

Assessment Level 2 (Assessment Level 1 Plus Appraisal Costs)

3.0 Appraisal Costs—General Definition

The sum of all costs associated with activities to measure, evaluate, or audit products, processes, or services to ensure conformance to internal and external customer requirements. Evaluation of products and services occurs at sequential stages, from design to first delivery and throughout the production or delivery process, to determine continued conformance to internal or external customer requirements. The appraisal costs include all costs incurred in the planned conduct of product and service appraisals to determine conformance to requirements.

3.1 Purchased Product and Service Appraisal Costs

Purchasing appraisal costs generally can be considered to be the costs incurred for the inspection and/or test of purchased supplies or services to determine acceptability for use. These activities can be performed as a receiving inspection function of the product or service as well as an inspection function at the product or service supplier's facility.

3.1.1 Incoming Inspections and Tests

Total costs for all normal or routine inspection activities and/or test activities of purchased materials, products, and services as a continuing part of a normal receiving inspection function to ensure conformance to standards and requirements.

Accounting: Verification of time card reporting.
Data Processing/MIS: Inspection of incoming data accuracy.
Engineering: Testing of new engineering equipment.
Operations: Inspection of incoming materials.
Purchasing: Development of incoming materials specifications.
Quality: Inspection of incoming materials.

Sales/Marketing: Inspection of sales brochures and other marketing literature.

3.1.2 Measurement Equipment
The cost of acquisition (depreciation or expense costs), calibration, and maintenance of measurement equipment, instruments, and gages used for appraisal of purchased products, materials, parts, assemblies, and supplies.

Accounting: Accounts payable activities related to the purchase of measurement equipment.

Data Processing/MIS: Computer costs incurred in the testing of purchased software.

Engineering: Equipment used in the testing of prototype components (that is, volt meters).

Operations: Equipment for incoming materials inspection.

Purchasing: Equipment for incoming material inspection.

Quality: Calibration of micrometers, calipers, and so on.

Sales/Marketing: Computer costs incurred in monitoring the performance of advertising.

3.1.3 Qualification of Supplier Products and Services
The cost of additional inspections or tests (including environmental tests) periodically required to qualify the use of production quantities of purchased goods or services. These are usually one-time costs, but they may be repeated during multiyear product or service acquisition situations.

Accounting: Reference checking of financial institutions to verify stability.

Data Processing/MIS: Review of supplier information-gathering procedures.

Engineering: First article inspection.

Operations: First article inspection.

Purchasing: Periodic testing of purchased goods.

Quality: Annual lab tests on purchased materials.

Sales/Marketing: Evaluation of advertising proposals.

3.1.4 Source Inspection Programs

All incurred costs for activities, including travel, to conduct progress reviews for product or service designs, and the qualification of supplier products or services at the supplier's location or at an independent test laboratory.

Accounting: Inspection of financial stability of suppliers.

Data Processing/MIS: Inspection of security procedures of data processing vendor.

Engineering: Inspection and qualification testing at supplier site.

Operations: Inspection and qualification testing at supplier site.

Purchasing: New vendor certification at supplier site.

Quality: Supplier certification associated expenses.

Sales/Marketing: Inspection of production process to ensure that customer requirements are being met.

3.2 Capability Evaluation Costs

Capability evaluation costs generally can be considered the costs of activities incurred for the inspections, tests, audits, or evaluations of internal or external operations or functions required to determine and ensure the acceptability of products or services. The evaluations can occur at each discrete step in the process, from start to the completion of production or service delivery. In each case where material losses are an integral part of the appraisal operation, such as machine set-up pieces or destructive testing, the cost of the losses is to be included.

3.2.1 Planned Inspections, Tests, and Audits

The cost of all planned inspection, test, and audit activities conducted on products or services at selected points or work areas throughout the overall process, including the point of final product or service acceptance. Also includes the total cost of any destructive test samples required. It does not include the cost of troubleshooting, rework, repair, or sorting rejected lots, all of which are defined as failure costs.

Includes checking labor done by other than inspectors as in-process evaluation, typically part of a production operator's job.

Product and service quality audits, personnel expenses as a result of performing quality audits on in-process or finished products. Inspection and test materials consumed or destroyed in control of quality, for example, by tear-down inspections, over-voltage stressing, drop testing, or life testing.

Accounting: Physical inventory audit.

Data Processing/MIS: Inspection of data entries and data flow procedures.

Engineering: Tear-down inspections.

Operations: Work-in-process inspection.

Purchasing: Verification of purchase order data accuracy.

Quality: Final inspection.

Sales/Marketing: Review of sales proposals.

3.2.2 Set-Up Inspections and Tests (First Piece)

The cost of all set-up or first-piece inspections and tests used to ensure that each combination of machine and tool is properly adjusted to produce acceptable products before the start of each production lot, or that processing equipment including acceptance and test devices are acceptable for the start of a new day (or other time period).

Accounting: Calculations for reports and presentations are complete.

Data Processing/MIS: Process and configuration control tests.

Engineering: Verification of blueprint accuracy prior to requesting a prototype be built.

Operations: Process setting inspection prior to the start of a new production run.

Purchasing: Verification of manufacturing requirements planning (MRP) inputs prior to processing run.

Quality: First-piece inspection.

Sales/Marketing: Sales demonstration equipment is properly set up and inspected prior to customer demonstrations.

3.2.3 Special Testing

The cost of all nonroutine inspection and test activities conducted as a part of the appraisal plan. These costs normally will include annual or semiannual sampling of sensitive products or services for more detailed and extensive evaluations to ensure continued conformance to critical environmental requirements.

Accounting: Year-end financial statement audit.

Data Processing/MIS: Testing costs of outdated system routings.

Engineering: Semiannual product testing.

Operations: Semiannual product testing.

Purchasing: Annual supplier evaluations.

Quality: Semiannual product testing.

Sales/Marketing: Review of client contact documentation.

3.2.4 Process Control Measurements for Products and Services

The cost of all planned measurements conducted on in-line product or service processes, equipment, and/or materials (for example, oven temperature, material density, or computer coding accuracy) to assure conformance to pre-established standards and requirements. Includes adjustments made to maintain continued acceptable results.

Accounting: Verification of time card accuracy prior to entering data into the system.

Data Processing/MIS: Synchronizing of data transfer rates.

Engineering: Time and motion study of production process.

Operations: Hourly monitoring of process controls (such as heats, speeds).

Purchasing: Verification of data accuracy.

Quality: Process control monitoring.

Sales/Marketing: Verification of sales order accuracy.

3.2.5 Laboratory Support

The total cost of any laboratory tests required in support of product or service appraisal plans.

Accounting: Audit by public accounting firm.

Data Processing/MIS: Independent verification of processing control and disaster recovery capabilities.

Engineering: Lab testing of material properties.

Operations: Lab testing of product capabilities.

Purchasing: Liaison activities with contract laboratory.

Quality: Liaison activities with contract laboratory.

Sales/Marketing: Research done by outside vendors to determine the effectiveness of marketing efforts.

3.2.6 Measurement (Inspection and Test) Equipment

Since any measurement or process control equipment required is an integral part of appraisal operations, its acquisition (depreciation or expense), calibration, and maintenance costs are all included. Include depreciation of capitalized equipment, cost of noncapitalized equipment, and maintenance and calibration labor.

Total depreciation allowances for all capitalized appraisal equipment, procurement, or build costs of all appraisal equipment and gages that are not capitalized, and the cost of all inspections, calibration, maintenance, and control of appraisal equipment, instruments, and gages used for the evaluation of support processes, product, or service for conformance to requirements.

Accounting: Clerical activities related to the acquisition and bookkeeping of measurement equipment.

Data Processing/MIS: Hardware test equipment depreciation.

Engineering: Equipment used in inspecting prototypes.

Operations: Calipers used for product testing.

Purchasing: Equipment used in supplier capability testing.

Quality: Depreciation of work-in-process testing equipment.

Sales/Marketing: Equipment used in customer capacity testing.

3.2.7 Outside Endorsements and Certifications

The total cost of required outside endorsements or certifications, such as Underwriters Laboratory (UL), American Society of Testing Materials (ASTM), or an agency of the U.S. government. Includes the cost of sample preparation, submittal, and any liaison support costs incurred for its final achievement.

Accounting: Certified Public Accountant or Certified Management Accountant certifications.

Data Processing/MIS: Certified Data Processor certification.

Engineering: UL certification.

Operations: Sample preparation for UL certification.

Purchasing: Endorsement of purchased materials by outside laboratory.

Quality: ASTM certification.

Sales/Marketing: Endorsement of product or service by consumer group. Certification of sales and marketing personnel by a professional group attesting to a level of competence and capability.

3.3 External Appraisal Costs

External appraisal costs are incurred anytime there is need for field setup or installation and check out prior to official acceptance by the customer, and also when there is need for field trials of new products or services.

3.3.1 Field Performance Evaluation

The total cost of all appraisal activities (inspections, tests, audits, and appraisal support activities) planned and conducted at site for installation and/or delivery of large, complex products, or the conduct of merchandised services (for example, repairs or leasing setups).

Accounting: Inspection of record keeping system implemented in production department.

Data Processing/MIS: Inspection of computer system installed at customer site.

Engineering: Inspection of product performance at customer site.

Operations: Visits to customer facilities to gain an understanding of how the product is interconnected with other products.

Purchasing: Examination of purchased components with internal customers.

Quality: Inspection of field installations.

Sales/Marketing: Administration of field evaluations with customers.

3.3.2 Special Product and Service Evaluations

Include life testing, life cycle costing, environmental, and reliability tests performed on production units.

Accounting: Analysis of pro forma financial statements under varying scenarios.

Data Processing/MIS: Estimation of data processing hardware and software requirements under varying growth scenarios.

Engineering: Environmental testing of prototypes.

Operations: Environmental testing of production units.

Purchasing: Reliability tests performed on routine material purchases.

Quality: Environmental tests on production units.

Sales/Marketing: Analysis of sales forecasts under varying scenarios.

3.3.3 Evaluation of Field Stock and Spare Parts

Include cost of evaluation, testing, or inspection of field stock for design or formulation changes, storage time (excessive shelf life), or other suspected problems.

Accounting: Verification of any changes or updates to processes or procedures effecting the control or management of assets, such as accounts receivable, inventory, or fixed assets.

Data Processing/MIS: Verification that remote job entry sites or remote operating sites are using the most recent codes, formats, and procedures.

Engineering: Inspection of blueprints to verify latest engineering changes.

Operations: Inspection of inventory to discard outdated items.

Purchasing: Verification of lead time data in MRP system.

Quality: Inspection of goods held at off-site warehouses.

Sales/Marketing: Inspection of brochures and sales literature held by sales agents in the field.

3.4 Review Test and Inspection Data on Products and Services

Costs incurred for regularly reviewing inspection and test data prior to release of the product for shipment or a service for delivery, such as to determine whether product or service requirements have been met.

Accounting: Review of incoming inspection data prior to authorization of payment.

Data Processing/MIS: Review of analysis of data integrity errors prior to release.

Engineering: Review of prototype test data prior to production release.

Operations: Review of product inspection data prior to release for shipment.

Purchasing: Review of source inspection data prior to acceptance for delivery and/or release to production.

Quality: Review of statistical process control (SPC) data prior to shipment.

3.5 Employee Performance Evaluations

The cost of all evaluation activities to determine the performance of personnel in relation to expected performance and/or the performance of outside human resources. Include the cost of forecasting human resource needs.

Accounting: Budget analysis of human resource requirements.

Data Processing/MIS: Annual performance review.

Engineering: Annual performance review.

Operations: Annual performance review.

Purchasing: Annual performance review.

Quality: Monthly efficiency evaluation of direct labor.

Sales/Marketing: Annual performance review.

3.6 Miscellaneous Quality Evaluations

The cost of all support and service area quality evaluations (audits) to assure the continued ability to supply acceptable products, services, or information to internal and external customers and consumers. Examples of areas include mail rooms, stores, packaging, and shipping.

Accounting: Accounts payable audit to ensure material supplies.

Data Processing/MIS: Hardware and software maintenance support.

Operations: Spare parts audit.

Purchasing: Verification of supplier delivery dates.

Sales/Marketing: Evaluation of forecasting system efficiency.

3.7 Other Appraisal Costs

Other appraisal costs associated with activities to measure, evaluate or audit products, processes, or services to ensure conformance to internal and external customer requirements, and identified by the assessment team as relevant to specific departments and the company.

Assessment Level 3 (Assessment Level 2 Plus Prevention Costs)

4.0 Prevention Costs—General Definition

The sum of all costs associated with the activities to prevent defects and poor quality in products or services by identifying and eliminating causes of failure before they occur or reoccur.

4.1 Internal and External Marketing, Customer, or User Analysis

Costs incurred from activities in the accumulation and continued evaluation of internal and external marketing, customer, or user requirements as well as their perceptions, including feedback on reliability and performance that affects their satisfaction with the products or services provided.

4.1.1 Internal and External Marketing, Customer or User Research

The cost of market research activities devoted to the identification of internal and external markets, customers, or users and the determination of requirements and attributes of the product or service that provide satisfaction.

Accounting: Meeting with senior management to determine managerial accounting requirements.

Data Processing/MIS: Meeting with customers to determine information requirements.

Engineering: Meeting with customers to establish new product specifications.

Operations: Meeting with the sales department to determine sales forecasts before the start of production scheduling.

Purchasing: Meeting with the manufacturing department to determine delivery priorities.

Quality: Meeting with customers to determine technical specification requirements.

Sales/Marketing: Surveying customer requirements.

4.1.2 Internal and External Marketing, Customer, or User Surveys
The cost of activities designed to obtain feedback from customers and their perception of product or service quality as delivered and used—from the viewpoint of their expectations and needs relative to competitive offerings.

Accounting: Survey of senior management to determine their perception of the adequacy of the information provided by the accounting department.

Data Processing/MIS: Survey of internal customers to determine the appropriateness of the services being provided by the data processing department.

Engineering: Survey of the production department to measure the quality of designs.

Operations: Survey of the company's customers to determine how they perceive the quality of the product.

Purchasing: Survey of the manufacturing department to measure the performance of the purchasing department.

Quality: Survey of customers to measure perceived quality of company's output.

Sales/Marketing: Survey of customers to determine their perceptions of the sales department's service.

**4.1.3 Marketing, Customer, or User Requirements
Specification and Review**
Costs incurred by activities in the review and evaluation of internal and external customer contracts and documents affecting product or service requirements (such as applicable industry standards, government regulations, or customer internal specifications) to determine the capability to meet the stated requirements—prior to acceptance of the customer's terms.

Accounting: Analysis of budget requests.

Data Processing/MIS: Review of customer requests to determine if capacity, systems, and staff are available.

Engineering: Verification of the technical information on sales contracts to assure manufacturability.

Operations: Review of customer requirements prior to ensure production capability.

Purchasing: Examination of sales contracts to verify that the quoted lead times are achievable.

Quality: Review of specification requirements prior to acceptance of customer order.

Sales/Marketing: Review of customer purchase orders prior to acceptance to ensure that the terms are consistent with company policy.

4.2 Define Product and Service Requirements

Costs incurred to translate internal or external marketing, customer, or user needs into reliable standards and requirements prior to the release of the authorization to create a product or service. These costs are normally planned and budgeted, and are applied to major design changes as well.

4.2.1 Progress Reviews for Product and Service Design

The total cost incurred for activities conducted to maximize conformance of product or service design to the internal or external customer needs with regard to function, configuration, reliability, safety, producibility, unit cost, serviceability, interchangeability, accuracy, timeliness, and maintainability. These formal reviews, including the planning of interim and final design progress reviews, occur prior to the release of the final design to fabricate prototype units, the start of trial production, or the initiation of a new service.

Accounting: Review of managerial accounting system design to ensure that customer requirements will be met.

Data Processing/MIS: Review of applications to verify that customer requirements will be met.

Engineering: Review of designs prior to release to manufacturing.

Operations: Review of designs prior to the start of making prototypes.

Purchasing: Review of bill of materials to ensure availability of materials.

Quality: Review of design specifications to ensure product will properly function.

Sales/Marketing: Review of marketing campaign design to ensure that the business goals are being addressed.

4.2.2 Support Activities for Product and Service Design

The total cost of all activities specifically required to provide tangible, meaningful, and useful inputs to the product or service design by other functions, departments, or organizations to meet customer requirements.

Accounting: Development of cost standards.

Data Processing/MIS: Evaluation of systems and processes to assist users in implementing current and future applications.

Engineering: Design document checking to ensure conformance to internal design standards.

Operations: Preproduction runs to examine manufacturing costs/cycle time.

Purchasing: Selection and design qualification of components and materials.

Quality: Failure mode and effects analysis.

Sales/Marketing: Analysis of customer misuse and abuse potential.

4.2.3 Qualification Testing of Products and Services

Costs incurred in the planning and conduct of the qualification testing of new products and services, and major changes to existing products and services. Include costs for the inspection and test of a sufficient quantity of qualification units under ambient conditions and worst case conditions. Qualification inspections and tests are conducted to verify that all product and service design requirements have been met or, when failures occur, to clearly identify where redesign activities are required. Qualification testing is performed on prototype units, pilot runs, a sample of the initial production run of new products or the initial use of a new service. (Some consider this an appraisal cost.)

Accounting: Testing of new payroll software package prior to use.

Data Processing/MIS: Alpha site testing of new applications.

Engineering: Testing of prototypes prior to release for production.

Operations: Manufacture of prototypes made for the intent of testing.

Purchasing: Acquisition of raw materials for prototype testing.

Quality: Preproduction testing.

Sales/Marketing: Testing of new order placement system.

4.2.4 Field Trials for Products and Services

The cost of planned observations and evaluation of end-product or service performance in trial situations—usually with the cooperation of loyal internal or external customers but also including sales into test markets. (Some consider this an appraisal cost).

Accounting: Recording the cost of field trials.

Data Processing/MIS: Beta site testing of new systems and procedures.

Engineering: Field trips to examine status of samples.

Operations: Production of prototypes for testing at customer sites.

Purchasing: Clerical activities related to the administration of travel arrangements.

Quality: Field evaluations.

Sales/Marketing: Administration of field trials with customers.

4.3 Internal and External Supplier Certification and Review

Costs incurred to ensure conformance to requirements of supplier parts, materials, or processes to minimize the impact of internal and external supplier nonconformances of delivered product or services.

4.3.1 Internal and External Supplier Review

The total cost of surveys to review and evaluate individual supplier's capabilities to meet requirements. Usually conducted by a team of qualified representatives from affected departments or organizations.

Accounting: Review of supplier's cost of quality.

Data Processing/MIS: Evaluation of vendor supplied applications and corporate generated data.

Engineering: Field trips to supplier locations to evaluate design and/or production capabilities.

Operations: Field trips to supplier locations to evaluate production capabilities.

Purchasing: Development and implementation of supplier review programs.

Quality: On-site supplier assessments.

Sales/Marketing: Review capabilities of marketing suppliers.

4.3.2 Internal and External Supplier Rating

The cost of developing and maintaining, as applicable, a system to ascertain each supplier's continued acceptability for future business. This rating system is based on actual supplier performance to established requirements, periodically analyzed and given a quantitative or qualitative rating.

Accounting: Review of supplier's billing accuracy as part of vendor certification process.

Data Processing/MIS: Development and maintenance of rating system to monitor incoming data accuracy.

Engineering: Rating vendors on the basis of efficiency of design.

Operations: Maintaining records on supplier performance as part of a rating program.

Purchasing: Development and implementation of supplier rating program.

Quality: Development and implementation of a supplier certification process.

Sales/Marketing: Rating of performance of marketing media

and supplier organizations, including advertising, trade shows, and outside sales representative firms.

4.3.3 Product and Service Purchase Order Review

The cost of review activities for purchase order, technical data, or other product or service acquisition information, usually by other than purchasing personnel, to ensure the ability to clearly and completely communicate accurate technical, quality and other requirements to internal and external suppliers.

Accounting: Verification of cost extensions on purchase orders.

Data Processing/MIS: Development of system to minimize purchase order data entry errors and assure consistency of data between suppliers and the organization.

Engineering: Review of technical information on purchase orders.

Operations: Verification of purchase order accuracy by the department making the requisition.

Quality: Appraisal of purchase order forms to ensure clarity.

Sales/Marketing: Review of technical information to confirm that components meet customer requirements.

4.3.4 Supplier Certification and Quality Planning

The total cost of planning for the incoming and source inspections and tests necessary to determine acceptability of supplier products and services. Includes the preparation of necessary documents, development costs for newly required inspection and test equipment, and preparation of check procedures or processes for services.

Accounting: Testing and verification of invoices submitted electronically by suppliers.

Data Processing/MIS: Development of quality assurance plans and procedures to verify incoming data accuracy.

Engineering: Preparation of technical inspection guidelines for incoming material.

Operations: Preparation of incoming material inspection guidelines.

Purchasing: Development of source inspection guidelines.

Quality: Preparation of incoming material inspection guidelines.

Sales/Marketing: Development of customer purchase order inspection guidelines.

4.4 Operations Performance Readiness Verification

Cost of activities assuring the capability and readiness of departmental or functional operations to perform and meet quality standards and customer product or service requirements, including quality control planning for the production activities, service delivery processes, and quality education of personnel.

4.4.1 Product and Service Process Capability Maintenance

The cost of activities established for the purpose of assuring the capability of new product and service methods, processes, equipment, machinery, and tools to initially and consistently perform within required limits.

Accounting: Development of guidebook on reporting (that is, scrap, overtime, rework).

Data Processing/MIS: Process and configuration control procedures.

Engineering: Time and motion studies.

Operations: Preventive maintenance on machinery and tools.

Purchasing: Development of purchasing procedures manual.

Quality: Process capability (C_p, C_{pk}) analysis.

Sales/Marketing: Development of position description manual.

4.4.2 Development of Product and Service Inspection and Measurement

The total cost for development of necessary product or service inspection, test, and audit procedures, appraisal documentation system, and workmanship or appearance standards to ensure the continued achievement of acceptable results. Include total design and development costs for new or special measurement and control techniques, gauges, and equipment. Include the cost of test equipment engineers, process engineers, gauge engineers, inspection equipment engineers, process planners, and designers.

Accounting: Development of audit procedures.

Data Processing/MIS: Development of data entry and output inspection procedures.

Engineering: Design of checking fixtures.

Operations: Development of inspection guidelines for production workers.

Purchasing: Development of purchase order audit procedures.

Quality: Development of inspection guidelines.

Sales/Marketing: Development of sales order audit procedure.

4.4.3 Operations Support Performance Readiness Verification

The total activity cost for planning and verifying the readiness of all activities required to provide support to product production and service delivery processes. As applicable, these product and service support activities include, but are not limited to, preparation of specifications and the construction or purchase of new production equipment, preparation of operator instructions, scheduling and control plans for supplies, laboratory analysis support, data processing support, and clerical support.

Accounting: Preparation of guidelines for accounting staff.

Data Processing/MIS: MRP runs to optimize planning of purchases and shop floor scheduling.

Engineering: Preparation of specifications of new production equipment.

Operations: Preparation of operator instructions, routings.

Purchasing: Vendor training and assistance.

Quality: Laboratory analysis support.

Sales/Marketing: Sales forecasting.

4.4.4 Skills Development, Education, and Training

Costs incurred in the development and conduct of training programs for the purpose of preventing errors and improving productivity by reducing the amount of wasted, redundant, nonvalue-added, and inefficient activities. Include education programs in subjects such as quality training, cost-of-poor-quality activity assessment training, process control, SPC, and problem-solving techniques.

Accounting: Continuing education course work on changing business and financial requirements.

Data Processing/MIS: Seminars for improving users' understanding of systems and applications.

Engineering: Course work in engineering methods.

Operations: Operator quality control classes.

Purchasing: Course work in negotiations.

Quality: Course work in how to teach SPC.

Sales/Marketing: Seminars in sales management.

4.5 Quality Management and Administration
Costs incurred in the overall management and administration of quality-related activities and functions within the departments and the business.

4.5.1 Management and Administrative Salaries
Compensation costs for personnel (for example, managers and directors, supervisors, and clerical staff) performing quality improvement management, support, and administrative activities.

Accounting: Administrative time relating to quality activities.

Data Processing/MIS: Administrative time relating to quality activities.

Engineering: Administrative time relating to quality activities.

Operations: Administrative time relating to quality activities.

Purchasing: Administrative time relating to quality activities.

Quality: Administrative quality control department personnel.

Sales/Marketing: Administrative time relating to quality activities.

4.5.2 Quality Process Expenses and Overhead
All other costs and expenses related to quality improvement not specifically covered elsewhere, such as heat, light, telephone, and overhead allocations.

Accounting: Quality support and administrative expenses.

Data Processing/MIS: Quality support and administrative expenses.

Engineering: Quality support and administrative expenses.

Operations: Quality support and administrative expenses.

Purchasing: Quality support and administrative expenses.

Quality: Overhead allocated and other costs attributable to the quality department.

Sales/Marketing: Quality support and administrative expenses.

4.5.3 Quality Process Planning

Costs incurred in quality procedure manual development and maintenance, inputs to proposals for selecting quality improvement projects, quality record keeping, strategic quality planning, and budget control for the quality improvement process.

Accounting: Development of budgets.

Data Processing/MIS: Clerical support for the development and updating of the quality control manual.

Engineering: Development of strategic plan for the engineering department.

Operations: Development/updating of operator guidelines.

Purchasing: Development of sourcing manual.

Quality: Development/updating of the quality manual.

Sales/Marketing: Development of strategic marketing plan.

4.5.4 Quality Performance Assessment

The cost of activities performed to evaluate the effectiveness of the quality management process. Include quality performance data collection, compilation, analysis, and issuance of reports designed to promote the continued improvement of quality performance. The cost-of-poor-quality activity assessment, cost-driver analysis, performance measurement of the improvement teams, and progress reports of the quality improvement process would be counted in this cost element.

Accounting: Administration and record keeping of the cost of quality.

Data Processing/MIS: Analysis of data accuracy.

Engineering: Analysis of drafting errors.

Operations: Compilation of scrap records.

Purchasing: Cost of quality participation.

Quality: Compilation of plant quality performance.

Sales/Marketing: Collection of performance data on pricing errors.

4.5.5 Quality Education

Costs incurred in initial and new employee indoctrination as well as continued quality education of all employees to maintain and improve the quality of products and services delivered to customers. Quality education programs emphasize the value of quality performance, the financial impact of eliminating poor quality activities and processes, and the role that each person plays in its achievement.

Accounting: Indoctrination of new employees on the importance of checking order entries.

Data Processing/MIS: Indoctrination of new employees regarding the importance of data entry accuracy.

Engineering: Indoctrination of new employees regarding the maintenance of drawings/files, and so on.

Operations: Indoctrination of new employees regarding work standards by stockroom supervisors.

Purchasing: Indoctrination of new employees regarding the emphasis of high quality in the purchase of components.

Quality: Quality awareness training.

Sales/Marketing: On-the-job training of new sales representatives with experienced employees.

4.5.6 Enterprise-Wide Quality Process

Costs incurred in the development and deployment of an enterprise-wide quality improvement process designed to promote awareness of improvement opportunities and provide individual opportunities for participation and contributions.

Accounting: Instruction to other departments on the relationship between quality and cost.

Data Processing/MIS: Development of program to inform other departments of the impact and importance of information.

Engineering: Involvement in quality circles and quality improvement teams.

Operations: Involvement in quality circles and quality improvement teams.

Purchasing: Development of multifunctional teams for the purpose of improving vendor quality.

Quality: Design and implementation of quality circles.

Sales/Marketing: Development of company-wide quality goals and objectives.

4.6 Employee Capability Testing

Costs incurred for activities in assuring the capability and readiness of the employees to meet quality standards and customer requirements.

4.6.1 Employee Hiring and Screening

The cost of ensuring that new employees have the ability to perform the job functions. This includes the development of interview guidelines as well as the conduct of applicant interviews, testing, and exit interviews. Include any outside testing and investigations (such as drug testing, psychological testing, background investigations). Include the cost of search firms for newly created positions.

Accounting: Interviewing of job applicants.

Data Processing/MIS: Processing of coded applicant screening examinations.

Engineering: Interviewing of job applicants.

Operations: Exit interviews of resigning employees.

Purchasing: Purchase of outside testing services.

Quality: Development of applicant screening exams.

Sales/Marketing: Interviewing of sales representative job applicants.

4.6.2 Job Descriptions

The cost of defining the responsibilities of individuals, departments, and positions. The goal of this activity is to assist in hiring individuals with the capabilities to meet the job requirements. This activity places specific responsibilities on individuals and/or departments and defines their objectives.

Accounting: Development of job descriptions.

Data Processing/MIS: Development of job descriptions.

Engineering: Development of individual job descriptions.
Operations: Development of job descriptions by position.
Purchasing: Development of departmental roles and objectives.
Quality: Development of job descriptions.
Sales/Marketing: Development of job descriptions.

4.7 Other Prevention Costs

Other activities identified by the assessment team that are or can be undertaken to prevent or eliminate the root causes of poor quality and its related costs to the business by preventing or eliminating nonconformances for internal and external customer requirements.

Notes

1. Cost-of-poor-quality elements for products and services are adapted from ASQC Quality Costs Committee, *Principles of Quality Costs, 2 ed.,* Jack Campanella (Milwaukee: Quality Press, 1990).

2. KPMG Peat Marwick, Robert S. Kaplan, Robin Cooper, and Maisel Consulting Group, *Implementing Activity-Based Cost Management: Moving from Analysis to Action,* a joint study by the Institute of Management Accountants (Montvale, N.J.: Institute of Management Accountants, 1992), 138.

3. KPMG Peat Marwick, *Implementing Activity-Based Cost Management,* 252.

4. KPMG Peat Marwick, *Implementing Activity-Based Cost Management,* 72.

Index